FROM RURAL CHINA
TO THE IVY LEAGUE

FROM RURAL CHINA TO THE IVY LEAGUE

Reminiscences of Transformations in Modern Chinese History

Yü Ying-shih

Translated by Michael S. Duke and Josephine Chiu-Duke

CAMBRIA
PRESS

Amherst, New York

Front cover photo courtesy of Tang Foundation.

Library of Congress Cataloging-in-Publication Data

Names: Yu, Yingshi, author. |
Duke, Michael S., translator. | Chiu-Duke, Josephine, 1951- translator. |
Title: From rural China to the Ivy League : reminiscences of transformations in modern
Chinese history / by Ying-shih Yu ; translated by Michael S. Duke, and Josephine Chiu-Duke.
Other titles: Yu Yingshi hui yi lu. English | Reminiscences
of transformations in modern Chinese history
Description: Amherst, New York : Cambria Press, [2021] | "Translated from the Chinese
version Yü Ying-shih Huiyilu (Taibei : Yunchen Culture Publishing Corporation, 2018)" |
Includes bibliographical references and index. |
Summary: " A leading authority in Chinese studies and hailed as the most important living
Chinese historian of our times, Professor Ying-shih Yu received the John W. Kluge Prize
for achievement in the Study of Humanity in 2006 and the first Tang Prize international
award in Sinology in 2014. These awards represent a recognition of his more than sixty-
year contribution to the fields of Chinese history, thought, politics, and culture during
which he published more than thirty books, forty-one monographs, and hundreds of
articles. Over the years his works have had great influence throughout the Chinese-
language world where he has been hailed as a paradigm of Chinese humanism. The book
covers Professor Yü's life and times from his childhood in rural China to his tenure as
a professor at Harvard University, with relevant discussions of later events. This book
is an invaluable record of a history of our times, witnessing the cultural, political, and
social transformations of what Professor Yu notes as the period of most violent turmoil
and social upheaval in modern Chinese history. His record of this complex period is now
made accessible to English-language readers with this book."-- Provided by publisher.

Identifiers: LCCN 2021002032 (print) | LCCN 2021002033 (ebook) |
ISBN 9781621966968 (library binding) | ISBN 9781621966258 (paperback) |
ISBN 9781621965985 (pdf) | ISBN 9781621965992 (epub)

Subjects: LCSH: Yu, Yingshi. | Historians--China--Biography. | Historiography--
China--History--20th century. | China--Intellectual life--1937-1948. |
China--Intellectual life--1949- | Sinologists--Massachusetts--Cambridge--
Biography. | Harvard-Yenching Institute--History--20th century.

Classification: LCC DS734.9.Y838 A3 2021 (print) | LCC DS734.9.Y838 (ebook) |
DDC 951.0072/02 [B]--dc23
LC record available at https://lccn.loc.gov/2021002032
LC ebook record available at https://lccn.loc.gov/2021002033

TABLE OF CONTENTS

LIST OF FIGURES

ONE OF FOUR POEMS FOR PROFESSOR QIAN MU'S NINETIETH BIRTHDAY

By the seaside looking back, separated from the past,
I still remember the wind on the water roiling the waves.[1]
In our haven it is difficult to find the three Chu families
    who vowed to overthrow tyrannical Qin;
But you once said that the Qin lasted only ten years.[2]
Like the ancient masters in Hejian
    you're still determined to elucidate the ancient principles,
And like Fusheng in the Han
    you still preserve the classics despite the changing times.[3]
Ashamed that I did not live up to the teachings
    you passed on to me then,
I can only strive to repay your eternal spring instructions
    with my remaining years.

I respectfully copied out this old poem in the *wuxu* year of the twenty-first century (2018) while remembering the past.

—Yü Ying-shih,
the 88-year-old man
from Qianshan (Anhui Province)

* * * * * *

This poem was originally composed in 1985. It is reproduced in this book in dedication to his beloved Professor Qian Mu (1895–1990).

NOTES

1. The wind refers to Professor Qian Mu's teachings, and the waves refer to the influence they had on Professor Yü.
2. The three Chu families are mentioned in the *Records of the Grand Historian* (*Shiji*), and they have become a symbol of determination to overthrow tyranny despite asymmetrical power. The Qin dynasty lasted from 221–206 BCE, but here the implication is that tyrannical regimes cannot last forever.
3. Hejian in Hebei was the home of Buddhist masters who interpreted Buddhist texts using Chinese terms in the third to fifth centuries. Fusheng (268–178 BCE) was a Qin-dynasty "erudite" famous for hiding the *Book of Documents* (*Shangshu*) in the walls of his family's house, thereby saving it from the Qin burning of the books.

Translators' Note

Professor Yü Ying-shih 余英時, a leading authority in the field of Chinese studies, received the John W. Kluge Prize for achievement in the Study of Humanity in 2006 and the first Tang Prize international award in Sinology in 2014. These awards represent recognition of his contributions, spanning more than sixty years, to the fields of Chinese history, thought, politics, and culture during which time he published more than thirty books, forty-one monographs, and hundreds of articles. They also serve to highlight his efforts to redefine the Chinese intellectual and cultural tradition and to imbue it with new life. These awards further serve to honor the way in which Professor Yü always put his intellectual convictions into practice through his criticism of the violent suppression of the Tiananmen democracy movement of 1989 and his decades-long commentaries on Radio Free Asia. Over the years his works have had great influence throughout the Chinese-language world, where he has been hailed as a paradigm of Chinese humanism.[1]

Professor Yü's reminiscences cover the period from his childhood in the rural Anhui Province in China to his professorship at Harvard University. His recollections were first published in Chinese and have been read extensively by Chinese-language readers, both in scrial form in the *Mingbao Monthly* and in book form. The Chinese version of this book sold more than 10,000 copies in the first month after its publication by Yunchen Publishing Company in Taipei, Taiwan, in late 2018. Such a phenomenon for books of this genre is rare, to say the least. Scholars in China who were not able to acquire it directly asked their friends in the United States to purchase the book through Taiwan's online book services and then mail it to Professor Yü to sign. The book was awarded the twelfth Hong Kong Book Prize in June 2019.[2]

It is an honor to be asked to translate this book, and we thank Professor Yü and Mrs. Monica Shu-ping Chen Yü for their assistance during the process. In our translation, we have tried to be faithful to Professor Yü's style of writing, which is sometimes very colloquial and sometimes in more formal classical Chinese. The difference between this translation and the original is that we have added endnotes concerning the many events and people mentioned that might not be familiar to some readers. In the notes, we have also added a few references to English-language works on which readers might want to follow up. Professor Yü listed many sources in parentheses in his text, and we have placed these in the endnotes with "Yü Ying-shih note" to indicate that these are his notes. We have provided Chinese characters for some words to indicate why we translate them the way we do; for example, the Chinese values mentioned in chapter 4, "Hong Kong and New Asia College": humanity (*ren* 仁), righteousness (*yi* 義), propriety (*li* 禮), wisdom (*zhi* 智), and honesty (*xin* 信). We have also provided the Chinese characters for important book and essay titles, like Qian Mu's *A General History of China* and Hu Shi's "What is Liberalism?" but have omitted them for works we consider self-explanatory or not sufficiently important. We hope these characters will be of assistance both to students learning Chinese and Chinese history as well as scholars who want to follow up on the books and essays mentioned.

We would like to express our gratitude to Professor David Der-wei Wang for his unfailing encouragement to publish this English-language version of Professor Yü's book and to Mr. Liao Zhifeng of Yunchen Publishing Company for providing us with a PDF copy of the Chinese version from which we translated. We also want to thank the Tang Prize Foundation for permission to reprint their photographs, Cambria Press's anonymous external readers for their positive and invaluable suggestions on improving our translation, and the Cambria Press team, especially the director Ms. Toni Tan, for all their efforts in skillfully guiding us through the editing and production process. The original Chinese title is *Yü Ying-shih Huiyilu* 余英時回憶錄 (Yü Ying-shih's memoir), but, with Professor Yü's permission, we have given it the present English title, though the word "memoir" will still be used in the main text. The publication of this book was aided by the generous support of the Chiang Ching-kuo Foundation for International Scholarly Exchange, for which we are most grateful.

Professor Yü Ying-shih (1930–2021) passed away peacefully in his sleep in the early hours of August 1, 2021. It has been an honor for us to know him and Mrs. Monica Shu-ping Chen Yü for the last seventeen years of his life. We also felt honored when he asked us to translate this book, and we are thankful for all the assistance we were given by Professor and Mrs. Yü during the process. It may be fairly said that Professor Yü Ying-shih was the greatest scholar of Chinese history and culture of our time. He was also a man of great kindness, humor, magnanimity, and integrity. His passing represents the end of an era in Chinese studies. We will never see his like again.

Josephine Chiu-Duke and Michael S. Duke

NOTES

1. For a more complete introduction to Professor Yü and his works, especially those in English, please see "Editorial Note" in the two-volume collection *Chinese History and Culture*, by Yü Ying-shih, with the editorial assistance of Josephine Chiu-Duke and Michael S. Duke (New York: Columbia University Press, 2016).
2. See Lianhe xinwen wang 聯合新聞網 United News network, "Yü Ying-shih Huiyilu huo Xianggang shujiang" 余英時回憶錄獲香港書獎, [Yü Ying-shih's memoir receives Hong Kong book prize], June 25, 2019.

FROM RURAL CHINA
TO THE IVY LEAGUE

FROM "INTERVIEWS" TO "MEMOIR"

This memoir is not something that I intended to write. It originated through a complicated process that I should make clear up front.

In the late autumn of 2007, when Mr. Li Huaiyu from Guangzhou visited the United States for the first time, he came straight to Princeton to interview me as we previously agreed on the phone. He told me that he had long since read my works and had always hoped for the opportunity to have a lengthy talk with me. At that time, he was still a newspaper reporter noted for his interviews of senior members of the academic and literary worlds; many of his published collections of interviews were already widely circulated. As soon as we met, he immediately asked me if I could give him a few days so that he could conduct a more thorough and detailed interview. He had two reasons: first, because I do not go to Mainland China to teach or conduct research, he would have no other opportunity to see me; and second, this visit to the United States was an extremely rare opportunity and it was highly unlikely he could come again. His dedication to his craft and his sincere attitude impressed me deeply; I was instantly moved and agreed to his in-depth interview.

Huaiyu interviewed me several times. The first time we talked for three or four days; he came to my home daily and stayed for around four or five hours. He tape-recorded our question-and-answer sessions in preparation for organizing them later when he returned to China. Before that, he also left Princeton to interview some other overseas Chinese scholars with whom he had appointments. His other interviewees were all friends of mine, so naturally they talked about me in their interviews, and he had collected a good deal more material about me. After he concluded the interviews with these other scholars, he visited Princeton again and wanted me to corroborate this new material. I cannot remember now how many times he visited Princeton, but what remains clear is the conscientious and serious attitude he exhibited in his work.

Next, I would like to discuss the scope and the main content of our dialogues. At first, I assumed that Huaiyu was probably concerned about my view of the present situation and future development of Mainland China. To my surprise, he started by asking about my childhood and then proceeded with his questions chronologically all the way up to the present. It was not, however, a simple and direct question-and-answer interview. When we came to certain people and events, Huaiyu felt the need to make further enquiries to clarify things. He would ask many questions from various angles, forcing me to search thoroughly through my memories to reconstruct past events. We would then continue our discussions until we were both satisfied with the results. The time we expended in this process often exceeded that of the usual question-and-answer interview. I must also point out that Huaiyu's persistent questioning greatly and unexpectedly revived my memories. Many long-forgotten events came to life again in the process of his unrelenting questioning.

By the end of the first day, I was already clearly aware that we were engaged in a kind of "oral history." I never had any desire to write an autobiography, and although oral history was very popular at the time, it did not appeal to me. Moved by Huaiyu's great enthusiasm and copious preparations, I did not have the heart to dampen his spirits. It also occurred to me that to take advantage of this opportunity to preserve an accurate record of my life might not necessarily be without its own significance. As to publishing it, I could wait and consider that at a later date.

Now, I would like to discuss the written text of our interview. After returning to Guangzhou, Huaiyu started to compose "A Record of Conversations" based on his tape recordings, but he did not merely transcribe the tapes of our interviews. He did a great deal of work to expand on his materials, including reading extensively on my works and those of my friends and teachers because they often preserved some accounts of my past. With this expanded foundation, he constructed a comparatively wide historical context into which he placed our "talks" in a logical structure that made reading them flow clearly and smoothly.

Huaiyu wrote two "conversation" drafts. The first draft had two parts. Part one had ten chapters with about 120,000 to 130,000 Chinese characters, mostly from the oral record. Part two was his own composition of "Notes from a Small Studio" ("Small Studio" referring to my study) —it was divided into twenty narrower topics based on "A Record of Conversations" and some other related materials; it contained a rather more intimate introduction about me and came in at around 60,000 to 70,000 characters. According to our original agreement, I would have to review and revise the drafts before we could consider whether and how they might be published. So Huaiyu sent me his first draft immediately after it was completed, but I was too busy with other writings and did not have the time to give it my full attention. So as to not to make him wait too long, I sent the revised version of the first three chapters back for him to consider. To my surprise, my revised and expanded version gave him the idea to rewrite the entire draft and even expand parts in the oral record into twenty chapters, making this version much more thorough and detailed than the original. He wanted me to revise and expand the entire draft, and then he would organize it and finish writing a final version.

At that time, I began to feel the need to give serious thought to the question of how this record of our conversations should actually be handled. My main considerations were as follows: If we proceeded according to Huaiyu's plan, the final volume would be a complete, accurate, and vivid "oral autobiography." The draft having taken such great effort and having already received enthusiastic support from the Yunchen Publishing Company meant that we could not just leave it after completion; the next thing to do would be to publish it as a book. This is where problems arose. As mentioned earlier, I never intended to write an autobiography, and that was because an autobiography would have to have as its narrative core my personal life and thought—and this was something I wanted to avoid at all costs. After giving the problem much consideration, I thought of a different narrative approach: change the original "oral autobiography" style into a "memoir" form. In other words, change the focus of the interviews from my individual life and thought to the changes in China and the world that I personally experienced in the last seventy to eighty years.

From the start of the Anti-Japanese War of Resistance in 1937, which was the beginning of the draft, to the present day is the period of the most violent turmoil and social upheaval in modern Chinese history. I felt very strongly that if we could present in these interviews the major changes that took place during this extraordinary period of history, it would be of far greater significance than merely tracing the development of my own life history. Huaiyu's second draft already contained the basic material, and I only had to shift the focus and add some details not covered in our interviews to change our "oral autobiography" into my conception of a memoir. Huaiyu most graciously agreed with my suggestion to change the focus, and so I started to write this memoir. However, I have to declare formally that because the memoir is constructed on the foundations of Huaiyu's second draft, it also should be included in its original "oral autobiography" category. In the final analysis, the difference between the oral autobiography and the memoir for this book can only be understood as a part-versus-whole relationship; the former is a constituent component of the latter.

Every memoir is different because of individual experiences. I have been engaged in research and teaching my whole life, and so my memories are all within the confines of academia, thought, and culture. It goes without saying that the changes in the world that I have experienced are within those realms. I hope that my recollections will be of some assistance to understanding the historical developments of that period. Some of my peers will also leave us their memories in different ways. The more memoirs, the better; together they can help us verify similarities and compare differences.

Let me give two interesting examples: Willard V. O. Quine (1908–2000) and Morton White (1917–2016) were both professors in the Department of Philosophy at Harvard University; not only did they work together for over twenty years but their thinking was nearly identical. In their later years, they both wrote autobiographies: *Time of My Life* by Quine and *A Philosopher's Story* by White.[1] These two books have similarities and differences, and reading them together gave me a sense of the development and activities of both the American philosophical world and the general academic world. I was of the same generation, even generally the same academic world, and I usually paid close attention to the direction of their thoughts; thus, I dare say that my understanding after reading their autobiographies was comparatively intimate and deep. These examples led me to believe that the more memoirs there are about a period of history, the more later generations will be able to understand the trends in their history.

This is another motive I have for publishing this memoir. As the saying goes, "toss out a brick and have jade thrown back" (*pao zhuan yin yu* 抛磚引玉); in other words, stimulate more scholars' interest in recollecting past events. If I am permitted to express another extravagant wish, I would hope that the course of my individual intellectual development recounted in this memoir, regardless of success or failure, may perhaps be utilized as a kind of reference by a new generation of young friends seeking knowledge.

Finally, I would like to express my most sincere appreciation to Mr. Liao Zhifeng. He has not only valued Li Huaiyu's "A Record of Conversations" from the start but also made certain that this memoir was published by Yunchen. What moved me most was that in mid-September of this year [2018] Zhifeng made a special trip to Princeton to see me about this book. In two long afternoon discussions, we talked over every possible issue, including proofreading the text, the length of this preface, organizing the structure of the book, selecting photographs, even writing the next volume, and so on. We were instantly like old friends, communicating perfectly, agreeing on many points and making decisions with but a single word. These were the most delightful two days I've had in the past few years.

Yü Ying-shih,
September 26, 2018

Notes

1. Willard V. O. Quine, *Time of My Life* (Cambridge, MA: MIT Press, 1985); and Morton White, *A Philosopher's Story* (University Park: Pennsylvania State University Press, 1999).

CHAPTER 1

RURAL LIFE IN QIANSHAN COUNTY, ANHUI PROVINCE

PART ONE: NINE YEARS IN QIANSHAN

I was born in Tianjin in 1930, but my registered hometown or ancestral origin was Qianshan County in Anhui Province. My hometown was not merely in name for the records because I did live in our family's ancestral home in Qianshan County for nine years, from 1937 to 1946. In order to explain why I would live in the rural countryside for such a long time, I need to explain my family background; to do so, I have to begin with the generation of my late father, Yu Xiezhong (1899–1980).[1]

According to my family's genealogical record, early on the Yü family settled in Guanzhuang Village (*xiang* 鄉) of Qianshan County (*xian* 縣) in Anhui Province. From the Ming dynasty into the Qing, however, the Yü family had never produced a successful provincial examination candidate (*juren* 舉人) or an "advanced scholar" (*jinshi* 進士), and so they stayed in the countryside and never moved to the big cities. It seems that my paternal grandfather was a "flowering talent" (*xiucai* 秀才; someone who passed the county-level imperial exam), but he never achieved any higher scholarly honors in the imperial examinations. He encouraged his four sons to pursue their studies, but only my father had better opportunities because he was the youngest. My father was born during the late Qing when there were no more imperial examinations (they were abolished in 1905), and so he could only work hard to receive a new modern-style education. On that account, he went from secondary school in Anqing (a prefecture-level city in Anhui) and Nanjing, and on to university in Beijing, graduating from the history department at Yanjing University. Under the direction of Professor Chen Yuan (Yuan-an, 1880–1971), my father wrote his doctoral dissertation "The Historiography of Liu Jizhi (661–721)," the celebrated Tang-dynasty historian.[2] However, my father was more interested in European and American history, and so he went to the United States and studied American history at Colgate College and Harvard University from 1926 to 1928.

My family were lower middle landlords, and the rents they collected every year were not enough to pay their expenses. Thus, the expenses for my father's schooling and overseas study were covered by borrowing money and selling some family land. He studied in the United States only for two years, received his MA degree, and returned home; the first thing he did was to start working to repay his debts. In 1929, he succeeded Jiang Tingfu (T. F. Tsiang, 1895–1965) as Chair of the History Department at Nankai University in Tianjin. He originally intended to serve in that capacity for a long time, but sadly my mother died giving birth to me, and it was too big a blow for my father. He left Tianjin a year after that.

After that, I remember living with father in Nanjing and Kaifeng. My father held the position of Special Committee Member in the Natural Resources Commission and did research on American history and international relations when we lived in Nanjing. A few years before the Anti-Japanese War of Resistance,[3] my father's good friend Xiao Yishan (1902–1978) took the position of the Dean of Arts at Henan University in

Kaifeng; he invited father to be the Chair of the Department of Literature and History. Fan Wenlan (1893–1969) was also in the department at that time, and they knew each other but could not be considered close friends.[4] Thus my memory contains many snippets of information about Henan University and Kaifeng.

In 1937, when the Anti-Japanese War of Resistance began, I remember our whole family taking a train from Kaifeng to Nanjing and then a steamship to Anqing in Anhui. We lived in Anqing until the end of the year when the Japanese army threatened our survival, which led to us returning to our old home in Guanzhuang Village in Qianshan County. My systematic memories really started from that time on, and to this day events occurring after that appear to me just as though they are right before my eyes.

I have related this story to show that my father's generation had only recently left the countryside to go out into the world, but their roots were still in their old village home. When the was crisis hit, father decided to move the entire family back to the countryside. My father himself moved with the national government to Chongqing, however, and I went back to our village home with my paternal uncle (my father's elder brother) and aunt (my uncle's wife). If my father and uncle's generation or several earlier generations had moved to the big cities long ago, I would never have had this chance to live in the countryside.

At that time, I was just seven years old. It was the first time I had returned to the rural village from the city; everything was new, and I was extremely excited, so my recollections are quite strong. I lived in the countryside for nine years separated by a great distance from my father, but his influence was still very much present. It was from him that I learned to value knowledge and learning. My father was influenced by people like Chen Yuan and Hong Ye (William Hung, 1893–1980) in the generation before him; he respected learned individuals and was always trying to advance his own studies.[5] Although he was a Counselor in the Examination Yuan during the Anti-Japanese War years, it was more or less a sinecure, and my father still had time to study and write. After the war, he was commissioned by Lieutenant General Du Yuming (1904–1981) in Shenyang (capital of Liaoning Province) to set up Northeast Zhongzheng University. This was the last thing he did in Mainland China, and it focused on research and education. My father also compiled a large *Xiyang tongshi* 西洋通史 (General history of the West) in several hundred thousand characters, and it inspired me very much.[6] I did not understand the content at first, but I began to gradually and came to have great respect for the work. It was probably one of the reasons that I came to study history and was fond of reading books on Western cultural history.

Guanzhuang was a typical remote and desolate rural mountain village. There was no public road to Anqing City at the time, and it took three days to walk there. I am quite certain that conditions in the Guanzhuang I saw then were not very different from the Guanzhuang of one or two hundred years earlier; it was only more rundown and more impoverished. It had no modern facilities or equipment such as running water, automobiles, or electricity; it was lighted only by oil lamps, and the village people continued to live primitive rural lives. At that time our village was basically an autonomous society that rarely had any dealings with the government. Individuals and families or clans were all mutually interconnected; geography and bloodlines weaved the entire village community into one large network. Everyone was either a relative or a friend, and they depended on clan rules to maintain order in their lives. Sometimes unavoidable conflicts would arise between families with different surnames or within the same family, but they could be satisfactorily mediated by the local gentry (*xiangshen* 鄉紳) or their own clan elders; they never took their complaints to the official government offices.

Living in the countryside for so many years, I fortuitously obtained an intimate understanding of traditional Chinese society, but that was something I realized only later. This period of experience made me somewhat different from other intellectual youths of the same generation. Many of my university classmates had grown up in the cities; when we talked about rural life in the villages, they had no direct, personal experience. They usually had only vague ideas about life in the countryside, and because of this it was easy for them to accept politically ideological propaganda. They believed that the relationship between landlords and peasants was one of exploitation and that the two social classes were pitted against each other in mutual hatred.

From what I saw, however, landlords and peasants were not two entirely different classes that were antagonistic and incapable of mutual tolerance. A system of perpetual tenancy was practiced in our area of Anhui Province. Once a tenant farmer had rented a landlord's land, the landlord could neither evict him nor oppress him. If the tenant farmer could not hand over sufficient produce (usually rice), the landlord would just let it go. I once saw a landlord come to collect rents (in kind) at my maternal uncle's home in neighboring Tongcheng County and watched the tenant farmers threshing (by beating) the unhulled rice. There was an art to how they did it. They did not beat it all out and left one-third of the grain on the threshing floor, but there was nothing the landlord could do about it. He also did not have a deep sense of class consciousness. Some of the tenant farmers who rented his land were also the landlord's elders, and at Chinese New Year and other festivals the landlord had to kowtow to them; this certainly mitigated their social class distinctions.

As I often say, China is such a huge society, bigger than all of Europe combined, and it is impossible for it to be the same everywhere. We cannot say that there was no conflict between landlords and tenants; such conflicts occurred everywhere, but did those conflicts rise to the level of so-called "class struggle"? What I saw was something else. Sometimes it was the tenant farmer who bullied the landlord; if the landlord was a widow with a child, there was nothing she could do about it. Of course, if the landlord was a retired official with great power, then he could oppress his tenants, and such things did happen. We should not lump all these different situations together.

The intuitive understanding that I gained from this life experience was of great help later when I began to study Chinese history and thought. This sort of understanding was not achieved by reading books. Thus, when I later read the investigations and surveys about China by some anthropologists and sociologists, they seemed quite beside the point to me. They did not really grasp the essential experience and the spirit of Chinese life; their research findings were only superficial and mere numbers, and that was because such sociological surveys are usually carried out in the form of questionnaires. The Chinese attitude toward such questionnaires is different from that of Westerners. Answers from Chinese respondents are often unreliable (whereas the responses from Westerners are generally honest); they have that tradition. Chinese people are afraid of making a mistake in their answers and getting into trouble later, and so to protect themselves there are some things they will not tell the truth about, or they will withhold and even misrepresent what they think. One anthropologist distributed a survey questionnaire to Chinese living in Indonesia and was very puzzled to discover that when he asked the same question twice, the second answer was different from the first.

My education then was characterized by "a lack of schooling." From 1937 to 1946, I very rarely went to regular school, though I did sporadically attend a few terms of elementary and middle school. Strictly speaking, not only did I not receive a complete modern education, I did not even receive a complete traditional education either. Most of my time from childhood to youth was spent between "the mountains and the streams," that is, in nature. The only thing related to my later studies was that I received some inspiration from reading classical Chinese prose and ancient history. I read some general texts like *Records of the Grand Historian* (*Shiji* 史記), *Intrigues of the Warring States* (*Zhanguoce* 戰國策), and *Finest of Ancient Prose* (*Guwen guanzhi* 古文觀止), but only selectively, not reciting or memorizing them from beginning to end. I did read the *Four Books* (*Sishu*

四書) but also not all the way through. In my written compositions, I used classical Chinese (*wenyan* 文言) since my teachers in the rural areas were all conservative and would not or could not write vernacular Chinese (*baihuawen* 白話文). I first encountered Tang-dynasty *shi* 詩 poetry and Song-dynasty *ci* 詞 poetry probably when I was around twelve or thirteen years old and liked them better because they were easy to remember. Soon after that, I mastered the *ping* 平 and the *ze* 仄 (level and oblique tones) of classical Chinese rhythmic poetry and tried my hand at composing five- and seven-character quatrains. In those days, I never even saw a Western-language book.

All throughout the Anti-Japanese War of Resistance, my father remained in Chongqing, and I lived with my second uncle, Yu Lizhong, and his family in the countryside. For the first time during the Lunar New Year of 1938, I saw my uncle writing Spring Festival couplets in large characters on red paper and pasting them on the central wall of the hall where the ancestors' memorial tablets were kept. One line had the five big characters "heaven, earth, country, parents, teachers" (*tian di guo qin shi* 天地國親師). My uncle explained that the line originally read "heaven, earth, ruler (*jun* 君), parents, teachers," but there was no longer an emperor and so he changed "ruler" to "country."

From 1945 to 1946, I lived for a year at my maternal uncle's home in neighboring Tongcheng County. That was the only "city" I remember from my youth, but it was really quite isolated and provincial. The people of Tongcheng were proud of their humanities, but they were still steeped in the classical Chinese "ancient-style prose" tradition of Fang Bao (1668–1749) and Yao Nai (1731–1815).[7] In Tongcheng I came under the influence of some distinguished literati living in a backwater and grew more interested in ancient poetry and prose. My second maternal uncle, Zhang Zhongyi, wrote poetry and was good at calligraphy. He was a descendent of Zhang Ying (1638–1708) and Zhang Tingyu (1672–1755) of the early Qing, and the Zhang family was a prestigious family in

Tongcheng and equal to the prominent Fang, Yao, Ma, and Zuo families, but by then they had fallen into decline.[8]

Because Second Uncle often met with famous literati in Tongcheng, I sometimes picked up some knowledge about poetry and prose from their conversations. To this day I still remember a seven-character quatrain he wrote on a portrait of Zhong Kui, the mythical vanquisher of evil spirits:

> An advanced scholar all your life with one jug of wine,
> In your ragged clothes, you wish for nothing more.
> Praising others gives you the utmost peace of mind;
> Hair and beard in wild disorder, demons fear to see you.

In his first draft, the last three characters in the first line were "but without a smooth career" (*shi bu you* 仕不優). When he showed it to a fellow poet friend of his, the man immediately pointed out to him that "but without a smooth career" should be changed to "one jug of wine" (*jiu yi ou* 酒一甌). Overjoyed, Second Uncle thanked him and dubbed him the "three-character master" (*san zi shi* 三字師). "With one jug of wine" was spontaneously formed and far superior to the stiffness of "but without a smooth career." I was enlightened on overhearing this process of revising a poem and came to understand that with lines of poetry one had to think very carefully like Jia Dao (779–843) whether to write "push" or "knock."[9]

Later on, I did research on Zhu Xi (1130–1200), Fang Yizhi (1610–1670), Dai Zhen (1724–1777), and Hu Shi (1891–1962), and all of them were from Anhui, but this had absolutely nothing to do with our shared locale because I have never had any deep sense of belonging to my province. It just happened that these men occupy very important positions in Chinese intellectual history, but when I studied them, I did not pay any attention to where they came from, and even less did I think of them as my fellow townsfolk whom I had to praise. Although Zhu Xi is said to be from Wuyuan County, Huizhou, he was actually born and raised in Fujian Province, and so in the Neo-Confucian School of Principle (*lixue* 理學) he is listed as being in the "Min School" (Min 閩 being the one-character form of Fujian). I simply never considered Zhu Xi's connection with Anhui. In fact, I had not planned to study Zhu Xi at all, but then writing a preface for *The Collected Works of Zhu Xi* (*Zhuzi wenji* 朱子文集) led me to write *The Historical World of Zhu Xi: A Study of the Political Culture of Song Intellectuals* (*Zhu Xi de lishi shijie: Songdai shidafu zhengzhi wenhua de yanjiu* 朱熹的歷史世界：宋代士大夫政治文化的研究).[10]

PART TWO: A LITERARY DISASTER

I lived in the countryside for nine years, and there are many things that I recall. For now I will relate two unusual experiences.

The first is the traditional-style private school (*sishu* 私塾). There were no modern elementary schools in the countryside, and so before the age of twelve I could only attend a traditional-style private school. After I turned twelve, I went to neighboring counties like Shucheng and Tongcheng to attend junior middle school. In the private school, one teacher taught ten to twenty students; all we read were traditional texts divided into three levels: primary, intermediate, and advanced. Primary texts were the *Hundred Family Surnames* (*Baijia xing* 百家) and the *Three Character Classic* (*Sanzi jing* 三字經); intermediate texts were the *Four Books* (*Sishu*) and the *Finest of Ancient Prose* (*Guwen guanzhi*); advanced texts included the *Zuo Commentary to the Spring and Autumn Annals* (*Zuozhuan* 左傳), *Records of the Grand Historian* (*Shiji*), *Intrigues of the Warring States* (*Zhanguoce*), and the *Book of Songs* (*Shijing* 詩經). In all, I probably attended three private schools, spending less than a year in each.

The best school was the one I attended when I was around eleven years old. The teacher's name was Liu Huimin; he was about forty years old, and his knowledge could be considered the best in our rural area because he had attended a new-style modern school earlier in Anqing. At first I was placed in the intermediate-level class with Mr. Liu, but he also allowed me to sit in on the advanced class. He taught in a lively fashion that was most captivating. In Mr. Liu's class, I gradually began to be able to ask questions and understand some hard-to-understand issues in the texts, and so he promoted me to the advanced class. Being under Mr. Liu's tutelage greatly benefited my training in classical literature.

Even more noteworthy is that he introduced us to the great realm of poetry writing. With the arrival of spring, Mr. Liu suddenly and very enthusiastically began writing poems, and he also guided the students in their practice compositions. He began with the four tones of *ping* 平, *shang* 上, *qu* 去, and *ru* 入 (level or even, falling and rising, falling, and entering) and so he taught us the four characters "Son (of) Heaven Sage Philosophy" (*tian zi sheng zhe* 天子聖哲), that were exactly the four tones. Then he taught us to use the 206 rhymes of classical poetry. Of course, we also had to recite from memory the five- and seven-character quatrains from the *Three Hundred Tang Poems* (*Tangshi sanbai shou* 唐詩三百首). I still remember two lines of poetry Mr. Liu wrote then:

> Spring flowers seem to feel for talented men,
> And they break out smiling beside our classroom.

It is not because these two lines are particularly brilliant, but I remember them because we soon discovered our teacher was then courting a young widow. Whenever this young woman happened to pass by our classroom, she would be smiling. When the poet mentions the smiling "spring flowers," he is alluding to her. Mr. Liu did eventually marry this young widow, but the denouement was not satisfactory—the couple's marriage did not seem to be a happy one.

The other encounter that I most vividly remember from my nine years in the countryside is the time I unintentionally precipitated a serious "literary disaster" and was almost executed because of it. My memory of this event, after sixty or seventy years, had already become pretty foggy, but when a Hong Kong TV station aired a documentary film about me (in January 2008), it brought the whole incident back to my mind.[11] The late Hong Kong director Weng Zhiyu (1968–2015) spared no effort in making this film. He took his camera crew on a special trip to Guanzhuang in Qianshan to interview relatives, clan members, and neighbors from my early years. I had been away from the countryside for more than sixty years, and there was no one left who was truly familiar with me. Nevertheless, there were still some people who remembered when I ran into this serious "literary disaster" at the age of thirteen or fourteen. When Mr. Weng returned, he told me what he had learned from those interviews and this helped me recall the incident.

During the eight-year Anti-Japanese War of Resistance, Anhui Province became part of the Gui or Guangxi clique's power base; Provincial Governor Li Pinxian (1892–1987) was a subordinate of Li Zongren (1890–1963), and Guangxi military units occupied various Anhui counties.[12] Around 1943, a battalion of Guangxi clique army troops were stationed in Guanzhuang in Qianshan. The battalion commander Du Jinting was likely involved in much bribery, corruption, abuse of the law, and bullying of the country people, who consequently seethed with discontent. I was then just about thirteen years old. I had never seen Commander Du and had never personally seen him breaking the law or committing crimes, but I had heard the village elders tell many stories, all of which were concrete and detailed, and so I felt very angry and indignant. I don't know what happened, but I suddenly decided to write a long letter to the government denouncing Commander Du for his many crimes. I wrote this accusatory letter purely to vent my anger and had no intention of sending it to the battalion commander's superiors. After I wrote the letter, I just left it on my desk and completely forgot about it.

By some curious coincidence, I had to go to Shucheng County for some reason which I cannot recall and was away from home for many days. It just happened that one of Commander Du's orderlies came to my home to inquire about something; he was taken into my study and unexpectedly discovered my accusation letter. Greatly alarmed, he took it and showed it to Commander Du. They say that after Du read it, he was both furious and very frightened. He doubted that the letter was written by a child; it must have been the local Guanzhuang gentry working together to denounce him and try to get him killed. On that account he sent his people to my home to arrest me so that he could interrogate me and find out the truth behind the letter. I was away from the village, so he called the prominent members of the village together and asked them face-to-face. These village gentry did not know anything about it, and naturally they all flatly denied doing it; they all said it was just a mischievous child fooling around. Someone told me afterwards that the local gentry prepared a sumptuous banquet that very night to help dispel the commander's worries. The commander got very drunk and then almost lost his voice from crying so loudly. He said that if the accusatory letter were a plot by the residents of Guanzhuang—since he would not be able to live anyway—he would have to go on a killing rampage and have everyone involved (myself included) executed by firing squad. This was of course a threat made in an extremely emotional state, but it certainly terrified our entire village.

About one or two days after all this happened when I was returning to Guanzhuang at night from Shucheng, I went down Guanzhuang Street, the only street in the village, and when people who knew me saw me, they look terrified, just as if they had seen a ghost. Two of the older ones urged me to hurry home and not remain on the street. This was because Du Jinting's battalion headquarters was nearby, and they were afraid his men would grab me and take me there. At that time I was completely in the dark about what had happened, and it wasn't until I ran home that I found out I had landed myself in big trouble and caused great difficulty for my whole family. My family was afraid that Commander Du would get wind of my return and send troops to capture me, so they spirited me off in the night to hide in the home of a clan elder brother, medical doctor Yu Pingge. Dr. Pingge and the rest of my family kept asking me why I wrote that troublesome accusatory letter, and I could not answer them. Quite a bit of time had already passed, and I was quite unable to recount my state of mind when I wrote the letter.

This event was a major turning point in my life. In one night, I had suddenly lost my childhood innocence and entered the adult world. This change did not come from me but rather it was forced on me by the people around. Clan elder brother Pingge was a man of over forty years old and was usually very serious and careful, not given to lax speech or careless laughter. When he received me that night, the first thing he said was (his general words): "Because you were young, I have always thought of you as a child. But now that you've done such a thing, you're already an adult. From now on, I'm going to treat you differently." It was not only he but also other older friends and relatives who completely changed their attitude toward me and began to treat me as an adult; they even jokingly called me "Little Mister" (*xiao xiansheng* 小先生). This sudden transformation ended my childhood. From then on, I was forced to be careful about everything I said and did to avoid people making fun of me. This unexpected incident forced me onto the path of "an elderly young man," and it was unnatural in the process of my maturation.

There was, however, a good ending to this incident. A little while later, Commander Du probably came to accept the village elders' explanation and believed that the letter was a prank played by a mischievous child. Nevertheless, he dispatched a rather well-educated political instructor to talk to us.[13] My clanspeople arranged for this political instructor to have dinner with me so that he could also test me on my knowledge of poetry. In the end, he was convinced that I had indeed written the offending letter and that I had no real intention of filing an accusation against Commander Du. I remember that when the political instructor left, he shook my hand firmly, expressing that he wanted to be friends with me despite the difference in our ages—and that was how the curtain fell on that farce.

PART THREE: THE NATURE OF THE MAY FOURTH MOVEMENT

Presented earlier was the general state of education and culture in Guanzhuang from 1937 to 1946. Today's reader might want to ask why

—twenty years after the May Fourth Movement—my hometown still had not made any contact with the new modern culture. To answer this question, I have to explain how I myself came to know about the May Fourth Movement. Given that May Fourth was the "prehistory" phase of my own education, I should also explain my understanding of its fundamental character.

The first time I heard the name Chen Duxiu (1979–1942) and the first time I encountered Hu Shi's vernacular poetry was probably when I was eleven or twelve years old and had just learned to read. Coincidentally, both men were from Anhui—Hu Shi came from Jixi County, and Chen Duxiu was born in Huaining County in Anqing (a county neighboring Qianshan). At this juncture, it would be an opportune time to sort out my understanding of the May Fourth Movement.[14]

The May Fourth Movement is too large a subject for a full-scale discussion here. I am only going to talk about the process of my changing understanding of the May Fourth Movement from the countryside to the present. I have been constantly changing and revising my understanding of the May Fourth Movement, and my final view is probably very different from today's mainstream view. I just wish to express my own viewpoint frankly; I neither believe it to be infallible nor have I any intention of persuading others to agree with my position.

The first time I learned of Chen Duxiu was when I heard that he once at a public gathering tried to undermine the traditional foundations of "filial piety" (xiao 孝) by writing that "parents' desire for sex is not because they want to have children." It was said that he openly advocated that "the greatest of the ten thousand evils is filial piety, and the best of the hundred forms of conduct is lewdness." In reality, these were false rumors spread by opposing conservative or reactionary factions and had no basis in fact. The first sentence was an altered version of Wang Chong's (27–100) famous words: "When husband and wife engage in sexual intercourse, it is not because they want to give birth to children. Their sexual desire being aroused they come together, and from that they give birth to children."[15] After this idea was elaborated on by Kong Rong (153–208) and Mi Heng (173–198) at the end of the Han dynasty (202 BCE–220 CE), it eventually spread throughout China, and in recent times it was wrongly attributed to Chen Duxiu. The second phrase turns an original Confucian maxim upside down with the malicious intent of falsely incriminating Chen Duxiu. Hu Shi in particular refuted these rumors about Chen in 1933 at the University of Chicago, when he gave a series of lectures entitled "The Chinese Renaissance." It is clear that Chen Duxiu was *persona non grata* in his hometown; as the Western people's saying goes, "a prophet has no honor in his own country."[16]

It was through his poetry and calligraphy that I first encountered Hu Shi. In the attic of my old home, I turned up a wall scroll that Hu had given to my father on which he had written one of his own five-character quatrains:

> Wind wafting over Serene Mirror Lake,
> Gives rise to light ripples on the surface.
> When the lake becomes even more mirror smooth,
> It is still hard to return to its former state.[17]

His calligraphy was very graceful with elongated characters, but they were not those of a calligrapher; they were typical literati characters. Because he had written it for my father, I felt a sense of closeness to Hu Shi. Later on, I discovered his *Experimental Collection* (*Changshi ji* 嘗試集) and, although I thought the new-style poetry quite novel, I did not really appreciate it.[18] I still preferred his old-style poetry or his simple old-style poems resembling ordinary speech like "Wind Wafting Over Serene Mirror Lake."

This was the limited extent of what I knew about Chen Duxiu and Hu Shi when I was in the countryside. I was completely unaware of the relationship between them and even less aware of "May Fourth." A poem Wang Xinggong (1887–1949) gave to Hu Shi has the following two lines:

> Valuing the beginning of national history

> pioneered in literary circles,
> In those days everyone talked about Chen and Hu.

Before 1946 I had not heard about the "literary revolution" created by Chen Duxiu and Hu Shi. It took time for the influence of the May Fourth Movement to spread. For example, *The Diary of Hu Shi* (*Hu Shi riji* 胡適日記) records that on July 24, 1922, during the Peking University preparatory examinations, a middle school (junior high) student from Fengtian (old name for Shenyang, also known as Mukden) asked Hu Shi "What is the May Fourth Movement?" Astonished, Hu went around to the other examination sites to enquire about this, and the invigilators told him that at least a dozen or so examinees did not know what the May Fourth Movement was. This was only three years after the May Fourth demonstrations of 1919, and quite a few students had already forgotten it or had basically never paid it any attention.[19] Thus we should not excessively exaggerate the influence of the May Fourth and imagine that immediately after the May Fourth Movement the spiritual countenance of all of China was completely renewed.

After 1946 when I returned to the city and attended upper middle school (senior high) and university, I came to understand the sequence of events in the May Fourth Movement. First off, at that time people in general did not understand the May Fourth Movement as limited to the patriotic student demonstration of the single day of May 4, 1919. We all considered the May Fourth Movement as equivalent to the literary and intellectual movements since 1917. The first point was that the vernacular language (*baihua* 白話) replaced classical Chinese (*wenyan*) as a medium of writing, combining both the elegant (elite) and the vulgar (popular). This was the so-called "literary revolution" brought about at Hu Shi's initiation and with Chen Duxiu's support. Second were the ceaseless attacks on the old Confucian code of ethics (*lijiao* 禮教) and the propagation of new ideas by Chen Duxiu, Hu Shi, and other scholars of their generation—through publications like *New Youth* (*Xin Qingnian* 新青年; also titled *La Jeunesse*) and *New Tide* (*Xin Chao* 新潮), also titled *The Renaissance*) and in the lecture halls of Peking University that stirred up the young students' passionate search for the new and for change. The "May Fourth" student demonstration happened precisely because the students' knowledge and thought underwent a fundamental transformation over a period of two to three years. When Sun Yat-sen (Sun Zhongshan, (1866–1925) observed the situation in Beijing from the south, he reached the same conclusion.

In 1919, Hu Shi wrote an essay entitled "The Meaning of the New Thought" ("Xin sixiang de yiyi" 新思想的意義) in which he advocated a program of four guiding principles of "studying problems, importing theories, re-organizing the national heritage, and rebuilding a civilization."[20] This was quite representative of contemporary thought and was generally acceptable to most people. In this essay, he used the term "New Thought Movement" to define the nature of the May Fourth Movement. Later some people also used "New Culture Movement" or "New Thought Movement," but they were actually more or less the same. In sum, most people understood the May Fourth Movement to be a movement for innovation in thought, culture, and knowledge that lasted over ten years from beginning to end and had a tremendous impact over the course of its long life.

The student protest on May 4, 1919, was a concrete example of the impact of this movement. If we try to understand this day as an isolated event, we have no way of explaining it. There are quite a few people today who emphasize this one day of student protest and define the May Fourth Movement as a "patriotic movement," but that makes one suspicious that they are deliberately hollowing out the spiritual content of May Fourth. The "patriotic" movement of Chinese intellectuals against the encroachment of foreign great powers broke out as early as the late Qing dynasty (1644–1911). Why should we wait until 1919 to date this? If the significance of the May Fourth Movement is "patriotism," then what is the difference between it and other similar movements like, for example, the Public Vehicle Petition of 1895 which pushed for reforms and against the Treaty of Shimonoseki? Thus, although I admit that "patriotism" was the fundamental motive force behind the entire May Fourth Movement (including the student demonstration on May 4, 1919), I have to point out that "patriotism" was the commonly shared sentiment of Chinese intellectuals ever since the second half of the nineteenth century—it was not a characteristic of the May Fourth Movement alone.[21]

The aforementioned represents my general understanding of the May Fourth Movement, and it has not changed greatly. On further analysis, however, the nature of the May Fourth Movement contains extremely complex questions, and my early and later views are thus dissimilar.

First, I would like to explain that when I returned to the city after the end of the Second World War, the earliest extracurricular book I read was *The Selected Writings of Hu Shi* (*Hu Shi wencun* 胡適文存).[22] I felt that the story of the origin of vernacular writing (*baihuawen*) was extremely interesting, and because of that I unintentionally began to accept Hu Shi's interpretation of the May Fourth Movement.

Early on when Hu Shi was advocating Chinese vernacular writing in the United States, he noticed how during the Italian Renaissance the written native Italian colloquial speech rose to replace Latin.[23] This phenomenon did not occur only in Italy but also other European nations. Hu Shi believed that because of this, it was of great significance to replace classical Chinese with the vernacular language and liberate China from the medieval to the modern world. In 1917 when Hu returned to Peking University to teach, vernacular writing had not only become popular throughout the nation and achieved unexpected success, but it also had a great influence on both learning and thought. In 1918 when Peking University students Fu Sinian (1896–1950), Gu Jiegang (1893–1980), and others were planning to publish a journal, *New Tide* (*Xinchao*), advocating new thought, Hu Shi did not have the least hesitation in giving it the English title "Renaissance."[24]

In the year 1919 when the student protest broke out, Hu was already conscious that he was promoting an important "Chinese Renaissance" movement. In addition to the vernacular replacing the classical language, he went on to emphasize that whether in the realms of thought, learning, or literature, a "Chinese Renaissance" had been going on constantly since the eleventh and twelfth centuries. Here are some examples he cited: Song-dynasty Neo-Confucianism was a liberation from medieval Buddhism, from withdrawal from worldly affairs to entering the secular world; from the Yuan and Ming dynasties on, the rise of vernacular fiction and drama laid down the foundations for the modern vernacular literature of the May Fourth period; the Qing-dynasty evidential investigation (*kaozheng xue* 考證學) was a new development of the "scientific method" in the realm of the Chinese humanities and it nicely coincided with the Italian humanist Lorenzo Valla's (1407–1457) detection of forgeries through textual criticism. In all these areas, the East and the West corresponded, and Hu Shi portrayed the May Fourth Movement as being similar to the European Renaissance. From then on, when he lectured in China and abroad, he always called the May Fourth Movement the "Chinese Renaissance."

At the same time, I had read *Outline of Qing Dynasty Scholarship* (*Qingdai xueshu gailun* 清代學術概論; 1920) by Liang Qichao (1873–1929), who compared Qing learning to the European Renaissance; because of this I became very convinced of the idea of a Chinese Renaissance.[25] This was why I decided to minor in European Renaissance and Reformation when I entered the Harvard University graduate school in 1956. I hoped to understand the process of change in twentieth-century Chinese thought and culture through studying the archetype of the European Renaissance.

After in-depth readings of several specialist studies by Western historians concerning the Renaissance, however, I discovered that the May Fourth Movement and the European Renaissance cannot be analyzed on equal terms. Their few superficial similarities cannot prevail over the substantial differences between these two big movements. Even with the idea that they began with vernacular languages replacing a classical language, one absolutely cannot draw indiscriminate analogies with the relations between European vernacular languages and Latin. The other differences between China and Europe in terms of thought and learning, each having their own distinct backgrounds, also override any similarities. In 1959 I published an article entitled "The Renaissance and the Humanist Thought Tide" ("Wenyi fuxing yu renwen sichao" 文藝 復興與人文思潮) in which I, for the first time, publicly expressed my doubts about the "Renaissance theory" about China.[26]

In 1933, Hu Shi gave a series of lectures entitled "The Chinese Renaissance" at the University of Chicago that were later published as a book with the same title. He used the following words to describe the movement of Peking University professors and students to promote the new tides of thought from 1917 through 1919: "It was a movement of freedom versus authority, reason versus tradition, praising the value of life and the individual human being in resistance to oppression." This description is more like a portrait of the eighteenth-century European Enlightenment, but it is not applicable to the Renaissance. It is also worth noting that it was precisely from the 1930s on that comparing the May Fourth Movement to the European Enlightenment began to be popular among Chinese intellectual circles, and soon the "Enlightenment theory" usurped the position of the "Renaissance theory." It was primarily the Chinese Marxists who promoted this new doctrine.

In eighteenth-century Europe, the voluminous works of Voltaire offered many sharp attacks on the darkness of the Middle Ages and the Catholic Church's oppression. Denis Diderot sent Voltaire a letter thanking him for exciting "in our hearts an intense hatred of lying, ignorance, hypocrisy, superstition, tyranny."[27] On this point, some of the writings of Chen Duxiu, Lu Xun (1881–1936), Hu Shi, Qian Xuantong (1887–1939), and others during the May Fourth period certainly also had similar effects.[28] Indeed, the May Fourth Movement can be said to have some elements that are comparable to the European Enlightenment: on the destructive side, there is the smashing of idols and the attacking the "Confucian Curiosity Shop" and the old Confucian code of ethics, while on the positive side there was the advocating for "progress," "reason," and "science." This is, I believe, because the proponents of the May Fourth Movement were all directly or indirectly influenced by Western Enlightenment thought.

However, if we look more deeply at the historical and cultural backgrounds of the European Enlightenment and the May Fourth Movement, we will see that they are utterly different. On no account should we maintain that the Chinese May Fourth is the equivalent of the European Enlightenment. I used to read widely on this subject in the research conclusions of the leading Western experts such as Carl L. Becker (1873–1945) and Peter Gay (1923–2015) of the United States. Peter Gay and I worked together at Yale University for ten years and had considerable private exchanges in which we discussed the question of the nature of the European Enlightenment. The final views that I arrived at then were more or less the same as my views on the "Chinese Renaissance theory," and so, in 1998, I published an essay entitled "Neither Renaissance Nor Enlightenment: A Historian's Reflections on the May Fourth Movement."[29] Simply put, the spiritual fountainhead of the Renaissance and the Enlightenment in Europe was the classical thought of ancient Greece and Rome; they were internal developments of European culture. By contrast, the May Fourth Movement was mainly a response to the incursions of Western culture into China. Although the elements intrinsic to Chinese culture did help in introducing and connecting with Western ideas, its spiritual fountainheads were not Confucian, Buddhist, or Daoist —they were Western.

I do not deny that the European Renaissance and Enlightenment both had some influence on the emergence of the new thought tides brought about by the May Fourth Movement, but the May Fourth Movement was a unique event in the modern history of Chinese thought and culture; nothing like it was seen in the West. If anyone insists that the May Fourth Movement and the European Renaissance and Enlightenment must be mutually comparable, they are falling into the trap of an extremely dangerous and completely unsupported historical presupposition. That is the so-called "law of historical inevitability" or the belief that all nations (*minzu* 民族) or civilizations must inevitably pass through the same stages of development—since the West developed one step earlier than China, then China naturally has to blindly follow suit, and every movement that has occurred in the West must definitely be repeated in China. Today's historical knowledge does not, however, permit us to accept such a presupposition blindly.

To sum up then, in my early years I did not have very strong negative reactions to the aforementioned comparisons. I even believed that there were reasons for holding such views and no reason to think that they could not coexist. After reading more deeply on studies of the Renaissance and the Enlightenment, I discovered that these comparisons contain more misguided than helpful information; what is gained by them certainly cannot make up for what is lost, and there is really no need to make these comparisons.

In the process of continuously revising my understanding of the May Fourth Movement, there was one change that is especially noteworthy. From my early years into middle age, I always accepted the popular view that the May Fourth Movement was completely opposed to the Chinese cultural tradition and specifically opposed to Confucianism. Because of this, from beginning to end the May Fourth Movement was a historical process of thoroughgoing radicalism, and the pace of its radicalization increased day by day. In the last decade, however, I have come to feel that this view needs to be reexamined. This tide of radical thinking was indubitably present in the May Fourth Movement, but it cannot represent the entire New Culture Movement or New Thought Movement. Even within *New Youth* magazine, after the student movement of May 4, 1919, its various leaders had already begun to separate into "left" and "right" factions—some like Chen Duxiu and Li Dazhao (1889–1927) moved toward the "political left," while others like Hu Shi and Tao Menghe (1887–1960) came to be regarded as politically "right wing."[30] This left-right split arose primarily due to their different attitudes toward political activities. The radical faction demanded "revolutionary action," while the moderate faction still wanted to continue their explorations in the literary, intellectual, and academic realms—they only wanted to comment critically on politics but not participate in it in practice.

In reality, once we consider the May Fourth Movement as a long-lasting movement of new culture or new thought (like what are known as the "Renaissance" and the "Enlightenment") and do not unduly emphasize its political aspects, we will immediately see that the aforementioned radicalization view is ill-founded.

In his 1919 essay, "The Meaning of New Thought" (mentioned earlier), Hu Shi only proposed that a "critical attitude" should be the common spirit of every participant in the New Thought Movement. He went on to emphasize that this "critical attitude" should be manifest in three areas: "studying problems, importing theories, and re-organizing the national heritage" ("rebuilding a civilization" was to be the ultimate outcome). *Hu Shi's Hand-Written Manuscripts* (*Hu Shi shougao* 胡適手稿) has a long unfinished essay from 1955 entitled "The Cleansing Power of Anti-Violence, Left Behind by the Chinese Renaissance Movement Over the Past Forty Years—The Historical Significance of the Chinese Communist Party's Liquidation of Hu Shi's Thought." In it, he has an even clearer elucidation of these three areas:[31]

> The first means to study the various questions of contemporary society, politics, religion, and literature; the second means to import foreign thought, scientific theories, and literature; the third means to carry out a systematic re-organization of all our old thought and learning, and this work can be called "re-organizing the national heritage."

From this explanation, we can immediately see that these three areas would all require the long-term efforts of countless numbers of intellectuals before they could obtain real achievements. We cannot imagine that everyone participating in this practical work would have to first adopt an anti-traditional and anti-Confucian ideological standpoint. Regardless of whether they are "studying problems, importing theories, [or] re-organizing the national heritage," it is sufficient to require that these knowledge workers have a "critical attitude." Their individual intellectual or belief orientations are completely irrelevant.

Firstly, let me give a few examples of "re-organizing the national heritage" to explain what I mean. In the so-called "New Culture Movement," the area that produced the most long-lasting scholarly achievements was that of "re-organizing the national heritage." Of the major scholars who emerged in this area, the overwhelming majority identified with the Chinese cultural tradition and Confucian values. The most celebrated among them were Liang Qichao, Wang Guowei (1877–1927), Chen Yinque (or Yinke, 1890–1969), Tang Yongtong (1893–1964), Qian Mu, and Feng Youlan (1895–1990).[32] Their scholarship is recognized throughout the world as having reached the highest levels of modern learning.

Wang Guowei is especially worthy of our attention.[33] In terms of thought and belief, he can be said to have been the most conservative, but when it came to the "scientific nature" of his writings, all of those purportedly radical scholars such as Hu Shi and Guo Moruo (1892–1978) had the utmost esteem for him. If we exclude these eminent scholars in the study of Chinese national culture (*guoxue* 國學) from the "new culture" because they were not anti-tradition and opposed to traditional Confucian morality, then the May Fourth Movement would be reduced to slogans emptily shouted in an academic wasteland.

Secondly, allow me to discuss another example outside the area of "reorganizing the national heritage." Liang Shuming's (1893–1988) lectures collected in a book entitled *Eastern and Western Cultures and Their Philosophies* (*Dong-Xi-fang wenhua ji qi zhexue* 東西方文化及其哲學) was a work that caused a stir for a time after the May Fourth Movement.[34] In scope it belonged to the realm of "studying problems." This series of lectures is based on a foundation of praise for Chinese culture and veneration of Confucius, and at the time it was regarded as an "anti–May Fourth" voice. However, in this book Liang Shuming repeatedly emphasized that China must completely accept the two marvelous trea-sures (*fabao* 法寶; a Buddhist term) of democracy and science before it would be able again to revitalize Chinese culture and allow it to occupy its rightful position in the modern world. I was once amazed to discover that in 1926 when Hu Shi lectured on the "Chinese Renaissance" at several British universities, he cited Liang Shuming and his works many times as an example of it. This demonstrates that the new generation of Chinese scholars had already accepted without the slightest doubt the mainstream values of Western culture. From this we can see that at least in Hu Shi's mind, even though Liang Shuming embraced Chinese culture and Confucianism, Liang could still be considered a "kindred spirit," that is, an organic member of Hu's "Chinese Renaissance."

Thirdly, let us consider briefly the journal *The Critical Review* (*Xueheng* 學衡; 1922–1933), launched by Mei Guangdi (1890–1945), Wu Mi (1894–1978), and others, in terms of "importing theories." This journal was published precisely to counter Hu Shi's movement for vernacular writing and was regarded from its inception as an opponent by the leaders of the May Fourth Movement. On closer observation, however, we can see that the situation was not that simple. *The Critical Review* spared no effort in its introduction to the theory of New Humanism by the American literary scholar and critic Irving Babbitt (1865–1933), and this had considerable influence on Chinese literary and intellectual circles after May Fourth.

Babbitt's humanism was an attempt to combine the spiritual or mental cultivation of Confucius's "teaching by being a personal role model" (*shen-jiao* 身教) with Western ideas of the "rule of law" (*fazhi* 法治) and democracy since the ancient Greeks. His celebrated 1924 book *Democracy and Leadership* especially developed these views.[35] He advocated Classicism in literature and criticized the Romanticism that has persisted since Jean-Jacques Rousseau (1712–1778). Although in the 1920s and 1930s, the "progressives" considered him to be a conservative, in the 1980s many of them, for example the historian Arthur Schlesinger, Jr.

(1917–2007) noted that Babbitt had some outstanding ideas that had been buried in oblivion for several decades.

When Babbitt's views were introduced to China, it was also a major event. It is especially worth mentioning that those who thought highly of Babbitt were not limited to Mei Guangdi, Wu Mi, and the like. Major followers of the vernacular literature movement, like Lin Yutang (1895–1976) and Liang Shiqiu (1903–1987), also greatly admired Babbitt and attended his classes at Harvard.[36] After seeking Wu Mi's permission, Liang Shiqiu collected all the articles about Babbitt and other similarly related works from *The Critical Review* and published them in a book entitled *The Humanism of Irving Babbitt* (*Baibide de renwen zhuyi* 白璧德的人文主義), and the publisher was none other than the Crescent Moon Bookstore, headquarters of the New Culture Movement. Babbitt's work was therefore an unequivocal part of the New Culture after the May Fourth Movement despite the fact that he advocated for Confucius and the Confucian tradition.

Mei Guangdi was a disciple of Babbitt's and strongly supported the central value of democracy. Mei criticized Hu Shi's ideas about literature in *The Critical Review*, but at the same time he wrote a letter to Hu and praised Hu's discussion of politics, which he noted were "mostly in accord with my views" and "of benefit to society." This clearly shows that in politics Mei was a moderate reformer. How then can we strike him out of the "new culture" or "new thought" with a single stroke simply because he did not approve of vernacular writing?

Lastly, I still want to add one more example to emphasize my point. I've already mentioned Liang Shiqiu's relationship with Irving Babbitt and his collaboration with *The Critical Review*. The experience of another Tsinghua University student, Xiao Gongquan (K. C. Hsiao, 1897–1981), reinforces my point even more. He participated in the May 4, 1919 student demonstrations, and then he went to Tianjin with other students to set up a newspaper and enthusiastically promoted the movement. Later on, he specialized in the study of political philosophy and had many accomplishments in the area of "importing theories." His two-volume *History of Chinese Political Thought* (*Zhongguo zhengzhi sixiangshi* 中國政治思想史) is a masterpiece in "re-organizing the national heritage."[37] Xiao Gongquan also wrote a great deal on education and constitutional democracy, and thus he also had outstanding achievements in the area of "studying problems."

There can be no doubt about Xiao's many contributions to the New Culture Movement, and yet if we examine his attitude toward Chinese culture and Confucius, we find him to be quite conservative. For example, he had great praise for the traditional Chinese family structure because both his parents died when he was very young, which resulted in his complete dependency on his uncle and aunt (his father's elder brother and his wife) for his upbringing as well as other extended family "brothers" for their support. He firmly stated that "I feel that the attacks on the old traditional family by the 'New Culture Movement' are too extreme." He also criticized the promotion of vernacular writing for going too far, and he disapproved even more so of the slogan "down with the Confucian Curiosity Shop." As for his literary tastes, he was extremely proficient in the composition of old-style poetry and lyrics (*shici* 詩詞), which he had loved since childhood. Given this, when Xiao Gongquan taught at Tsinghua University, he and Wu Mi became close friends. Wu Mi said that when the two of them "discussed the Way, literature, and events, they were always in close agreement because they both tended toward the active idealism of the West."

I believe that these examples amply demonstrate that participants in the New Culture Movement did not necessarily have to be anti-traditional, anti-Confucian radicals. On the contrary, the individuals who made genuine contributions to the "New Culture" were those scholars who were both the most rational and the most willing to work hard over the long term. In the end, those who wildly shouted radical slogans often went into political activism and made few accomplishments in the "New Culture."

I have now given an extremely brief and simple account of my understanding of the May Fourth Movement as well as my earlier and later
views of it. My current understanding can be summarized as follows:
The core problem of the so-called "New Culture Movement" of the
May Fourth period was how to receive and accept several central ideas
and values of the modern West and make them relate to China's traditional culture in order to lead China into comprehensive modernization
without losing its original cultural identity. The earliest expression of
this position was stated in Hu Shi's preface to his 1917 Columbia University doctoral dissertation, "The Development of the Logical Method in
Ancient China."[38] The exploration of this problem began in the late
Qing, but only before and after the "May Fourth" did it become explicit
and grow into a large-scale, systematic, long-term movement. This was
because the intellectual leaders of the May Fourth period already had
direct understanding of Western knowledge and thought, a situation
completely different from their predecessors, like Liang Qichao, who
had only indirect knowledge passed on from Japan. From this we can
see that considered as a movement of intellectual or cultural innovation,
"May Fourth" occurred at a particular turning point in modern Chinese
history, and its spiritual resources came from the West. By contrast, the
European Renaissance and Enlightenment were internal developments
in Western culture, and their spiritual resources came from a revival of
classical Greek and Roman culture. This is why I firmly maintain that
the May Fourth Movement cannot be mutually compared with these
two European movements.

The May Fourth Movement and the two European movements do have
a certain number of areas in which they are superficially similar. The
reason for these superficial resemblances is not hard to understand. The
intellectual leaders of the "May Fourth" generation came to maturity
under the intense stimulation of modern Western culture. Many of
the concepts and the language they employed were indirectly passed
down from the European Renaissance and Enlightenment. Moreover,
because they were inspired by modern Western history, they often

could not help hoping that China would also create its own Renaissance and Enlightenment. In the final analysis, it would be better to examine linguistic and psychological factors as to why the May Fourth Movement shared some characteristics of the two Western movements; after all, China did not share the same conditions as Europe, which would lead to Chinese history following the same path as Europe's.

In discussing the central ideas and values of the modern West, we must mention especially the two that are known to everyone: "democracy" and "science." In 1918, Chen Duxiu published an article entitled "A Reply to Criminal Accusations Against this Magazine" (*Benzhi zui-an zhi dabianshu* 本誌罪案之答辯書) in which he wrote that there were two big charges against *New Youth*: the first was supporting Mr. Democracy (*Demokelaxi xiansheng* 德莫克拉西先生), and the second was supporting Mr. Science (*Saiyisi xiansheng* 賽因斯先生).[39] For ninety years now, "democracy" and "science" have always been held up as two major "values" that China must pursue. Of course, there are some other values that are related to these two. For example, "freedom" or "liberty" (*ziyou* 自由) is a necessary precondition for "democracy" and "science," and "human rights" (*renquan* 人權) constitute the ultimate goal to be achieved through "democracy." In short, Chen Duxiu's selection of these two major "values" as the central objectives of the "New Culture Movement" or the "New Thought Tide" was collectively acknowledged by his contemporary Chinese intellectual circles—and Chen's essay was written even before the May Fourth student movement broke out.

It must be pointed out that the introduction of the concepts of science and democracy into China also began as early as the second half of the nineteenth century. What I want to emphasize, though, is that Chen Duxiu's introduction of the two major "values" of "Mr. Democracy" (*De xiansheng*) and "Mr. Science" (*Sai xiansheng*) in this unusual manner had its own symbolic significance; that is, from that time on, "democracy" and "science" became officially naturalized "citizens" of China and inseparable elements of a modernized China. During the late Qing, "science" was still known as "Western learning" (*Xixue* 西學), but it was changed to our common modern term *kexue* 科學 after the Xinhai Revolution of 1911. Similarly, Zhang Zhidong (1837–1909), the famous Qing official and reformer, wrote of it as "Western politics" or "Western government" (*Xizheng* 西政), but after the collapse of the imperial system, groups that were either striving to gain political power or to protect their political power all spoke of "democracy" to increase their appeal, and this demonstrated that "democracy" had already been Sinicized.

Today if we look back at May Fourth in the broadest sense, we cannot but admit that "democracy" and "science" together are the most important legacies the movement bequeathed to us. Although Mr. Democracy and Mr. Science have been naturalized Chinese "citizens" for a long time now, they still have not generally settled down and set up shop in the great land of China. "Science" in China has been primarily manifest as "technology," a "skill" or "technique" (*yi* 藝), but not a "Way" or "principle" (*dao* 道). The spirit of truth for truth's sake has not yet been sufficiently established. The status of "democracy" is one of "respect" but not "intimacy," and we frequently hear loud demands that its citizenship be revoked and that it be sent back to the West. Precisely because of this situation, I cannot help lamenting that the "May Fourth has not yet been completed." Speaking from the point of view of its "not yet being completed," the May Fourth Movement, as a stirring campaign that surged forward with great momentum, is not only rich in historical significance but also radiant with genuinely familiar meaning for us today.

NOTES

1. The pinyin romanization system is used throughout this translation with the exception of well-known figures like Sun Yat-sen and Chiang Kai-shek. In keeping with this, we have used Yu Xiezhong rather than Yü Xiezhong for Yü Ying-shih's father, but we have retained "Yü" for Yü Ying-shih because he is so named in many other English books. Yu Ying-shih is used only on page iv to accord with the Library of Congress Cataloging-in-Publication Data system.

2. Chen Yuan was a well-known scholar of Chinese history, president of several Chinese universities, and the first director of the Harvard-Yenching Institute at Yenching University.

3. In China the Second World War is referred to as the Anti-Japanese War of Resistance, or simply the War of Resistance. For a thorough study, see Hans van de Ven, *China at War: Triumph and Tragedy in the Emergence of the New China* (Cambridge, MA: Harvard University Press, 2018).

4. Fan Wenlan was a Marxist historian of China and the author of a multivolume *Zhongguo tongshi* 中國通史 [General history of China] (Beijing: Renmin chubanshe, 1956) and many other books on Chinese history.

5. Hong Ye (William Hung) was a Chinese historian who taught at Yenching and Harvard universities; he is well-known for his work on Du Fu, and for editing the Harvard-Yenching Index Series.

6. The *Xiyang tongshi* (Taipei: Qimeng shuju, 1928) has been republished many times.

7. Fang Bao and Yao Nai were Qing-dynasty scholars and poets of the Tongcheng School of simple and unadorned ancient prose writing.

8. Both Zhang Ying and his second son Zhang Tingyu were prominent officials in the Qing dynasty.

9. A well-known allusion to the meticulous poetry of Jia Dao, who found it hard to decide whether to write "push" or "knock" on a gate in one of his poems.

10. See Yü Ying-shih, *Zhuzi wenji, xu* 朱子文集, 序 [Preface to Zhu Xi's essays], in *Zhuzi wenji*, vol. 1, ed. Chen Junmin, (Taipei: Defu wenjiao jijinhui, 2000), 13–26. Yü Ying-shih, *Zhu Xi de lishi shijie: Songdai shidafu zhengzhi wenhua de yanjiu* [Historical world of Zhu Xi: a study of the political culture of Song intellectuals] (Taipei: Yunchen, 2003; Beijing: Sanlian, 2011).

11. Weng Zhiyu (1968–2015), "Jiechu huaren" [Outstanding Chinese], January 6, 2008, http://appl.rthk.org.hk/php/tvarchivecatalog/episode.php?progid=554&tvcat=2.

12. Li Zongren (Li Tsung-jen) was a leader of the Guangxi warlord clique along with Huang Shaohong and Bai Chongxi; Li was later vice president and acting president of the Republic of China. See David Bonavia, *China's Warlords* (New York: Oxford University Press. 1995); and Li Tsung-jen, and Tong Te-kong, *The Memoirs of Li Tsung-jen* (Boulder, CO: Westview Press. 1979).

13. A "political instructor" is an officer in charge of political propaganda.

14. Chen Duxiu and Hu Shi were the two most important leaders of the May Fourth Movement, but Chen was a radical and Hu was a moderate. See Chou Ts'e-tsung, *The May Fourth Movement: Intellectual Revolution in Modern China* (Cambridge, MA: Harvard University Press, 1960).

15. Wang Chong (27–ca. 97?), *Balanced Inquiries* (*Lunheng* 論衡) quotation is from the "Tendencies of Things," 物勢 *Wushi* chapter, see https://ctext.org/lunheng/wu-shi/zh?searchu=夫婦合氣，非當時欲得生子，情欲動而合，合而生子矣%E3%80%82.

16. Hu Shi, *The Chinese Renaissance: The Haskell Lectures, 1933* (Chicago, IL: University of Chicago Press, 1934). John 4:44: "Now Jesus himself had pointed out that a prophet has no honour in his own country."

17. Jingpinghu 鏡平湖 (Mirror-Smooth Lake; literally meaning a lake smooth as a mirror) is a popular scenic spot in Jiangsu Province. This poem is collected in Hu Shi, *Hu Shi Jingxuan ji* (Beijing: Yanshan, 2013).

18. See a recent publication of Hu Shi's *Changshi ji* (Xinbeishi: Huamulan wenhua, 2016).

19. See Chou Ts'e-tsung, *The May Fourth Movement*, for the distinction between the demonstration of May 4, 1919, and the overall New Culture Movement.

20. "Xin sixiang de yiyi" was originally published in *Xin Qingnian*, 7, no. 1 (December 1, 1919).

21. Yü Ying-shih uses *zhishiren* 知識人—people with knowledge—rather than the usual *zhishi fenzi* 知識份子, but we will usually translate it as "intellectual."

22. Since the 1921 edition published by Beida chubanbu (Beiping), there have been many subsequent editions of Hu Shi's selected writings. For example, *Hu Shi wencun, ba juan* (Taipei: Yuandong, 1985).

23. Yü Ying-shih note: Hu Shi originally used the term "dialect or patois" (*tuyu* 土語), and I have previously used it, but now I have

replaced it with "native colloquial" (*bentu suyu* 本土俗語) to accommodate readers in Taiwan.

24. Fu Sinian was one of the student leaders of the May Fourth Movement, a celebrated educator, one of the founders of the Institute of History and Philology of the Academia Sinica, acting president of Peking University (1945–1946), and president of National Taiwan University (1949–1950). Gu Jiegang was a famous Chinese historian, editor of the multivolume *Gushi Bian* [Debates on ancient Chinese history], and a leading "doubter" of antiquity. See Wang Fan-shen, *Fu Ssu-nien: A life in Chinese History and Politics* (New York: Cambridge University Press, 2000); and Laurence A. Schneider, *Ku Chieh-kang and China's New History: Nationalism and the Quest for Alternative Traditions* (Berkeley: University of California Press, 1971).

25. Liang Qichao was a scholar and major reformer of the late Qing and early Republican period. His *Qingdai xueshu gailun* [Outline of Qing dynasty scholarship] (Taipei: Zhonghua shuju, 1959) was very influential. It has been translated by Immanuel C. Y. Hsü as *Intellectual Trends in the Ch'ing Period* (Cambridge, MA: Harvard University Press, 1959).

26. "Wenyi fuxing yu renwen sichao" [Renaissance and humanistic thought tides] was published in *Xinya shuyuan xueshu niankan* [New Asia College academic annual] 1, (October 1959).

27. Yü Ying-shih note: Quoted in Carl L. Becker, *The Heavenly City of the Eighteenth-Century Philosophers* (New Haven, CT: Yale University Press, 1932), 92.

28. A friend of Lu Xun's, Qian Xuantong was a Professor of Literature at Peking University, who advocated the abolition of classical Chinese. See Chou Ts'e-tsung, *The May Fourth Movement.*

29. This article was originally published in Milena Doleželová-Velingerová and Oldrich Král, eds., *The Appropriation of Cultural Capital: China's May Fourth Cultural Project* (Cambridge, MA: Harvard University Asia Center, 2001), 299–324. It was more recently reprinted in Yü Ying-shih, *Chinese History and Culture*, Vol. 2: *Seventeenth Century through Twentieth Century* (New York: Columbia University Press, 2016), 198–218.

30. Li Dazhao was a cofounder, with Chen Duxiu, of the Chinese Communist Party in 1921. He was executed in April 1927 on the orders of warlord Zhang Zuolin. Tao Menghe was a sociologist who remained in China after 1949 and died before the Cultural Revolution. See Maurice Meisner, *Li Ta-Chao and the Origins of Chinese Marxism* (Cambridge, MA: Harvard University Press, 1967).

31. Yü Ying-shih note: *Hu Shi's Hand-Written Manuscripts* (Taipei: Hu Shi jinian guan, 1966–1970).
32. A historian, Qian Mu was founder and president of the New Asia College in Hong Kong, and the author of the widely read *Guoshi dagang* [A general history of China] (Chongqing: Shangwu yinshuguan, 1943). English readers may be interested in Ch'ien Mu, *Traditional Government in Imperial China: a Critical Analysis*, translated by Chün-tu Hsueh and George O. Totten (Hong Kong: Chinese University Press and New York: St. Martin's Press, 1982); and Jerry Dennerline, *Qian Mu and the World of Seven Mansions* (New Haven, CT: Yale University Press, 1988).
33. Wang Guowei was a poet and a most important scholar who made significant contributions to the study of the *jiaguwen* "oracle bones," the *Dream of the Red Chamber*, and Chinese drama and poetry criticism. See Joey Bonney, *Wang Kuo-wei: An Intellectual Biography* (Cambridge, MA: Harvard University Press, 1986).
34. Liang Shuming, *Dong-Xi-fang wenhua ji qi zhexue* (Shanghai: Shangwu Yinshuguan, 1921). See also Guy S. Alitto, *The Last Confucian: Liang Shuming and the Chinese Dilemma of Modernity* (Berkeley: University of California Press, 1979).
35. Irving, Babbitt, *Democracy and Leadership* (Boston: Houghton Mifflin 1924).
36. Lin Yutang was well known for his popular books like *My Country and My People* (New York: Reynal & Hitchcock, Inc., 1935). Liang Shiqiu was a Professor of English at Peking University and editor of the *Crescent Moon Monthly*. See Chou Ts'e-tsung, *The May Fourth Movement*.
37. Published in 1945 by Shangwu Yinshuguan of Chongqing, volume 1 is available in English translation by Frederick W. Mote as *A History of Chinese Political Thought, Volume 1: From the Beginning to the Sixth Century AD* (Princeton, NJ: Princeton University Press, 1979).
38. Hu Shi, *The Development of the Logical Method in Ancient China* (London: K. Paul, Trench, Trubner and Co and Shanghai: The Oriental Book Co, 1922).
39. In *Xin Qingnian*, 6, no. 1 (January 15, 1919).

CHAPTER 2

COMMUNISM AND THE ANTI-JAPANESE WAR OF RESISTANCE

PART ONE: HOW I LEARNED TO UNDERSTAND COMMUNISM

The rise of communism was the most important event in twentieth-century Chinese history. Not only did it determine the fate of the entire Chinese nation, but it also transformed the personal lives of every individual Chinese person, myself included. From 1949 onward, when I was nineteen, I began my self-exile and spent more than twenty years living a stateless life because of this significant change in China. I cannot, of course, make a complete and deep analysis of this major event, but I would like to look back on the way, step by step, that I came to understand communism starting from my childhood years. I will examine this in the same way that I discussed the May Fourth Movement earlier. I must emphasize, however, that what I am expressing here is essentially my own particular point of view based on what I personally heard and saw.

The first systematic memories I have of my childhood begin in 1937, the year the Anti-Japanese War of Resistance erupted and I returned to the countryside. In my nine years in the countryside, however, I never heard the word "communism." I only knew that Chen Duxiu and Hu Shi were famous cultural figures, but I had absolutely no idea that Chen Duxiu was also one of the founders of the Chinese Communist Party. This was probably because no one in our rural area had received a modern education or encountered the popular currents of new thought or the new terms from the cities. Qianshan County was situated in the mountains, and Guanzhuang Village was even more inaccessible; even so, the fate of our rural area became indissolubly linked with an armed military force that was intimately related to communism—the New Fourth Army.[1] The older people of the village were probably quite aware that it was part of the armed forces of the Chinese Communist Party, but as far as what the "ism" that the CCP pursued was all about, they did not seem to be able to articulate that clearly and they did not seem to be interested in inquiring about it either. Since I was only a child, no one told me that the New Fourth Army was simply the Chinese Communist Party's army. As a result, before I returned to the city, "communism" and "Communist Party" were both words that I had never heard.

In 1938, an armed force active in the Qianshan region was incorporated into the Fourth Detachment of the New Fourth Army. This armed group was widely known for kidnapping and murder, and many people in Guanzhuang and the surrounding area had fallen victim to them. Why was this Fourth Detachment so vicious then? To answer this, its historical background needs to be examined.[2]

This armed group was first organized by Gao Jingting (1907–1939), the son of a moderately well-off family from Guangshan County in Xinyang, Henan Province. As a youth, Gao refused to study; instead he went around with other delinquent ruffians, breaking the law and committing various crimes. By the time he entered his twenties, he grew increasingly bold and started to commit serious criminal offenses from murder to theft. Eventually he could not remain in his own region, and so he gathered a gang of marginal village characters and scarpered into the Dabie Mountain Range on the borders of the Henan, Anhui, and Hubei Provinces. There they hid out and carried on their banditry. The country folk in those mountain regions were simple, honest, unsophisticated, and timid, and Gao and his gang could take whatever they wanted from these pitiful people.

At the same time, Gao and his gang also stole many guns and expanded their cohort of followers. By the mid-1930s they numbered about one thousand and called themselves the "Seventy-Fifth Division." In three or four more years, their numbers reached several thousand and they expanded into the Twenty-Eighth Army. This military unit sported the banners of the Red Army (Hongjun 紅軍) in carrying out their activities, but whether or not they had any kind of official relationship with the Red Army was something that outsiders had no way of knowing. When the Anti-Japanese War of Resistance began and the Chinese Communist Party (Gongchandang 共產黨 or CCP) and the Nationalist Party (Guomindang 國民黨 or KMT) began to cooperate again, the CCP officially established the New Fourth Army and incorporated Gao Jingting's forces as their Fourth Detachment, appointing Gao as Detachment Commander.

I began to hear vivid descriptions of Gao Jingting and his gang's slaughter of the common people when I first returned to the countryside. People talked about this continuously, and because of that a very strong fear of them developed in my childhood mind.

The largest and most brutal massacre took place on February 15, 1935, and so the villagers called it the "2-15 Incident." On that day, Gao Jingting dispatched more than five hundred of his followers to Gaozhuang Village and other nearby villages to kidnap people. They grabbed anyone who was well enough off to feed themselves, took a total of three hundred plus hostages, and pressed them to pay a collective ransom of a hundred thousand silver dollars. Of course, this figure far exceeded their ability to pay. After their extortion failed and they did not get what they wanted, the kidnappers went into a rage, lined up the hostages, and massacred them. Only one or two of the younger people were lucky enough to escape, and the true story of the massacre was exposed.

Word of the 2-15 Incident not only circulated widely in Qianshan but also sent shock waves throughout the south where it was reported in the *Shanghai News* (*Shenbao* 申報) in Shanghai and the *Central Daily* (*Zhongyang Ribao* 中央日報) in Nanjing. This was because one of the victims of the massacre, Yu Yimi (1873–1935), was an important personage in Anhui Province. Mr. Yu was a member of my clan and a generation above me. He was a successful examination candidate who was chosen to enter the Imperial Academy in the late Qing and served in several offices, from district magistrate (*Zhixian* 知縣) to circuit magistrate (*daoyin* 道尹). After the establishment of the Republic, he was very highly regarded in Anhui Province. At first he was chosen to be the Head of the Provincial Legislative Council (the Provincial Assembly) and later moved to the executive branch and served as Chief of the Finance Bureau, Head of the Political Affairs Bureau, and for a while Protector of the Governor of Anhui Province. His reputation as an official was excellent; he was upright in his personal conduct and especially respected for his honesty and incorruptibility. After he retired in the 1930s, due to his straitened financial situation he could not afford to live in the city and so he moved from Anqing back to Linjia Chong Village (neighboring Guanzhuang Village) in Qianshan County. His murder was especially harrowing because one son and one grandson were also killed with him, and the newspaper accounts of the killings of these three members of one family were particularly gruesome.

When I returned to Guanzhuang, it was only two years after the terrible 2-15 Massacre, and so it was still a recent event, and for that reason also the one topic the village people talked about most. Because Gao Jingting always flew the banners of the "Red Army" and "Revolution" and was later incorporated into the New Fourth Army, the blame for the 2-15 Massacre was chalked up to the Red Army or the New Fourth Army.

According to recent historical sources concerning Gao Jingting, however, it is Gao himself who bears the responsibility for his ruthless activities.[3] This is because after Gao was incorporated into the Fourth Detachment of the New Fourth Army, he did not accept the leadership of Ye Ting (1896–1946), Xiang Ying (1898–1941), and other Chinese Communist Party military leaders. He disobeyed their orders and went on single-mindedly building up his power and territorial base of operations. The Communist Party Central eventually sent a group of men to Hefei and arrested Gao Jingting and executed him after a three-day struggle session. The charges against him were not massacring the common people, however, but rather for not following Yan-an's leadership, for setting up a "mountain stronghold" or "independent fiefdom" (*shantou zhuyi* 山頭主義) and for practicing "factionalism" or "sectarianism" (*zongpai zhuyi* 宗派主義).

Unfortunately, after the execution of Gao Jingting, the military discipline of the Fourth Detachment of the New Fourth Army did not improve; they continued murdering people just as before. One such murder was of a clan elder brother, whose corpse I saw with my own eyes after he was killed. I recounted earlier how I hid out for a while in the home of Dr. Yu Pingge when I suffered a "literary disaster." Elder Brother Pingge was a respected doctor in our village and Guanzhuang's only doctor. He had a stubborn temperament and refused to be ordered around. According to an account revealed later by someone with inside knowledge of the event, people from the Fourth Detachment repeatedly tried to force him to cooperate with them, but he resolutely refused. One night they dragged him out of his house, slit his throat, and left him to die beside the well outside of the family gate. When I heard about it early the next morning, I ran over and saw his corpse still lying there. This awful tragedy took place during my adolescence (probably in 1944), and my memory of it is fresh to this day.

If the behavior of the Fourth Detachment of the New Fourth Army operating in the Qianshan region was representative of the Chinese Communist Party's armed forces, then what it primarily impressed upon

the common people there was a sense of fear and not one iota of an ideal
to look forward to. For the entire nine years I was in the countryside,
I never once heard that this armed force represented the future hope
of China and a new world rising to replace the old. It was not until I
returned to the city in 1946 that I first heard that communism had such
an ideal and that some people were appealing to Chinese youth to work
for the realization of that ideal.

However, because the city I lived in after the war was Shenyang, right
from the beginning a dark shadow was cast over this ideal in my mind.
And why was that? Because I arrived in Shenyang just shortly after
the withdrawal of the Soviet Red Army, whose raping and pillaging
throughout the Northeast had already given rise to widespread anger
among the people. From my classmates who were from that region, I heard
almost endless stories of hair-raising atrocities committed by the Soviet
Red Army. At that time, the left-wing intellectuals were all proclaiming
with one voice that the Soviet Union had already entered the paradise
of communism and that their today was our tomorrow. The Soviet Red
Army came from the communist paradise, but their behavior was so
appalling that there was no way I could have any faith in communism.

The earliest contact I had with the theory of communism was after I
moved from Shenyang back to Beiping (Beijing after 1949). At the end
of 1947, Shenyang was already surrounded by the Chinese Communist
army, and we had to leave. We lived in Beiping for eleven months
(December 1947 to October 1948); when the situation in North China
followed the same disastrous path as that of the Northeast, our whole
family had to leave Beiping for exile in Shanghai. During those eleven
months in Beiping, however, I stayed home, unable to attend school,
with nothing to do, and so I occasionally met with some Beiping college
students and finally learned about the most sensitive issues of the time. I
also liked to read some of the more widely circulated periodicals like *The
Observer* (*Guancha* 觀察), *Independent Commentaries on Current Affairs*
(*Duli shilun* 獨立時論), *New Path* (*Xinlu* 新路), and the like. All this

made me begin to think about topics such as communism, socialism, and liberalism. I will discuss this in detail later.[4]

In recalling my intellectual journey of 1948 in Beiping, I must mention Wang Zhitian, my older male cousin (my father's sister's son). He was ten years older than I and was then in his third year in the law department of Peking University. We knew for some time that around 1937 he had already joined the Chinese Communist Party's Young Pioneers. It was not until after 1949 that I discovered that he was an undercover CCP member and in charge of the CCP's underground organization at Peking University. Beiping's student demonstrations were all collaboratively set in motion by him and his "comrades," but whenever there were large student protest demonstrations in the streets, he never participated. He was usually at our house eating and chatting. At the time we jokingly called him a "professional student," but he just laughed it off.[5] In 1946 while in the Northeast, he often traveled back and forth between Beiping and Shenyang ostensibly as a "travelling salesman" for the purpose of buying and selling Western medicine to make a little money to support his aging mother. I remember when he was in Shenyang, he would often invite many of his friends to meet in our home, and they would close the door and talk in our big living room for three or four hours at a time. In August 1949 when I returned to Beiping, he told me that the people he met with in our home then were all important underground CCP leaders who had shifted their base of activities to Shenyang because the situation was too precarious in Beiping and their personal safety was not guaranteed.

I had great respect for him because he was a very earnest, sincere person and certainly had a zeal for searching out a new direction for China. I felt that he had genuine affection for our family (his maternal uncle's family) and did not resent us because our political views were different from his. I still remember the summer of 1948 when he took me and another young relative on a hike around the Beiping suburbs for three days and three nights. We walked to the Summer Palace, the

Jade Spring Hill (west of the palace), the Fragrant Mountain (in the northwest), and other scenic spots. We did not have any money, but we each carried a blanket and every night we would bed down and sleep out in the open. That was a very pleasant trip, and I remember it today as if it just happened.

Wang Zhitian's faith was very sincere, and he was the first person who tried to inculcate in me the ideals of communism. There was a mutual trust between us, and I very much respected his opinions, and so I began to study and contemplate the various schools of thought popular at that time. He introduced me to Ai Siqi's (1910–1966) *Philosophy for the Masses* (*Dazhong zhexue* 大眾哲學). In this sense, he was one of my "enlighteners," but as the saying goes "you can lead a horse to water, but you can't make it drink." The result of my explorations did not lead to my complete acceptance of communism. I was certainly opposed to a minority of capitalists monopolizing the wealth of society, and so I tended toward a system of fair and equitable distribution. At the same time, I was also willing to accept that some large-scale enterprises (like the railroads) that impacted the lives of the entire populace should be operated by the government. From the beginning, however, I believed that "freedom" (*ziyou*) is a necessary core value that any modern society must not be without. At the time, many people were discussing President Franklin D. Roosevelt's "Four Freedoms" speech, which I agreed with completely.[6]

In the process of exchanging ideas with my older cousin, I discovered that he did not belong to the extremely radical crowd. For example, his attitude to Hu Shi, President of Peking University, was not like most left-wing students—he did not blindly denounce Hu Shi and sometimes even regarded him in an unbiased manner. He naturally criticized Hu for being pro-American, but on more than one occasion he praised Hu's 1947 proposed "Ten-year Plan to Fight for Academic Independence" ("Zhengqu xueshu duli de shinian jihua" 爭取學術獨立的十年計畫).[7] In his efforts to convince me of his beliefs, Wang Zhitian occasionally employed the intellectual weapons of dialectics and materialism. In the end, though, he was merely a practitioner and not a theoretician. I remember he once proclaimed to me the "truth" that "everything in the universe changes." So I asked him a question: This "truth" must also be something in the universe, so does it itself change or not? This question caught him off guard, and he very frankly admitted that his theoretical training was insufficient for him immediately to give a satisfactory answer to it. That was his way of "saying you do not know when you do not know" (*bu zhi wei bu zhi* 不知為不知), [8] and this made me aware of something about his beliefs about communism.

Wang Zhitian's beliefs were not based on rational understanding; one could even say that he actually had very little comprehension of the whole overall system of communism. This is not unlike other intellectuals of his generation within the Chinese Communist Party, who came to a new awareness after the Cultural Revolution and admitted in unison that in the beginning their faith was chosen more or less inevitably because of a "misunderstanding."[9]

In August 1949 I returned from Shanghai to Beiping to enter Yanjing University, and Wang Zhitian was already one of Peng Zhen's (1902– 1997) important cadres.[10] He was responsible for the youth organizations and activities of the entire city and regularly visited various universities to make contact with Party and Corps (*tuan* 團) organizations. Once he came to Yanjing University and looked me up on the way, but we did not meet up. After that someone told me that "Comrade Xiang Ziming was looking for you today; he says he's a relative of yours." At first I was at a loss when I heard that name, but after a few minutes I realized that it was my cousin's Party name. By that time, he was a very busy and important man, and I never again had the opportunity for any in-depth conversations with him. Much later, at the beginning of the Cultural Revolution, the overseas Chinese periodicals reported on the so-called "Beijing Changguanlou Incident" (*Beijing Changguanlou shijian*) and wrote that he opposed Mao Zedong's opinions. It goes without saying that he must have already become a target of "revolution" and "dictatorship."[11]

The last time I met with my cousin Wang Zhitian was in New York in the 1980s. At that time, he was visiting various American universities as the Acting Party Secretary of Peking University. He was splendidly received at the campuses of the University of California, Berkeley, and Harvard University. We had prearranged our meeting, so we had two days of very lengthy conversations in New York. This was the first time we had met in over thirty years, and we both felt quite emotional and had an indescribable sense of sorrow. Although he was there on an official visit and was given deferential treatment wherever he went, he was in rather low spirits. From our discussions, I learned that after the Cultural Revolution he was not very highly thought of by the Party Central leadership, his post at Peking University was an empty position, and he was Acting Party Secretary only in name. More importantly, he had obviously become very skeptical about his early beliefs. He did not utter a word of remorse, but his wife (another true believer in those earlier days) told me quite frankly, "You (mainly referring to my father) were farsighted and lucky to get out early." Wang Zhitian stood there and tacitly agreed with what she was saying. To avoid causing him further pain, I did not delve any further into the issue, and our feelings were silently understood.

Finally, there was still one more thing that left a deep impression on me. On the way to New York's Chinatown to have dinner, we passed by a very large bronze statue of Confucius. When Wang Zhitian saw it, he suddenly became extremely excited and insisted that we had to take a picture in front of the statue to commemorate the occasion. In the earlier years when his beliefs were strong, this would have been unimaginable, but now his innermost feelings were motivated by an irrepressible impulse. It was very clear that after his thorough disillusionment with his early beliefs, his system of values seemed to have returned to two sources. The first was the Western mainstream values that were popular ever since the "May Fourth Movement"—democracy and freedom. This was understandable because the "revolution" that he joined originally carried the banners of "democracy" and "freedom" to attract China's intellectual youth. The second was the Chinese cultural tradition, the part that primarily advocated respecting and valuing human beings. This was why he had a deep respect for Confucius.

This was how I came to understand communism from 1937 to 1949. My nine years of life in the countryside was the first stage during which I had contact with the Fourth Detachment of the New Fourth Army and their nefarious activities in my rural village. At that time, I did not know that the Fourth Detachment of the New Fourth Army represented the communist movement; I had not even heard the word "communism," much less understood what it meant. It was not until the second stage beginning in 1946 when I returned to the city that I finally understood that communism was a worldwide revolutionary movement, that it comprised a complete system of complex theories and had more than a century of revolutionary experience, and that in 1917 it had been implemented in the Soviet Union. At that time Chinese left-wing intellectuals universally believed that the Chinese revolution had to follow the path of the Soviet Union and that this was the only way forward; the United States of America represented the last stage of decadent, stagnating capitalism and would soon die out. I heard these opinions expressed many times in Beiping, but it was very difficult for me to make a judgment at the time.

The individual events just related are quite limited, but they are my real-life experiences and very different from empty armchair discussions.

At the conclusion of this section, I would like to offer a few reflections. Since the process of my understanding of communism was so difficult, I believe other people's situations may have been similar. How, then, was this -ism or ideology (*zhuyi* 主義) coming from outside of China able to spread so widely and so quickly in China?

The historical elements behind the rise of communism in China are extremely complex, and I cannot carry out a full discussion here. The most important motive force was obviously nationalism, which was stimulated especially by the invasion of China by the Japanese military. The Xi'an Incident of 1936 and the Marco Polo Bridge Incident of 1937 were two key turning points (I will discuss these later when I discuss the Anti-Japanese War of Resistance).[12] That the Communist revolutionary movement whose appeal was "internationalism" finally had to rely on the motive force of nationalism to accomplish its goals is one of the great paradoxes of history. What I want to talk about here, however, is not the later course of history but rather to begin at the beginning. That is, why did Chinese intellectuals at the end of the Qing dynasty and the beginning of the Republic so enthusiastically introduce communism into China? In the final analysis, how did these early introducers of communism actually understand it?

I believe that traditional Chinese thought with Confucianism as its core facilitated the easy acceptance of a communist (or socialist) consciousness by late Qing intellectuals. In the first place, Confucianism emphasized the concept of "equal" or "equity" or "equality" (*jun* 均) as the saying by Confucius notes that "[what worries the head of a state or a noble family] is not poverty but inequality (*or* uneven distribution)."[13] From the concept to its institutionalization, later generations had policies such as "equal fields" (*juntian* 均田), "uniform taxation" (*junshui* 均稅), "equal labor (*or* corvée) obligations" (*junyi* 均役), and so on. The concept of "equality" was also transmitted from Confucianism to Daoism and from the elite ranks of culture down to the level of popular culture. Thus, the *Scripture of Great Peace* (*Taipingjing* 太平經) of the Eastern Han period understood the concept of Great Peace as "great equality" (*da pingjun* 大平均). We can say that the idea of egalitarianism in China goes back to the distant past, has lasted a long time, and is all pervasive; it established a kind of psychological basis for Chinese intellectuals to accept communism, and because of it they almost immediately responded positively to it.

Under the framework of "egalitarian" thought, what the scholar officials were most indignant about was "land annexation by powerful and wealthy local families," that is, extremely unequal distribution of land that produced a situation in which "the land of the wealthy joins north and south, while the poor have not enough land to dig a hole."[14] From Dong Zhongshu (ca. 179–ca. 104 BCE) of the Han dynasty on, innumerable memorials are clear evidence of this. This tradition of opposing "land annexation" continued through the Tang and Song dynasties and later periods. In general, the "scholar" (*shi* 士) class sympathized with the poor while disdaining or despising the rich.

Another Confucian value that wielded great influence was prioritizing the "common good" or the "public" (*gong* 公) over "self-interest" or the "private" (*si* 私). Scholar officials always advocated that anything for the sake of the "public" is good whereas anything done in "self-interest" is bad. They especially valued the concept of "Great Unity" from the "Ceremonial Usages" (Li yun 禮運) chapter of the *Book of Rites* (*Liji* 禮 記). In the modern era, the reformer Kang Youwei (1858–1927) wrote a *Book of Great Unity* (*Datong shu* 大同書), and the revolutionary Sun Yat-sen proclaimed a slogan from the *Book of Rites* that "all Under Heaven is Public" (*tianxia weigong* 天下為公). This ideology also formed part of the foundation for the acceptance of the ideal of communism by late Qing intellectuals.

The late Qing intellectuals' embrace of communism through the facilitation of Chinese traditional thought had its advantageous side, but it was not without its price. The greatest cost was that they misunderstood or misinterpreted modern theories from the West. These late Qing intellectuals first encountered the works of Karl Marx, Friedrich Engels, and others from Japanese scholars, of whom the most influential was Marxist economist Hajime Kawakami (1879–1946). Kawakami had a fairly accurate understanding of Western political thought because Western thought had reached Japan much earlier than China and because Japan was ahead of other Asian nations when it came to modernization. How much of Marx's thoughts, Engels's ideas, or the concept of socialism itself was understood by Kawakami's Chinese followers, including Li

Dazhao, is, however, very questionable. Allow me to provide a few examples to illustrate.

I remember that Liu Shipei (1884–1919) was closely associated with the earliest Chinese translation of the *Communist Manifesto*. At the time Liu also advocated anarchism because he admired the essay "On Having No Ruler" ("Wujun lun" 無君論) by the Eastern Jin thinker Bao Jingyan (4th century CE).[15] During that period, many people such as Zhang Taiyan (1868–1936), Wu Zhihui (1865–1953), and Li Shizeng (1881–1973) were anarchists.[16] Quite a few people who initially believed in communism also believed in anarchism, but they could not distinguish between the two. How could people who did not understand these concepts judge whether China could implement communism?

Then there was also Liang Shuming who wrote in his memoir that in his early years he instantly opposed capitalism when he first heard that it protected private property and declared he would rather choose socialism. He had probably never heard of John Locke's (1632–1704) views on how private property is the foundation of civilization and the guarantor of individual liberty. Liang had no understanding at all what "capitalism" meant, but because the "common good" and "self-interest" (public versus private) were central to his value system, as soon as he heard the word "private" he was filled with righteous indignation, believing that only the "public" or "common good" could be positive.[17]

Finally, there was Huang Kan (1886–1935) who, under the penname Yunpi, published an article in *Minbao* (no. 17, 1907) entitled "Lament for the Impoverished," in which he called for revolution. The gist of his article is as follows: The poor fall into poverty because the rich take their property away from them, and this constituted inequality. Based on this, he called upon all poor people to annihilate the rich. As he wrote, "Take revenge on your enemies, return to the truth of equality, and be willing to die in order to achieve equality." If the revolution succeeds, it will mean "good fortune for the poor," but if it fails, "then we can regard our sacred land as a gigantic burial mound" and all the people—rich and poor—can be buried there together. This essay was quite the sensation at the time among the revolutionary camp. It was obviously influenced by communism and the slogan "proletarians of all countries, unite!" (the last line of the *Communist Manifesto*).

From these factual examples, we can see that when Chinese intellectuals first decided that communism was the key to saving the nation, it was mainly due to a misconception. They had not done any serious research into whether this system of ideas was in any way suitable as a cure for China's afflictions. It was simply because some elements (e.g., "equity," the "common good") of communism seemed at first blush to be close to the concepts and values of the Chinese tradition with which they were familiar, they unhesitatingly regarded it as "the truth" and were willing to dedicate their lives to it. Similar misconceptions and illusions continued to appear after May Fourth. One example is maintaining that only communism gives people "true democracy," "true freedom," and "true equality." In sum, this choice can be said to have brought together all the iron in the nine continents (the known world) to forge a colossal blunder.

Looking back today, what saddens me the most is that China has paid a most terrible price for this choice, and yet after discovering this great mistake, China has actually gone backwards. The market system, private property, and class distinctions have returned but in an unfair, dishonest, uncivilized, and illegal fashion, so much so that corruption and embezzlement are intrinsic characteristics of this flawed societal system. Former Premier Zhao Ziyang (1919–2005)[18] called this system "crony capitalism" [literally capitalism run by the rich and the powerful officials (*quangui* 權貴)] because in it the "part of the people who became rich first" (paraphrasing Deng Xiaoping) did not rise legitimately through thrift and hard work. Their enrichment was closely linked to political power, through which they were afforded various special privileges and extralegal benefits—some people even transformed public property into their private property. In the system that germinated from this freakish seed, taking advantage of one's position to push people around is normalized, and the level of injustice steadily rises each day.

This is exactly what is so saddening—before suffering destruction by violent revolution, China had long since developed a market mechanism that functioned normally. According to my research, by the late Ming dynasty (1368–1644) at the latest, this market system had already created an enormous amount of wealth, changed China's social structure, and altered the Chinese value system.[19] In terms of values, the "public" or "common good" and the "private" or "self-interest" were no longer incompatible or irreconcilable but had become mutually interrelated. In fact, in the sixteenth century, scholar-merchant Yu Xie (1496–1583) stated: "Common good can be established only if self-interest is realized in the first place." The iconoclastic scholar Li Zhi (1527–1602) also discovered the superiority of "self-interest," and thus he openly declared that "As for self-interest (si), it is in the human heart-mind (xin). A person must have self-interest and then his heart-mind will appear. If he has no self-interest, then he has no heart-mind."[20] According to this, every person is a "selfish" (si 私) individual, and his heart-mind necessarily represents his individual "selfishness or selfish motives" (literally, "selfish mind" sixin 私心). In today's philosophical discussions of the individual's "identity" or "selfhood," we can find very solid evidence to support this opinion. We can see that the past idea of human selfishness being caused because of private property simply cannot be supported; the exact opposite is true—human beings need to have "self-interest" or a "selfish mind" first before they can move on to accumulate private property.

At this time, "wealth" (fu 富) was also recognized in a positive sense. From the sixteenth through the eighteenth centuries, in local regions many different kinds of material social benefits—like printing books, building bridges, constructing temples, writing genealogies, establishing clan charitable estates, and such matters—all depended on monetary donations by merchants. Whenever there was a famine or some town or village was in crisis (e.g., in an invasion by Japanese pirates), it was always the merchants who donated large sums of money. As such, from the Ming dynasty on, statements like "enriching the people is the key foundation of a region" (*fumin shi yifang zhi yuanqi*, 富民是一方之元氣) and "storing wealth among the people" (*cangfu yu min*, 藏富於民) and other similar ideas were especially popular. According to my research, then, from the sixteenth century on, Chinese society was steadily developing in a new direction. If it had not been for the wanton destruction by violent revolution, China today might be a civilized society that is "wealthy yet observant of the rites" and might not have taken the road of "crony capitalism" and fallen to into the corrupt condition whereby "if one's aim is wealth, one cannot be benevolent."[21]

PART TWO: BACKGROUND OF THE ANTI-JAPANESE WAR OF RESISTANCE

The Anti-Japanese War of Resistance (1937–1945) was a significant earthshaking event in twentieth-century Chinese history. The old order (social, cultural, and economic), which was already teetering on the verge of collapse, broke down completely under the massive onslaught of the Japanese military invasion. After the Meiji Restoration, Japan became a mighty industrial nation with considerable military power. In terms of intellect and knowhow, Japan expanded its reach beyond Asia to Europe to study modern Western civilization comprehensively; the Japanese also became proficient in Western "barbarity" or what was generally called "imperialist expansion and encroachment."[22] What is called "imperialism" basically arose from the various dominant Western maritime nations fighting over world markets and resources. England was the most advanced and successful, and so there were British colonies throughout the world. Other Western nations such as France, Holland, Spain, Portugal, and others strove to outdo one another and expand everywhere. Germany was unified later when all the colonies had already been carved up among the other powers, which was why Germany initiated two world wars. Japan's rise came even later, and since it too lacked natural resources, the Japanese set their sights on invading the Asian continent, first the Korean peninsula and then China. In 1592, the warlord Toyotomi Hideyoshi (1536–1598, reigned 1590–1598) dispatched 160,000 troops across the ocean to occupy Hancheng (modern Seoul) and then prepared to attack and seize Beijing. Although Toyotomi's invasion did not achieve its objective because of his early death, it nevertheless served as a model for the Japanese militarism three hundred years later.

From the Anglo-Japanese Alliance (Ying-Ri Tongmeng or Nichi-Ei Dōmei) of 1902, we can see that England already recognized Japan's hegemonic position in East Asia. In 1905 Japan defeated Russia in northeast China and took possession of all Russian interests there, controlling the Liaodong Peninsula, including the two great ports of Lüshun (or the Lüshunkou District, or Port Arthur) and Dalian, and operating the South Manchurian Railway from Changchun to Dalian. All this greatly strengthened the foundations of Japan's hegemony. After Japan annexed Korea in 1910, it immediately turned toward the three provinces of Northeast China—Liaoning, Jilin, and Heilongjiang—so-called Manchuria.

Because the warlord Zhang Zuolin (1875–1928), "the King of Manchuria," refused to submit completely to Japan's control and manipulation, in 1928 the Japanese Kwantung Army planted a bomb and killed him.[23] On September 18, 1931, on the pretext of the "Mukden Incident," the Kwantung Army began their full-scale invasion and occupation of Manchuria; in Chinese history this is known as the "September 18 Incident." Today scholars of Japanese history have proven that this was a premeditated operation for which the Japanese army had been planning a long time and that this was definitely not the result of "random events."

Why did the Japanese begin invading China in 1931? The reason is very simple: After the Nationalist Party's Northern Expedition (a 1926–1928 campaign led by Chiang Kai-shek against various local warlords), the Nationalist Party [KMT] established its capital in Nanjing. In November 1931, Zhang Zuolin's son Zhang Xueliang (1901–2001) accepted the authority of the Nationalist Party government (under Chiang Kai-shek,

1887–1975), and the Nationalist "white sun on a blue background" flag was raised in Manchuria. The Japanese military authorities probably felt that if they did not move quickly, China might very possibly become a powerful and united modern nation.

Similarly, the Marco Polo (Lugou) Bridge Incident of July 7, 1937, in Beiping also cannot be understood as a result of "random events." Again, the Japanese army felt much pressure to take swift action to forestall China. Why? Because in the decade from 1928 to 1937, the Nationalist Party government had invested great effort in modernizing many areas, including its military. In the 1930s, as Japan intensified its invasion, the Nanjing government seemed to have chosen a policy of "non-resistance" and repeatedly made concessions, which led to criticism from their left-wing faction and fast-growing student-movement groups. In actuality, however, the Nationalist government was actively training a new-style army (having hired German military advisors to assist them) while also setting up a National Resources Commission and mobilizing scientists in many fields to work on building up the economy. Most importantly, they established various core industries such as steel, electricity, machinery, and arms manufacturing, among others. In 1936 when Wen Yiduo (1899–1946) was on his way to Anyang in Henan to survey oracle-bone excavations, he visited a military training school at Luoyang. On his return to Tsinghua University, he told the students that in Luoyang, unlike Beiping, he had seen the government preparing to resist Japan. He told the students, "We should not completely lose hope in the government."[24] This was the context of Japan's invasion of China in 1937.

Public opinion forced Chiang Kai-shek to make the final decision to fight against Japan, but Chinese preparations were woefully inadequate and the sacrifices were enormous. The 1937 Battle of Shanghai, Song Hu kang-ri, or "8-1-3" for August 13, 1937, lasted three months. More than half of the new elite officers and troops that Chiang had trained in the past decade were killed, as the Japanese army bragged that they would conquer all of China in only three months. To prove to the international community that Japan's wild assertions were not to be believed, Chiang Kai-shek was willing to accept any price to defend to the end the Shanghai front. After this battle, new troop replacements became a serious problem. Later on, although the National Revolutionary Army was still able to score some victories, there were many defeats and retreats, and all they could do was "trade space to gain time." Just as Hu Shi said in a speech on December 6, 1944, at Harvard University, "China's problem in this war was that a country that was not well prepared in science and technology was, nevertheless, forced to engage with a first-class military and industrial power, Japan, in a modern war."[25]

The result of the Anti-Japanese War of Resistance was a catastrophe of enormous proportions which China had not experienced in thousands of years. Take my hometown as an example; when I returned at the beginning of winter 1937, it was still peaceful, but in a short time a large number of Guangxi troops were garrisoned there or would pass through. There was little or no military discipline, and these troops harassed the villagers so much that there was hardly a day without trouble. Exacerbating the situation was the increasing activity of the New Fourth Army setting up guerrilla bases, which often affected Guanzhuang. Later, there were also roaming bandits who kept us in a constant state of trepidation. At nights toward the end of the Anti-Japanese War of Resistance, I often saw flashlights flickering in the hills behind our village; the villagers all knew that they belonged to bandits spying for an opportunity to come down from the hills and pillage our homes. Social order in the countryside worsened visibly with each day during the war. According to the older villagers, they remembered a time, during the end of the Qing dynasty and the beginning of the Republic era, when the country people carried silver ingots or silver dollars to Anqing, Wuhu, and other prefectural cities and did not have to worry about running into bandits on the roads there.

This widespread disruption of order in the countryside paved the way for the vast upheaval, complete turmoil, and total confusion after the war. At this point, I would like to quote from the final work, *China: A New History*, of leading American Sinologist John King Fairbank (1907–1991) to delineate the disastrous consequences of the Anti-Japanese War of Resistance:

> Without the devastating Japanese invasion, the Nanjing government might gradually have led the way in China's modernization. As it turned out, however, resisting Japan gave Mao and the CCP their chance to establish a new autocratic power in the countryside, excluding the elements of a nascent urban civil society that were still developing under the Nationalists. In conditions of wartime, the CCP was buildling a new type of Chinese state geared for class warfare. In the twentieth century, Chinese revolutionaries were thus preparing to assault and reorder a class structure that went back at least 3,000 years.[26]

Why would I quote Fairbank's proclamation here? Because from the 1930s on, Fairbank had always detested the Nationalist Party and sympathized with the Chinese Communist Party. In his later years, however, he changed his position. This book was completed on September 11, 1991; the next morning, he sent the original manuscript to the publishers, and two days later he passed away. This book can be said to hold his "final conclusions." Fairbank was an American, so he could transcend internal Chinese political wrangling and probably be somewhat more objective in his judgments.

It is obvious that the Chinese Communist Party benefited the most from the Anti-Japanese War of Resistance. The Chinese communists fled from Jiangxi to northern Shaanxi, but they were unable to shake off the feeling that a crisis was imminent. Lin Biao (1907–1971) doubted whether the "red flag can still fly for long."[27] For this reason, beginning in the early 1930s, the Chinese Communist Party launched anti-Japanese movements in several large cities to force the Nationalist Party to abandon its policy of "pacifying the interior before resisting outside aggression." Anti–

Chiang Kai-shek societies, political celebrities, and leftist university students took on this task, causing the outcry against the Japanese to grow louder each day. In 1936, the communists persuaded Zhang Xueliang and Yang Hucheng, of the northeast and northwest armies respectively, to pull off the sensational Xi-an Incident, which gave the communists an opportunity to catch their breath. If the war had not broken out, however, the Chinese Communist Party would not have been able to spread out and set up guerrilla units and regional power bases. It was not until the complete unfolding of the Anti-Japanese War of Resistance that the Chinese Communist Party recovered from their precarious position, like a dragon returning to the ocean.

Chiang Kai-shek and the Nationalist Party saw this, but with Japan coming down so hard, there was nothing they could do but resist. At the same time, Wang Jingwei (1883–1944), Zhou Fohai (1897–1948), and others were obstinately suing for peace and, regardless of the risks, they recklessly moved to Japanese-occupied territory and set up a puppet regime in Nanjing. They did this because they estimated that if the war went on for long it would necessarily give the Chinese Communist Party an opportunity to expand its power and influence and ultimately deliver China to the Soviet Union. Explicit corroboration for all this can be found in Zhou Fohai's diary.[28] At the time of the Nanjing-Wuhan split between the Wang and Chiang governments, Wang Jingwei was a leader of the left-wing faction of the Nationalist Party and had the closest relationship with the Chinese Communist Party. Zhou Fohai was even one of the leaders of the Chinese Communist Party when it was founded in 1921, and Chen Gongbo (1892–1946) had also been a member of the Chinese Communist Party for a time.[29] It was precisely because they had a deeper understanding of the Chinese communists that their anxiety was far greater than others. They were so anxious to sue for peace because they believed that it was the only way to save China from falling into the trap of the Soviet Union's totalitarian system. Their illusions that Japan would make peace were completely baseless, but their estimation that the

Chinese communists would take advantage of the war to seize political power throughout the entire country was completely accurate.

According to relatively conservative numbers, from 1937 to 1945 the number of Chinese Communist Party members grew from forty thousand to 1.2 million.[30] These numbers are the strongest evidence that the war against Japan gave the Chinese Communist Party the opportunity to expand its power and influence substantially. After the outbreak of war, a political regime that was initially besieged in a small corner of northern Shaanxi was actually able to spread rapidly throughout the country. By the end of 1940, the population under the control of the Chinese Communist Party was nearly 100 million.[31]

In the Anti-Japanese War of Resistance, the central government's armed forces—the National Revolutionary Army—bore the brunt of fighting on the advanced front positions while the Chinese Communist army carried out mobile or guerrilla warfare from the sides to impede the Japanese army.

There are two battles in the Anti-Japanese War of Resistance about which the Chinese Communist Party has fomented the most fervent propaganda: one is the September 1937 Battle of Pingxingguan commanded by Lin Biao, and the other is the August 1940 Hundred Regiments Offensive commanded by Peng Dehuai (1898–1974). Historian Yang Kuisong has written an account of the Battle of Pingxingguan.[32] The National Revolutionary Army had gathered at Pingxingguan and were prepared to defend to the death the mountain pass. The communist troops were ordered to defend the right flank, but at the last minute the communist side decided to take 4,000 troops and lie in wait in a nearby ravine so that they could ambush a Japanese force of 700 replenishment troops with heavy supply wagons. Only a hundred of the Japanese troops were combat soldiers; the others were non-combat troops. Even though this was the case, the communist troops had to fight for more than ten hours and suffered four hundred casualties before they were finally able to defeat the Japanese force. The propaganda about this battle in the interior of China was tremendous, and many young people who did not understand what had actually happened came to believe firmly that the Chinese Communist army was able to defeat Japan. Based on this misconception, they trekked to Yan'an in a continuous stream. It is hard to say, though, that the battle had any great significance for the war against Japan.

The Hundred Regiments Offensive was not meant to be a direct confrontation; its original goal was just to damage roads and railroad tracks to break out of the Japanese army's blockade. At the beginning of the battle, the Japanese troops were taken by surprise and their losses were heavy. Peng Dehuai then expanded his troops to around a hundred regiments. However, this battle led the Japanese army to launch a campaign lasting three years to annihilate the Chinese Communist base of operations in North China, causing the communist-occupied area to shrink, making the situation extremely difficult for them. Given the situation, even though Mao Zedong (1893–1976) was at the time privately very dissatisfied about the battle and believed it to have been a strategic mistake, he had to praise it publicly. After the 1959 Lushan Conference, leading the Hundred Regiments Offensive was one of the criminal charges against Peng Dehuai. In the same manner, after Lin Biao turned against Mao, the Battle of Pingxingguan also suddenly became a source of denunciation—significant only in a negative way.[33]

In sum, the aforementioned facts offer ample evidence to explain how the Japanese army's all-out war against China offered the Chinese Communist Party a one-in-a-million opportunity to turn defeat into victory and finally capture all under Heaven.

In conclusion, I would like to add a little more. Under the pretext of the 1945 Yalta Agreement, and only after the first atomic bomb fell on Hiroshima, the Soviet Union sent Russian troops flooding into China's Northeast. This further reinforced conditions for the Chinese Communist Party to seize power throughout China.[34] The Soviet Union then reneged on their promise to leave China within three months and delayed for eight to nine months before they finally withdrew completely from the Northeast. During this long period of time, the Soviets set up complete land, sea, and air blockades to prevent National Army troops from entering the Northeast while they were secretly transporting large numbers of Chinese Communist troops and cadres to the Northeast to set up camps and establish operational bases. By the time the National Army entered the Northeast in April 1946, the Chinese Communist army already had 400,000 to 500,000 troops stationed throughout the Northeast, and their superiority was such that they could simply "wait at their ease for an exhausted enemy." Allow me to quote here a passage by a communist cadre who entered the Northeast at that time:

> Both the Nationalist Party and the Chinese Communist Party were determined to win the Northeast. When we left Yan'an, Party Central leaders told us if we win the Northeast we win the whole country. Because of the external environment of the Northeast borders on the Soviet Union, the victory of our revolution and the future construction of our nation will have to depend on our "big brother." In our interior environment we are richly provided with natural resources and industrial facilities [...]

> Later events also confirmed that the three great campaigns to liberate the entire country, especially the powerful Liaoshen Campaign [of September to November 1948] and Pingjin Campaign [of 29 November 1948 to 31 January 1949], were all fought by the Fourth Army from the Northeast [...]

> As soon as the Anti-Japanese War of Resistance ended in victory, the Nationalist Party borrowed American warships to ship their crack troops, the New First Army and the New Sixth Army and so on, to the Northeast while their other troops also came north through the Shanhai Pass from Beiping and Tianjin, but after all they were too late. Before they arrived our armies from Hebei, Rehe (northern Hebei), and Liaoning had already entered Shenyang. At the same time we also transferred 110,000 soldiers from Shandong,

northern Jiangsu, and other areas to head into the Northeast by land and sea.

Party Central also sent nearly two-thirds (20) of the Central [Committee] members and alternative members together with 20,000 cadres of various ranks to work in the Northeast.[35]

From this, we can see that the eight-year Anti-Japanese War of Resistance and the postwar occupation of the Northeast region by the Soviet Union decided the fate of the Chinese nation in the second half of the twentieth century. According to a report, "When Tanaka apologized for the crimes of aggression against China during the Japanese War, Mao said that if Japan had not invaded China, and that there would be no victory for the Communist Party, there would be no talks today." He was not just being polite. These words came from the bottom of his heart.[36]

Notes

1. The New Fourth Army was a unit of the National Revolutionary Army of the Republic of China established in 1937. In contrast to most of the National Revolutionary Army, it was controlled by the Chinese Communist Party (Gongchandang) rather than the Nationalist Party (Guomindang). See Gregor Benton, *New Fourth Army: Communist Resistance Along the Yangtze and the Huai, 1938–1941* (Berkeley: University of California Press, 1999).

2. Yü Ying-shih note: I must note that the following discussion of the activities of Gao Jingting is primarily based on a long essay by a member of my clan, the late Yü Shiyi, entitled "The Whole Story of Gao Jingting's Rampages in the Region of the Dabie Mountain Range on the Borders of Henan, Anhui and Hubei Provinces, His Fall, and the Reversal of the Verdict" ("Gao Jingting weihuo Dabieshan qu ji qi fuwang yu fan-an shimo"). This essay was later published in *Beijing Spring* (*Beijing zhi chun*) in New York and in *Chinese People* (*Zhongguo renwu*) in Taiwan. I am relying on a photocopy of the original draft because I have not seen the printed versions.

3. See Geng Rong, "Qiangsheng, zai zheli huixiang: Gao Jinting jiangjun zhuanlüe" [The sound of gunfire echoing here: Biography of General Gao Jingting"], *Xinhua wenzhai* [China digest], July 8, 1989.

4. *New Path* is our translation; it was a weekly that began in 1948.

5. The term "professional student" is applied to someone who spies on other students for a political party, usually the Chinese Communist Party or the Guomindang.

6. Franklin D. Roosevelt's "four freedoms" were freedom of speech, freedom of worship, freedom from want, and freedom from fear. The speech was the State of the Union address on January 6, 1941.

7. The proposal was originally published in *Zhongyang ribao* [Central daily] on September 28, 1947. The full text is available at https://zh.wikisource.org/zh-hant/爭取學術獨立的十年計畫.

8. In *Lunyu* 2.17, Confucius tells a disciple what it is to know: "To say you know when you know, and to say you do not when you do not, that is knowledge." D. C. Lau, *Confucius: The Analects* (Harmondsworth, Middlesex, England: Penguin Books, 1979), 65. (Hereafter Lau, *Analects*.)

9. For some examples, see Cheng Nien, *Life and Death in Shanghai*, (New York: Grove Press, [1986] 2010); Yue Daiyun and Carolyn Wakeman, *To the Storm: Odyssey of a Revolutionary Chinese Woman* (Berkeley, CA: University of California Press, 1985); Li Zhisui, *The Private Life of Chairman Mao: The Memoirs of Mao's Personal Physician* (New York: Random House, 1985).

10. Peng Zhen was a major organizational figure in the Chinese Communist Party in Beijing after 1949. He was mayor of Beijing from 1951 to 1966, but he was purged by Mao Zedong during the Cultural Revolution and later rehabilitated by Deng Xiaoping when he presided over many legal reforms. See Pitman B. Potter, *From Leninist Discipline to Socialist Legalism: Peng Zhen on Law and Political Authority in the PRC* (Stanford, CA: Stanford University Press, 2003).

11. The Beijing Changguanlou Incident was one of the internal Chinese Communist Party purges during the Cultural Revolution. For details, see https://zh.wikipedia.org/wiki/畅观楼事件.

12. In the Xi-an Incident, Generals Zhang Xueliang and Yang Hucheng took Chiang Kai-shek prisoner to force him to focus on fighting Japan rather than destroying the Chinese Communists. In the Marco Polo Bridge Incident (also called Lugou Bridge Incident or Seven-seven Incident) of July 7, 1937, Chinese troops fought with Japanese invaders in what is considered the beginning of the Anti-Japanese War of Resistance.

13. *Lunyu* 16.1. Lau, *Analects*, 138; Simon Leys, *The Analects of Confucius* (New York: W. W. Norton, 1997), 80–81. We have combined these two translations.

14. *History of the Former Han Dynasty (Hanshu)*, "Shihuo zhi," 23. https://ctext.org/han-shu/shi-huo-zhi

15. Liu Shipei was a linguist, anarchist, and a revolutionary. Bao Jingyan was a Daoist and perhaps China's first anarchist.

16. Zhang Taiyan (Zhang Binglin) was an influential philologist and revolutionary political activist. Wu Zhihui was a linguist who became an anarchist in France; he was a prominent member of the 1920s Guomindang. Li Shizhen and Wu Zhihui founded the Chinese anarchist movement, but Li was also a prominent member of the 1920s Guomindang. Huang, Kan was a philologist, revolutionary, and popular professor.

17. Liang Shuming, *Yi wang tan jiu lu* (Taipei: Li Ao, 1990). For an overview of Liang's ideas, see Guy S. Alitto, *The Last Confucian*, (Berkeley: University of California Press, 1979).

18. Zhao Ziyang was the third premier of the People's Republic. He spear-headed Deng Xiaoping's reforms until he was removed from office for supporting the students during the 1989 democratic movement. See Zhao Ziyang, *Prisoner of the State: The Secret Journal of Premier Zhao Ziyang*, trans. and ed. by Bao Pu, Renee Chiang, and Adi Ignatius (New York: Simon and Schuster. 2009).

19. Yü Ying-shih note: Yü Ying-shih, *Xiandai ruxue lun* (River Edge, NJ: Bafang wenhua, 1996; Shanghai: Shanghai renmin, 1998, first and second editions). Translators' note: For an English-language article on some of this research, see "Business Culture and Chinese Traditions: Toward a Study of the Evolution of Merchant Culture in Chinese History," in Yü Ying-shih, *Chinese History and Culture*, Vol. 1: *Sixth Century B.C.E. to Seventeenth Century*, 2016), 222–272. For the English version of Yü's classic book on this subject, see *The Religious Ethic and Mercantile Spirit in Early Modern China*, translated by Yim-tze Kwong, edited with introduction by Hoyt Cleveland Tillman (New York: Columbia University Press, 2021). The Yu Xie quote is Yü Ying-shih's translation from this essay. Original from Li Weizhen, *Taibi shanfang ji*, 105:28a.

20. Li Zhi, *Cangshu* (Beijing: Zhonghua shuju, 1959), *juan* 32, p. 544.

21. In *Lunyu* 1.15, Confucius said it is better to be "poor yet delighting in the Way, [and] wealthy yet observant of the rites." Lau, *Analects*, 61. According to Mencius, "Yang Hu said, 'If one's aim is wealth one cannot be benevolent; if one's aim is benevolence one cannot be wealthy.'" *Mengzi* 3A.3 "Duke Wen of Teng, Part One, D. C. Lau, *Mencius* (Harmondsworth, Middlesex, England: Penguin Books, 1970), 97. (Hereafter Lau, *Mencius*.)

22. Datsu-a Ron (脱亞論) was a proposal calling for Japan to leave Asia behind and learn from the West. It was published in the Japanese newspaper *Current Events* (Jiji Shimpo 時事新報) on March 16, 1885. See https://ja. wikipedia.org/wiki/脱亞論 for details.

23. Zhang Zuolin was the warlord ruler of Manchuria from 1916 to 1928. The Kwantung Army was the largest unit in the Imperial Japanese Army. See Kwong Chi Man, *War and Geopolitics in Interwar Manchuria: Zhang Zuolin and the Fengtian Clique during the Northern Expedition* (Leiden and Boston: Brill, 2017).

24. Yü Ying-shih note: Wen Liming and Hou Jukun, ed., *Wen Yiduo nianpu changbian* (Hankou: Hubei renmin, 1994), 486. Translators' note: Wen Yiduo was a modern poet, a classical Chinese literature scholar, and

a member of the Crescent Moon Society and the Chinese Democratic League; he was assassinated by Guomindang agents in July 1946.

25. Yü Ying-shih note: Cao Boyan ed., *Hu Shi riji quanji*, vol. 8 (Taipei: Lianjing chuban shiye gufen youxian gongsi, 2004), 203.

26. Professor Yü cites a translation, but we have quoted the original: John King Fairbank, *China: A New History* (Cambridge, MA: Belknap Press of Harvard University Press, 1992), 311.

27. Lin Biao was a leading general in the Chinese Communist army. Instrumental in their victory in the Civil War, he was Mao Zedong's designated successor during the Cultural Revolution, but then he botched an assassination attempt on Mao and died in a plane crash trying to escape. One of many useful books on Lin Biao is by Jaap van Ginneken, *The Rise and Fall of Lin Piao*, translated (from the Dutch) by Danielle Adkinson (New York: Avon, 1977).

28. Yü Ying-shih note: Cai Dejin, ed., *Zhou Fohai riji quanbian* (Beijing: Zhongguo wenlian, 2003). Translators' note: Wang Jingwei died shortly after the war ended. Zhou Fohai held many high posts in Wang's government. He was found guilty of treason was sentenced to death, but this was commuted, and he died in prison. See Gerald E. Bunker, *Peace Conspiracy: Wang Ching-Wei and the China War, 1937–1941* (Cambridge, MA: Harvard University Press, 1972).

29. Chen Gongbo was President of Wang Jingwei's Nanjing puppet government. He escaped to Japan after the war, but was extradited back to China, where he was tried, convicted, and executed by firing squad. See David P. Barrett and Larry N. Shyu, eds., *Chinese Collaboration with Japan, 1932–1945: The Limits of Accommodation* (Stanford, CA: Stanford University Press 2001).

30. Yü Ying-shih note: Fairbank, *China: A New History*, 316. According to Chen Yongfa, the Chinese Communist army numbered only around 40, 000 in 1937. See Chen Yongfa, *Zhongguo Gongchandang geming qishinian*, revised version, vol. 1 (Taipei: Lianjing, 2001), 341.

31. Yü Ying-shih note: Chen, *Zhongguo Gongchandang geming qishinian*, 341.

32. Yü Ying-shih note: Yang Kuisong, "*Youguan Pingxingguan zhandou de jige wenti*," *Dangshi yanjiu ziliao* 黨史研究資料, No. 2 (1996). Translators' note: Full Chinese version at https://web.archive.org/web/20070531205 006/http://www.yangkuisong.net/ztlw/sjyj/000223.htm. Partial English translation at https://forum.axishistory.com/viewtopic.php?p=1066435 #1066435.

33. At the Lushan Conference, Peng Dehuai was purged because of his criticism of the Great Leap Forward, and Lin Biao was promoted to Peng's position. See Jürgen Domes, *Peng Te-huai: The Man and the Image* (London: Hurst, 1985); and Roderick MacFarquhar, *The Great Leap Forward, 1958–1960* (New York: Columbia University Press, 1983).

34. The Yalta Conference of February 4–11, 1945, was a meeting of the leaders of the United States, United Kingdom, and Soviet Union to plan for the post-WWII world. Stalin agreed to enter the war against Japan three months after the defeat of Germany. See United States Department of State, *Foreign Relations of the United States. Conferences at Malta and Yalta, 1945* (Washington, DC: U.S. Government Printing Office, 1945), 547–996.

35. Yü Ying-shih note: He Fang, *Cong Yan-an yilu zoulai de fansi: He Fang zishu* (Hong Kong: Mingbao, 2007), 155.

36. See "Talk: Mao Zedong/Archive 3," https://zh.wikipedia.org/wiki/Talk:毛泽东/存档3.

CHAPTER 3

NORTHEAST ZHONGZHENG UNIVERSITY AND YANJING UNIVERSITY

PART ONE: STUDYING IN NORTHEAST ZHONGZHENG UNIVERSITY

In the summer of 1946, I returned to Anqing from Tongcheng, then headed to Beiping via Nanjing, and finally settled down in Shenyang. At that time only a year had passed since the victory in the Anti-Japanese War of Resistance, and the great majority of the Chinese people thought they would be able to have a few peaceful years, but in less than three years China was involved in a change so great that it would turn their entire worlds upside down.

My father, Yu Xiezhong, and Lieutenant General Du Yuming were old friends of many years. After the victorious war, Du was transferred to the Northeast to handle military affairs, and he strongly urged my father to go with him. This was primarily to prepare for a new university, the Northeast Zhongzheng University, which opened in 1946. The university appointed Zhang Zhongfu (1901–1977) as president. His specialty was the history of the Republic of China's foreign affairs. He and my father had once worked together at Nankai University. Zhang later served as Chairman of the Department of Politics at Peking University; when the Anti-Japanese War of Resistance began, he joined the government and worked in foreign affairs. After his appointment at Northeast Zhongzheng University, he was dispatched to work at the United Nations. Zhang was thus president of the university in name only, and my father as Dean of Arts took over Zhang's university administrative work.

By that time I was already sixteen years old, but I had only studied for about two years in a private school and two years in a temporary middle school in Anhui. I had left halfway through and never finished an entire year from beginning to end. My educational level was probably somewhere between the second and third year of junior middle school. My English vocabulary was extremely limited; in a short two- or three-page essay, there were usually more than eighty words I did not know; and I knew even less in the areas of mathematics, physics, and chemistry. I was, however, already at the age when I should be taking the university entrance examinations. I therefore enrolled in a Northeast Zhongzheng University preparatory class (the equivalent of grade three in senior middle school) and found tutors to provide extra remedial lessons; I was hoping that after one year of these combined efforts I would be able to pass the university entrance examinations.

To this day, I still remember the two teachers who taught me my remedial lessons. The first was Teacher Liu who taught me mathematics, physics, and chemistry; he was from the Northeast and taught university preparatory classes. His teaching was very organized, and within three or four months I achieved a general understanding not only of algebra, trigonometry, and geometry but also physics and chemistry. Of course, these were all eleventh-hour efforts. With Buddha's mercy, I was hoping to get through the examinations. Teacher Liu eventually moved to live in Taiwan. We lost contact, and it is a pity that I have even forgotten his personal name.

The second remedial instructor was Shen Bolong, who taught me the *Records of the Grand Historian* (*Shiji*). He only made it through "The Basic Annals of Xiang Yu" ("Xiang Yu Benji" 項羽本紀) and "The Hereditary House of Chen She" ("Chen She Shijia" 陳涉世家).[1] I still remember the vivid, lively way that he told the story of Xiang Yu's (ca. 232–202 BCE) Hongmen Banquet. He explained in a clear, straightforward manner that the sentence, "Oh, what a heap of stuff you have, Chen She, now you're a king! Such a big place!" was in the vernacular language of the time. I originally thought that the father and son Sima Tan (c. 169–110 BCE) and Sima Qian (c.145–86 BCE) only wrote carefully composed elegant and refined words, but after he disabused me of that idea, I began to pay attention to the fact that the ancient classics and histories have many instances of faithfully recorded colloquial speech, and the boundary between classical and vernacular Chinese is not that easy to distinguish. Several decades later when I wrote an essay entitled "The Seating Order at the Hongmen Banquet," the seeds of which were probably sewn by Mr. Shen's lectures.[2]

Not long after, I finally heard indirectly that he [Shen Bolong] was in fact the very prominent Shen Qiwu (1902–1969). It is probable that during the Anti-Japanese War of Resistance he had some relationship with the Japanese or the puppet government, and so he changed his name and went into hiding in the Northeast. Very few people know the name Shen Qiwu today, but in the 1930s and 1940s he was very active in literary circles. He and Yu Pingbo (1900–1990), Jiang Shaoyuan (1898–1983), and Fei Ming (1901–1967) were known as "the four major disciples of the Bitter Rain Studio" (i.e., followers of Zhou Zuoren).[3] The writings collected in Shen Qiwu's 1932 *Recent Prose Anthology* (*Jindai sanwen chao* 近代散文抄) are primarily the short essays of the Gong-an and Jinling prose schools of the late Qing. In his preface to the work, Zhou Zuoren (1885–1967) had great praise for Shen's insightful selection of essays.[4] According to contemporary critics, Shen's essays imitated and successfully captured the spirit embraced by Zhou Zuoren, but Shen later offended Zhou and was expelled from his circle of students. In his later years Zhou wrote a book of essays entitled *Recollections from the Knowledge Studio* (*Zhitang Huixiang lu* 知堂回想錄), which contains an essay entitled "The New Year's Day Assassin" ("Yuandan de cike" 元旦的 刺客) that mentions Shen Qiwu as being present during that assassination attempt and possibly getting wounded.[5] I learned about all this many years later, but at the time I was quite surprised to learn that my teacher Shen had been a famous writer as well as a disciple of Zhou Zuoren.

During that period, there were quite a few people with backgrounds similar to Shen Qiwu's who had come to Shenyang to live. One of them was Chen Qitian (1900–1975), Dean of the School of Law at Yanjing University.[6] On December 8, 1941, the day after the Japanese surprise attack on Pearl Harbor, Chen and several other leaders of Yanjing University, including Zhao Zichen (Tzu-ch'en, T.C. Chao, 1888–1979), Lu Zhiwei (C.W. Luh, 1894–1970), Zhang Dongsun (1886–1973), and Zhao Chengxin (1907–1959), were arrested by the Japanese military authorities. After being held in custody for half a year, Chen was sentenced to one year in prison and two year's probation.[7] He eventually compromised with the Japanese, and so after the Chinese victory he had to escape to the Northeast. When I knew him, he was doing research in my father's Northeast Political and Economic Research Institute and looking quite dispirited; anyone who did not know the inside story could never have imagined how bossy and domineering he had been in his years at Yanjing University. His 1937 book *A Brief Study of Shanxi Banking* (*Shanxi piaozhuang kaolüe*) is still worth consulting even today.[8] When he served as the Dean of the School of Law, however, his power was such that it raised many eyebrows. For example, in May 1932, Xiao Gongquan arrived at his Office right at the appointed time to speak with him, but he kept Xiao waiting outside for half an hour before granting him an audience and addressing him in a very rude manner. From this we can infer that Chen Qitian was extremely haughty.[9]

When I was in the preparatory class of Northeast Zhongzheng University, I was mainly cramming classes in mathematics, physics, and chemistry, but I still remember a Chinese literature teacher, Wang Senran (1895–1984), who taught very enthusiastically. He was also a painter and held an exhibition in Shenyang. In a remarkable coincidence, at the end of the 1970s one of my relatives in Beijing asked a friend to bring me a gift, which was a painting by his elderly next-door neighbor who was a very famous painter. When I unwrapped it, I was astonished to see that it was a work by Wang Senran. Such a coincidence can probably only be attributed to fate, and it is a shame that I never had the chance to see him again.[10]

In the summer of 1947, I passed the examinations and entered the history department at Northeast Zhongzheng University. It must have been because my peers in the Northeast received a poor education under the puppet state of Manchukuo, which resulted in most of them not being able to pass the Republic of China examinations, thereby reducing my competition. It was surprising that I was on the list of accepted candidates. I chose history as my major because I was not good in mathematics, physics, and chemistry and because of my father's influence. At Yanjing University my father concentrated on Western history, and then later at Harvard he studied American history under Professor Arthur M. Schlesinger (1888–1965). When my father came back to China, he taught Western history and American history at Nankai University. The majority of the books in our family library were on the history of the West and, although I could not read them, they still had an influence over me, leading to my intense desire to study Western history. My extracurricular reading began with the works of Liang Qichao and Hu Shi, and these sowed the seeds of my love of Chinese intellectual history. The first-year course on general history of China at Northeast Zhongzheng University was taught by a young lecturer, who used as his textbook Qian Mu's 1943 *A General History of China* (*Guoshi dagang* 國史大綱). This was the first time I encountered Professor Qian's scholarly work. Because of this, even though I only studied at that new university for only three months, the path I would take for my whole life was more or less decided there and then.[11]

Northeast Zhongzheng University was located right outside the pass where the fires of war raged all around, yet in its first year some famous professors actually accepted appointments there, though some did in a visiting capacity only. The one who made the deepest impression on me was Liang Shiqiu. He was teaching at Peking University, and my father offered him a very generous compensation package to come to Shenyang and teach for a month and a half. I already knew that he was Lu Xun's arch enemy, and I had read his *The Art of Reviling* (*Ma ren de yishu* 罵人的藝術).[12] My father held a banquet for him, and I was able to attend. His humorous remarks and satirical witticisms often made the whole room burst into laughter, but he always maintained a straight face. Such occasions to hear him speak always gave his audience great pleasure. Another esteemed person was Professor Sun Guohua (1902–1958). He was a famous psychology scholar of the Behaviorism School and was formerly Chairman of the Department of Psychology at Tsinghua University for many years. Toward the end of the 1920s— because the timing coincided with a break at Tsinghua University and because he liked it in Shenyang—Sun taught at Northeast Zhongzheng University. At the time he was on leave from Tsinghua University and brought his whole family.

Finally, I would like to mention Gao Heng (Gao Jinsheng, 1900–1986), who was from the Northeast. A personal friend of my father's, he accepted the position of Chairman of the Chinese Literature Department at Northeast Zhongzheng University. He came from the Tsinghua University Institute of Chinese National Culture where he studied under Liang Qichao and Wang Guowei. Gao Heng was very well respected in national culture studies (*guoxue*) circles, even though he did not have much of a name yet. He was an upright and sagacious scholar. I never studied with him, but his presence commanded my respect. He was extremely serious and not given to lax speech or careless laughter. Occasionally he would ask me a question, and I would always answer very respectfully, without daring to be presumptuous.

One incident made me admire and respect Gao Heng even more. When I took the Northeast Zhongzheng University entrance examination in the summer of 1947, he happened to be the invigilator. I have no idea what caused him to be suspicious, but he suddenly walked over to my desk and snatched up my exam paper to see if there was something hidden under it. Luckily, I hadn't the slightest intention of cheating or he would have expelled me from the examination. The fact that I was his friend's son was of no consideration; he was as unmoveable as a mountain when it came to maintaining his principles.

Toward the end of the Cultural Revolution, Gao Heng suddenly came to be highly thought of. He annotated many newly discovered texts, such as the Mawangdui *Laozi*.[13] I never doubted his integrity in the least. He must have been convinced by some moral persuasion to have been willing to contribute to the "revolution" with his research. Later when I read in the *Continuation of Wu Mi's Diary* (*Wu Mi riji xubian*) and learned that in the early 1950s in Chongqing he still had not given any indication of following the herd, I became even more convinced that my original assessment of him was correct.[14] In Shenyang, though, I never would have conceived that in the 1970s Gao Heng would play a role in using scholarship for political motives.

The fighting between the armies of the Nationalist Party and the Chinese Communist Party changed greatly in the summer of 1947. In May and June of that year, the Chinese Communist army launched a full-scale attack on Siping (or Sipingkai in western Jilin), and the National Army under the direction of Chen Mingren (1903–1974) steadfastly defended to the death its position and defeated the Communist army at the end of June. When the papers printed a picture of the dirty and miserable-looking Commander Chen, it made a deep impression on me. This was a battle in which casualties on both sides were disastrously high, and it was the last time the National Army was victorious in the Northeast. In July the

Communist army had already shifted from a defensive position to an offensive one, and by October Shenyang was already surrounded.

In the beginning of November, the Chinese Communist army occupied Shenyang. When I flew from Shenyang back to Beiping in the middle of October, I had narrowly escaped death. There were only three planes available at the Shenyang airport, and my father was put on the first plane while I was put on the third one. Just as I was waiting in line to board the plane, my father suddenly called me over to the first plane because there happened to be an empty seat. At the last minute, then, I got on the first plane. The third plane was lost in a crash.

Part Two: Living at Leisure in Beiping

From the end of October 1947 to October 1948, I lived in Beiping with nothing to do. In the spring of 1948, I was not able to transfer to any university. In the fall I passed the examination to enter the first-year class at Furen Catholic University in Beiping, but Beiping was surrounded by the Chinese Communist army, and so my father decided to move south to Shanghai, and I never entered Furen University. Nevertheless, this year still had special significance for me because this was when I encountered currents of contemporary Chinese popular thought.

The Northeast Zhongzheng University students who were from the Northeast bitterly deplored the savage violence of the Soviet army, and so there was no opportunity for any leftist thought to develop. When the students occasionally marched and demonstrated, their protests were mostly targeted at the Soviet army. An example is the Zhang Shenfu (1898–1946) Incident, which was a protest against the Soviet army's killing of a Chinese engineer.[15] The intellectual environment in Beiping was completely different; as soon as I arrived, I had to face the conflicts in contemporary ideologies.

It was at this time that I read Ai Siqi's *Philosophy for the Masses* (*Dazhong zhexue*). This is a book of propaganda, promoting dialectical materialism, written in accessible language and using simple examples to indoctrinate young people. From worldview to everyday life philosophy, the whole book advocated a single closed system. The book quoted from "Ka-er" and "Yi-li-qi." When I first read the book, I simply could not understand it, but after reading on I eventually realized that it referred to Karl (Marx) and (Vladimir) Ilyich (Lenin). The three characters Ai 艾 Si 思 qi 奇 meant love (*ai* 愛), (*Makesi* 馬克思) *si* 思 for Marx and (*Yiliqi* 伊里奇) for Ilyich (Lenin). *Philosophy for the Masses* had considerable influence among the youth of the time. Although it did not make me a believer, it did stimulate my thinking in that it touched upon some issues to which I had previously not paid any attention. Reading this book was the first time that I encountered Marxist-Leninist thinking.[16]

What had the greatest influence on my thinking at this time would have to be Chu Anping's (1909–1966?) weekly *The Observer* (*Guancha*) and the combined *Observer Collection* (*Guancha congshu* [觀察叢書]).[17] This was of course because in my heart of hearts I accepted universal values such as democracy, freedom, tolerance, equality, human rights, and the like that derived from the May Fourth Movement. I remember in the summer of 1948 when I read Hu Shi's essay "What is Liberalism?" ("Ziyou zhuyi shi shenme?" 自由主義是什麼?) in the "Opinion" (*shilun* 時論) section of the *Independent Commentaries on Current Affairs* (*Duli pinglun*), I was extremely excited because Hu Shi emphasized that the fight for freedom (or liberty) in China had a very long and glorious history. He pointed to Confucius's saying that "the practice of benevolence depends on oneself alone" (*wei ren you ji* 為仁由己) as simply another way of talking about "freedom."[18] I found this to be very persuasive. I have always believed that since China is a large and ancient civilized country, it must comprise elements that are sensible, rational, and in conformity with human nature, and that if they are suitably modified, they can converge with universal values and provide an impetus for China's modernization. I cannot accept the extremist view that the Chinese tradition contains only negative elements such as dictatorship, inequality, and oppression.

The Observer was a publication that I simply had to read every week. Its fundamental position may be said to have been liberal, and on that account it followed an open and pluralistic editorial policy, incorporating many diverse and even conflicting points of view. For a young person like me who had only just begun to think about the big issues of politics, economics, society, and such, it was just the right sort of material for cultivating practical thought. I continually had to form my own independent judgments, but whether they were right or wrong is another question. At that time, proposals for violent revolution or peaceful reform were in constant competition, and, being influenced by Hu Shi, I preferred peaceful reform. As such, I especially appreciated Fei Xiaotong's (1910–2005) two books *From the Soil* (*Xiangtu Zhongguo* 鄉土中國) and *Rural Recovery* (*Xiangtu Chongjian* 鄉土重建) as well as *Imperial Power and Gentry Power* (*Huangquan yu Shenquan* 皇權與紳權) edited by Fei and Wu Han (1909–1969) because they brought up historical questions that were of interest to me.[19]

Fei Xiaotong studied in England and had some knowledge of the process by which the gentry class was transformed from feudal landowners into corporate entrepreneurs in recent English history. In his *Rural Recovery*, he tried to employ the English model to lay out a path for the peaceful evolution of the Chinese landlord class. He had conducted onsite research in the countryside (Jiang village), so his descriptions of the lives of the landlords were generally quite objective, and this was mainly why I was drawn to his work at the time. Violent revolution prevailed in the end, and Fei's analyses and discussions of rural China were all for naught.

In 1979 a delegation from the Chinese Academy of Social Sciences visited Yale University, and Fei Xiaotong was one of the delegates. This was the first and only time that I ever met him. I told him that early on I had read his works, and he complied with the Chinese government's official regulations by quickly saying that those mistaken ideas were not worth mentioning. I could not help blurting out, "if you had not written those things, you would not be here today." He could only smile in embarrassment. To be fair, up until 1948, Fei Xiaotong was one of a very small minority of representative Chinese sociologists, and his English-language publications were highly thought of by international scholars in his field. In the autumn of 1955, when I audited Talcott Parsons's (1902–1979) course "Social Systems" at Harvard University, the reference works on Chinese subjects included Fei Xiaotong and Chih-i Chang's coauthored *Earthbound China: A Study of Rural Economy in Yunnan* and a 1946 article by Fei on the Chinese "Peasantry and Gentry" in the *American Journal of Sociology*.[20] Unfortunately, Fei's academic life was put on hold in the 1950s. The English-language book *Towards a People's Anthropology*,[21] which he published in China in his later years was quite unreadable, and the occasional random essays he published in Chinese journals were lackluster; none of these works could compare with the *Guancha* and *Dagong bao* era, which is a great pity.[22]

Lastly, I would like to discuss the *New Path* (*Xinlu*) weekly. This publication was managed and supported financially by Qian Changzhao (1899–1988). As director of the Nationalist government's National Resources Commission, Qian had no problem obtaining the funds for the publication. He had studied in England and was influenced by the Fabian Society, so he leaned toward democratic socialism. The *New Path* was founded in Beiping in the summer of 1948 with Wu Jingchao (1901–1968), a professor of sociology at Tsinghua University, as chief editor; Wu also contributed quite a few articles. Liu Dazhong (1914–1975) of Tsinghua University and Jiang Shuojie (1918–1993) of Peking University enthusiastically contributed articles on economics.[23] In the 1970s, I often had the opportunity to meet with Liu and Jiang in the United States and Taipei, and we would reminisce about the *New Path* of those days.

In the summer of 1975, Liu Dazhong accepted the offer from the board of directors of New Asia College to be my successor as dean of the college. After he returned to Cornell University, he received the terrible news that he was in the final stages of cancer. In August that year, I received the shocking news that he and his wife had committed suicide together.

I learned quite a bit about socialism, capitalism, economic freedom, social equality, and such matters from the *New Path* weekly, which broadened my vision of the world. In the early 1950s, when I wrote books like *On Democratic Revolution* (*Minzhu geming lun* 民主革命論) and *Between Freedom and Equality* (*Ziyou yu pingdeng zhi jian* 自由與平等之間), which were superficial and not worth reading, the origin of my thought could be traced back to my leisurely life in Beiping in 1948.[24]

During the time I was in Beiping, I did not, of course, spend all my days greatly concerned with intellectual issues. As an ancient cultural city, Beiping certainly had an inexhaustible number of interesting places, and I would occasionally gallivant outside the city walls to the Summer Palace, the Jade Spring Hill, the Fragrant Mountain, and other scenic spots. One of my greatest pleasures, unforgettable to this day, was browsing in secondhand bookshops, such as the ones in the Liulichang District famed for its books and arts and crafts, as well as those at the Longfu Temple, Dong-an Market, and other small book stalls—these were places where one could enjoy oneself to the point of forgetting to go home. It made me happy for many days when I found an old book I was looking for and learned how little the seller wanted for it. In the evenings, listening to Peking opera for free was also a great pleasure. Peking opera performances generally began at seven or eight o'clock; some of my friends who knew the ropes told me that if I slipped into the theatre after ten o'clock, there would not be anyone at the door taking tickets, and I could saunter straight in and could even find a good seat. I watched quite a few plays for free, including works like *Mount Dingjun* (*Dingjun shan* 定軍山) with Tan Fuying (1906–1977) in it; the best plays were always performed at the end of the evening's bill.[25] This was the aspect of cultural life in old Beiping that everyone loved most and never wanted to end. In October of 1978 when I returned after twenty-nine years to a newly named Beijing, I felt it had become a completely unfamiliar place.

While in Beiping I never participated in any student demonstrations nor did I join any student organizations, but occasionally if I heard about lectures on a topic in which I was interested, then I would certainly attend. For example, when Yang Zhensheng (1890–1956)[26] lectured at Peking University on Lu Xun's old-style poetry, I listened with great interest and pleasure. This also gave me an opportunity to interact with the university students and get a feel for the intellectual pulse. I can honestly say that the youth of that period were in general very dissatisfied with the corruption and ineffectiveness of the Nationalist Party, but with the exception of underground Chinese Communist Party members, very few students approved of or identified themselves with the Soviet Union's "dictatorship of the proletariat." What most believed in were the universal May Fourth values of democracy, freedom, tolerance, and equality. At the time, the Chinese Communist Party was flying the flag of "New Democracy" (*xin minzhu zhuyi* 新民主主義). Notably, Mao Zedong's essay "On the People's Democratic Dictatorship" ("Lun renmin minzhu zhuanzheng" 論人民民主專政) was not published until June 30, 1949—after the Communist armies had taken Nanjing and Shanghai.[27]

Another major reason why intellectual youth and the democratic political parties were opposed to the Nationalist Party was because it was a "one-party dictatorship." The reason they wanted to overthrow the Nationalist Party regime was certainly not because they wanted to replace an ineffective "one-party dictatorship" with an effective "one-party dictatorship." Chu An-ping expressed this sentiment very clearly in 1947 in his celebrated essay "China's Political Situation" ("Zhongguo de zhengju"):

> As we are now struggling for freedom under the control of the Nationalist Party, it is a question of "a great deal" (*duo* 多) or "a little bit" (*shao* 少) of "freedom"; if the Communist Party takes power, this question of "freedom" will become a question of "having any" (*you* 有) or "having no" (*wu* 無) "freedom."[28]

To overthrow one regime was not to be regretted much, but the intellectual class of that time had never expected that the ensuing total chaos would lead to the sacrifice of the emerging model of civil society, which had been building up gradually since the founding of the Republic.

Part Three: In Shanghai 1948 to 1949

In the last weeks of October 1948 when we left Beiping for Shanghai, the Communist armies already controlled north China. On October 22, when Hu Shi flew back to Beiping from Nanjing, he wrote in his diary: "Returning this time after being away for thirty-six days, I have a sense of impending doom regarding these momentous changes; the situation has really deteriorated so much!"[29] It was because of these conditions that my father decided to move temporarily to Shanghai. By then the trains were no longer coming in and airplanes would not allow any luggage, and so we decided to take a boat from Tianjin; it was the first time I ever travelled on a boat. My own experience of living in Shanghai for those nine plus months was pretty depressing. Unlike in Beiping both the people and the place were unfamiliar, and since I could not speak the Shanghai dialect, I could not go anywhere. These few months just happened to be the crucial period in China's complete upheaval, and it was here that I saw firsthand the Nationalist Party's collapse and the Chinese Communist troops' entry into the city.

Now, as far as my memory will allow, I will briefly discuss the main tendencies of the time.

Not long after we arrived in Shanghai, the Huaihai Campaign came to an end.[30] The Nationalist Party's modernized elite troops were almost completely wiped out by the campaign, and calls for peace talks arose again once the campaign was over. After Chiang Kai-shek stepped down in January 1949, Li Zongren as acting president reopened negotiations with the Chinese Communist Party. The peace talks broke down in mid-April, but China was in a state of cease-fire. The general public, of course, hoped that peace would be achieved, but people with a deep understanding of the two parties and their fundamental nature as "dictatorships" certainly held out no hope for peace. On February 4, Fu Sinian sent a letter to Li Zongren in which he wrote:

> The Chinese Communist Party was originally a war party. Having been so warlike in the past and now in a winning position, there is certainly no way to achieve peace with them.[31]

Based on this, he concluded that: (1) the Chinese Communist Party would discuss peace only with local authorities, so as to completely annihilate the central government regime; (2) the Chinese Communist Party would definitely follow the Soviet [party] line; (3) as far as possible the Chinese Communist Party would do their best to destroy all former military commanders [of the Nationalist Army] and all intellectual leaders. These predictions by Fu Sinian were later proven to be very accurate.

Although the war temporarily halted, the living conditions of most people, especially those living in the cities, continued to worsen rapidly. In Shanghai I experienced two extraordinary situations. To this day, as soon as I think back on them, it feels as if they just happened.

The first was inflation. At that time, the currency issued by the Nationalist Government [in 1948] was devalued countless times in a single day. Thus, as soon as the residents of Shanghai had any paper money, they rushed to the black market to buy silver dollars. There were two types of silver dollar coins in general circulation at the time: one with Yuan Shikai's (1859–1916) image called "Big Head Yuan" and one bearing Sun Yat-sen's image called "Little Head Sun."[32] The black-market money traders all worked their silver-counting abacuses with click-clacks as they shouted over and over "big head, little head, buying in, selling out!" Every morning I would leave home with a couple of silver dollars in my hand, go to the black market, and exchange them for paper currency, then run as fast as possible to the market to buy the necessary food for the day. I had to run fast because if I were slow, the money in my hand would lose much of its value on the way. This was such a long time ago and my memory is vague, but if I recall correctly, the price of one sesame flatbread (*shaobing* 燒餅) would sell for as high as several ten thousand paper dollars. This was a clear symptom of economic collapse.

The second was the rampant organized crime. The civil war threw communications between the cities and the countryside into constant chaos. This impacted the shipment of goods and disrupted the supply of daily necessities to the cities, which meant that supply could not meet demand. The situation was exploited by organized crime gangs which rushed in to dominate the markets—they seized all material goods and then sold them at exorbitant prices. These organized criminal elements were active everywhere in Shanghai; people called them the "Yellow Ox Party," and many urbanites joked that they were the third major party outside of the Nationalists and the Chinese Communists. One situation which I encountered personally was having to buy scalped tickets. When you went to see a movie in Shanghai then, you could not buy a ticket at the movie-theatre box office because all the tickets had already been bought up by the Yellow Ox Party. Every time I wanted to buy a ticket, I had to purchase it in front of the theatre from one of the scalpers of the "Yellow Ox Party," and the price was always several times higher than the regular movie-theatre price.[33] This shows how the market and ordinary life in society were in complete disarray. The Shanghai police department was also in cahoots with the organized crime gangs and had lost the ability to maintain social order.

Just from these two situations, it is plain to see that it was impossible for the Nationalist Party rule to continue. The peace negotiations broke down; and on April 21, 1949, the Communist army crossed the Yangzi and very quickly broke through the defenses at Nanjing. After one month the same fate befell Shanghai. To borrow the Chinese Communist Party terminology, I "was liberated" (*bei jiefang* 被解放) in Shanghai. At the time I was neither frightened nor excited; I regarded the change of regime as an ordinary occurrence. Xiao Gongquan recorded that before he left Shanghai, he heard people say "The Chinese Communist Party is coming? There's nothing to be afraid of!"[34] I can bear witness to the veracity of this statement. It was probably a so-called case of "having already lost the hearts of the people" as often described in Chinese history. After the Huaihai Campaign, Yin Haiguang (1919–1969) wrote an editorial in the *Central Daily* in which he called out for "putting the people's hearts in order immediately," (i.e., recapturing the hearts and minds of the people), but it was already too late.[35]

A couple of months after their takeover of Shanghai, the Chinese Communist Party's control gradually changed from relaxed to strict. My father had already begun to hear that the new regime was inquiring about him because of his relationship with General Du Yuming in the Northeast (discussed earlier). The situation suddenly became extremely tense, so my father had to leave Shanghai immediately. During the months of peace negotiations, my father had already discussed with friends and relatives many times the possibility of going to Taiwan or Hong Kong. From what we heard at the time, living in Hong Kong was very expensive and we could not afford it, but Taiwan was a completely unfamiliar place and our safety was not guaranteed. Given these factors we had put off our search for refuge, but now circumstances forced us to leave. There only seemed to be one dangerous route left: take a boat to the Zhoushan islands (in Zhejiang) and then transfer to Taiwan. This was a dangerous route not only because of the unpredictability of the wind and waves but also because pirates often roamed those waters. Because time was of the essence, my father took my stepmother and younger brother and hurriedly set off. I was the only one who could settle matters at our house for my father: our rented house had to be subleased, our rental deposit had to be retrieved, and our books and other miscellaneous items had to be packed up and shipped back to Beiping. As the eldest son, it was my duty to see to these matters. Seeing them off at the Yangshupu Pier was like a life-and-death parting, and I have never forgotten the day.[36]

They left at the beginning of June [1949], and at the end of the month I sat for the Yanjing University entrance examination in Shanghai. As luck would have it, I passed the exam to become a second-year transfer student. About a month later I took the train back to Beiping.

Part Four: Things Seen and Heard at Yanjing University

My family had a house in Beiping situated at 17 Jiaodaokou North Warden's Office Lane (*hutong* 胡同). There were usually several relatives living there, and the house would bustle with activity. Upon my return to Beiping, I went to my family home first to see my family again. Yanjing University was far off in the western suburbs, so I had to stay at the university most of the time and only went home during the weekends. At first I went back and forth on a pedicab, but later it became more convenient when I started to ride a bicycle.

I had been away from Beiping for over nine months, and when I returned, the atmosphere was completely different. By then it was already settled that Beiping would be the nation's capital (replacing Nanjing), and the important members of the Chinese Communist Party and the democratic parties were all gathered there waiting for office appointments and competing for housing. Two lines from a poem by Du Fu (712–770) accurately describes Beiping at that time: "The mansions of the princes and aristocracy all have new masters, and the civil and military livery are all different from former times."[37] Not much later when all the official appointments were made, the following jingle was heard throughout Beiping (the word *shunkouliu* 順口溜 [jingle] did not exist at the time): "To make early revolution is not as good as to make late revolution, to make late revolution is not as good as not to make revolution, not to make revolution is not as good as to foment counterrevolution." This reflected the sentiments of the old revolutionary cadres (the ones who made "early revolution") and was meant to project the Chinese Communist Party's "united front"; that is, to give many high-level offices to surrendered officials and generals of the Nationalist Party as well as other non-party individuals. The Chinese Communist Party cadres were full of dissatisfaction and carried out many serious protests, causing the party to organize and send out many operatives to persuade them to change positions.

My cousin Wang Zhitian (whose Party name was Xiang Ziming) told me in private that Mao Zedong, at a party meeting, had explained the situation as follows: Mao said that to exclude non-party people from joining the government was the so-called "closed-door exclusionism." In the Three Kingdoms period, Guan Yu (Guan Gong, d. 220) was just such a typical "closed-door exclusionist." He refused to unite with the Sun family of the Wu Kingdom to fight together against the Cao family of the Wei Kingdom, and as a result he lost Jingzhou and was defeated at Mai City (both in Hubei). This was a clever explanation and so I still remember it, and it is precisely what the *Book of Songs* (*Shijing*) and the *Analects* mean when they speak of "artful words, like organ reeds" and "cunning words and an ingratiating face."[38] The Chinese Communist Party dictatorship could not keep an open door for long, and in a few short years "closed-door exclusionism" succeeded finally and completely.

The aforementioned events involve the worlds of the powerful; what follows are two stories about ordinary society. The first story is about the time I was on my way to Yanjing University from the city and struck up a conversation with the pedicab driver. Offhandedly, I remarked that "now you have all been emancipated (*fanshen* 翻身, literally "turned over") and did not expect that this would set off a litany of complaints. He said, "Emancipated (turned over)? I've been turned over from my bed onto the floor." It turned out that all businesses in the city were doing very badly and he had very few pedicab customers. It was no wonder he had such an adverse reaction to being called "emancipated." The second story involves my cousin Wang Zhihua (Xiang Ziming's second younger sister), who worked as a clerk in a bank. One day she came to our house on North Warden's Office Lane angry and in tears. We asked her what happened. She told us that a large sum of money was missing from the bank that day, and so the CCP Secretary insisted that all the bank employees—except the Party and Corps members—submit to a body search. The reason for this was very simple, the CCP Secretary said, for people who entered the Party or its associations had already gone through various tests, and so there were already reliable guarantees of their exemplary moral character. People who had not yet entered the Party or its Corps were called "the masses" (*qunzhong* 群眾, a term still used today), and they were one or two ranks below the Party and Corps members both politically and morally (it goes without saying that Party members were a rank higher than Corps members). In Shanghai, Gu Jiegang was also forced to endure the overbearing and bullying behavior of Chinese Communist Party cadres, and he wrote that "they consider themselves to be conquerors and so they compel others to be conquered."[39] From this we can see that the "same ill wind was blowing" in both the north and the south.

These may not have been big issues, but they made a very deep impression on me, and I have not forgotten them some fifty or sixty years later. When I had the chance later to read the diaries of Gu Jiegang and Deng Zhicheng (1887–1960), I saw that they were basically in accord with my memories. In short, the people of both Beiping and Shanghai had lost all faith in the Nationalist Party, but they also had misgivings about the Chinese Communist Party. Those who were happy about the CCP's victory were the revolutionaries and their fellow travelers, not the general population. This was the real situation that I witnessed firsthand.

I was extremely fond of Yanjing University, not only because it was my father's alma mater but also because of its serene, beautiful campus, which was one of the top in all of China. I was assigned to a dormitory room, which was connected to the Number Two Dining Hall, and shared it with another new student. This building was very close to the Weiming Lake, and in my free time I used to walk around the lake or sit by it; in the winter when the lake froze over, I would go there at night with other students to learn how to ice skate. In November 1978, when the American Academy of Sciences sent me as part of the Han Dynasty

Research Inspection Team to visit Peking University and we happened to go by Weiming Lake, I left the group and went over to the Number Two Dining Hall to have a quick look around .... I could hardly bear the contrast between the past and the present.[40]

Yanjing University was founded and financed by an American Christian church consortium. The founder, John Leighton Stuart (1876–1962), was the American ambassador to China after the war, and he was in charge of university affairs. When I arrived at Yanjing University, Mao Zedong's essay "Farewell, Leighton Stuart!" ("Bie le, Situ Leideng!") had only just been published (August 18, 1949), and the university's situation seemed to be very difficult, but none of us new students felt uneasy about it.[41] When I entered Yanjing University, there was no sense of any foreign Christian church influence; on the contrary, the Chinese political atmosphere was exceptionally potent. In the past, what the university professors and students disliked the most was the presence of the Nationalist Party and the Three People's Principles Youth Corps on the campus; and so before 1949, members of democratic liberal groups kept demanding that Nationalist Party associations leave the campus. Surprisingly, by the time I entered Yanjing University, all extracurricular activities had come under the control of Chinese Communist Party Corps (specialized academic curricula still appeared to be arranged by the university departments). For example, if Qian Junrui (1908–1985) or Ai Siqi or someone else came to give a lecture, or if a "struggle session" (*douzheng* 鬥爭) had to be carried out against some troublemaker, then all classes would be canceled so that the teachers and students could participate.[42]

PART FIVE: SCHOLARS OF YANJING UNIVERSITY

The year 1949 was the beginning of the end for Yanjing University; three years later it no longer existed. I have already written elsewhere about the last days of Yanjing University, and I do not wish to repeat it here. I would simply like to introduce a few Yanjing University professors and discuss the impact that Yanjing University had on me.[43]

The first person I met from Yanjing University was Professor Nie Chongqi (1903–1962). I had met him one year earlier, before I entered Yanjing University, when our whole family went on an excursion to the Summer Palace and planned to stay overnight. Nie and my father had been schoolmates, so we made a special detour to Yanjing University to visit him and borrow some sheets and blankets. When I arrived at Yanjing University, it had been a year since we had last met and he did not remember me, so I had to introduce myself before he finally realized that I was the son of his old friend. Nie was from Shandong and had succeeded through hard work; he was a specialist on Song-dynasty history and the bureaucratic systems of successive dynasties. Later when I was at Harvard, my father's teacher (Grand Teacher or *Tai laoshi* to me) William Hung (Hong Ye, 1893–1980) told me that Nie made the most important contribution to the compilation of the Harvard-Yenching Institute Index Series and made it a point to praise Nie's moral character. In the fall of 1948, Professor Nie came to Harvard for a one-year visit, but because the situation in Beiping was so tense and he was worried about his eldest brother and his family, he hurried home in December. Professor Hung said that Nie was, as the Chinese saying goes, "without peer in filial piety and friendship" (*xiaoyou wushuang* 孝友無雙).

Professor Yang Liansheng (Yang Lien-sheng, 1914–1990) was teaching at Harvard while Nie was visiting. Yang was annotating the official terms of the Ming dynasty in Matteo Ricci's (1552–1610) China travel diaries, and Nie was of great help. These bureaucratic terms in popular usage and their Romanization into Western languages by Ricci and others are extremely difficult to identify. If it were not for Professor Nie with his thorough knowledge of the Ming dynasty's official system and its many historical anecdotes, it would have been virtually impossible to reconstruct the terms in Ricci's work. When Professor Yang published his English-language book, *Topics in Chinese History*, he especially thanked Nie Chongqi.[44]

During the fall term of 1949, Professor Nie did not offer his Song-dynasty history course; instead, he offered a requisite course "Modern Chinese History" that began with the Opium Wars. As a textbook he used Fan Wenlan's *Modern Chinese History* (*Zhongguo jindaishi* 中國近代史).[45] Shao Dongfang located this book in the East Asian Library at Stanford University and sent me a photocopy of the title page.[46] Initially I thought that Professor Nie was teaching this course unwillingly and was just doing it to cope with the exigencies of the times. It was not until I recently read the fifth volume of the *Diary of Deng Zhicheng* that I learned that as early as February 15, 1949, Professor Nie had already expressed his desire to teach this new course, and so it is clear that he taught it completely of his own volition. Deng Zhicheng even ridiculed Nie, saying that he "could even be said to be making a determined effort at political reform." My current conjecture is that Nie probably already recognized that this course in "Modern Chinese History" was going to become increasingly important, and rather than letting someone with insufficient training in historiography teach it and turn it into a purely political course, it would be better for him to assume the responsibility and maintain academic standards.

There is evidence to support my conjecture because, although he did not teach the course in a way that contradicted the basic [Communist Party] line of the textbook, Nie expended a great deal of effort on certain details, delved deeply into the original source materials, and highlighted important facts. To this day I vaguely recall the parts about Zeng Guofan (1811–1872) fighting against the Heavenly Kingdom of the Taipings.[47] Nie was naturally critical of Zeng Guofan, but he told the story from beginning to end in accord with the facts, and he had obviously read many sources, some of which were not mentioned in the textbook. He related how Zeng organized local military units and suffered defeat repeatedly in the beginning, and how Zeng almost committed suicide once. Nie also did not use emotionally ladened slogans like "traitor to China" (*Hanjian* 漢奸) or "executioner" (*kuaizishou* 劊子手).

In addition to "Modern Chinese History," I also took a course on historiographical theory and methodology called "Philosophy of History" taught by Professor Weng Dujian (1906–1986). He had been a very talented student in the history department of Yanjing University. After graduation he went to Harvard, studied Mongolian language and Yuan-dynasty history, and received his PhD. He was extremely fond of learning languages; after returning home he studied Manchu while teaching himself Russian.

In the "Philosophy of History" course, Professor Weng assigned the Chinese translation of Georgi V. Plekhanov's (1856–1918) *The Development of the Monist View of History* (*Lun yiyuan lishiguan zhi fazhan* 論一元歷史觀之發展). He said he was trying to read it in the original Russian.[48] I had already heard of the importance of this work by Plekhanov in the history of Russian Marxism. Although Plekhanov was politically opposed to Lenin, Lenin still admitted that this book had educated an entire generation of Russian readers. The work traces the origin of the Marxist view of historical materialism. Besides the ideas of French materialist Paul T. d'Holbach (1723–1789), German philosopher Georg W.F. Hegel (1770–1831), and from utopian socialism, Plekhanov also emphasized the contributions of the French historians Francois Guizot (1787–1874), Augustin Thierry (1795–1856), and Francis-August Mignet (1796–1884), who interpreted the process of history as a struggle over material interests between various classes in society, thereby paving the way for Karl Marx's theory of class struggle. Plekhanov believed that Marx had not only fully absorbed the ideas of these thinkers but also had swept away their liabilities, thereby establishing the foundations of social science. On this account, Plekhanov compared Marx to Nicolaus Copernicus (1473–1543) and Charles Darwin (1809–1882).

Plekhanov's book and Professor Weng's explanations certainly opened up a new world of thought for me, and they also aroused my curiosity, especially about the ideas of the French historians. I must admit that my understanding at the time was rather fuzzy, but my interest was very strong. Later I would frequently read up on European intellectual history because of this early experience.

In his class, Professor Weng also introduced us to *A History of Western Philosophy* by Bertrand Russell (1872–1970) and had us read the English version. He said that Russell's work had two strong points. First, its title, *A History of Western Philosophy*, is an expression of modesty because it does not take an arrogant Eurocentric position; and second, Russell pays attention to the relationship between philosophy, society, and political background—a special characteristic of his book.[49]

Professor Weng's course did not turn me into a historical materialist or a monist, but it probably influenced my future research on intellectual history, specifically in not focusing on abstract concepts alone but also seeking out the complex elements in the political, social, economic, and cultural contexts of any concept. We had to write an essay for our final examination, and my essay "A Study of the Decline of the School of Mozi's Thought" ("Moxue shuaiwei kao" 墨學衰微考) was on the social changes from the Warring States period to the Qin and Han dynasties.

Before the semester ended, Professor Weng was rather unexpectedly appointed as director of the Beijing Cultural and Education Bureau. I say this was unexpected because he had never demonstrated any political inclinations during class and had also never uttered a word of political propaganda. He asked our class who wanted to accompany him to serve in the bureau. Apparently, nobody responded. We had no idea at all that he and the Chinese Communist Party had already reached such a level of mutual trust. It was not until I read the *Diary of Deng Zhicheng* that I learned that Weng despised the Nationalist Party and had sympathized with left-wing intellectuals and students for a very long time. He seems to have been able to play it safe, without bringing any attention to himself during the Nationalist Party era. Later on under the Chinese Communist Party rule, he became an official and in the end emerged unscathed without any trouble. He was the only professor that I saw again after I left Yanjing University. In the fall of 1986, he visited the

United States with his daughter and son-in-law. They drove from Boston to Yale University and spent an afternoon at my home. At the time, he was very gloomy about China's political situation. He told me that he had joined the Chinese Communist Party because it would afford him quite a number of benefits in his old age.

The third course I enrolled in was "Second-Year English," which was taught by Professor Zhao Luorui (1912–1998) from the Department of Western Languages.[50] In two prefaces to Wu Ningkun's (1920–2019) books, *A Single Tear* (*Yi di lei*) and *Lonely Zither* (*Guqin*), I have already written quite a bit about the bitter experiences of Professor Zhao and her husband Chen Mengjia (1911–1966), so I will not say more here.[51] Professor Zhao taught the course in English and required students to speak English in her class. I had never done this before and found it to be very difficult at first. After a month or so, my spoken English as well as my reading and writing showed obvious improvement, though I was still far from being fluent. Nevertheless, that course was a good foundation for my English-language skills, so that semester continues to be a memorable one for me.

The fourth course I took was "Guided Readings in European History." The teacher in charge was a lecturer (or a teaching assistant; I can't remember for sure). The course involved one-on-one guidance, similar to a tutorial in the West. It was only when I read the *Diary of Deng Zhicheng* did I learn that my teacher's full name was Li Wenjin. She was extremely good-natured and very patient in working with me on my readings. Because I was a transfer student who entered in the second year, she spent some time telling me quite a few stories about the university and its history department. She was the one who told me that when Jian Bozan (1898–1968) compiled historical materials on the Boxers of 1900, he included *Gengzi xiao xia ji*, an early Qing record of painting and calligraphy as a reference book. According to her, at that time there were the so-called "Four Big Vacuum Tubes" at Yanjing University, and Jian Bozan was one of them. They were called "vacuum tubes" because their scholarship was considered shallow or empty (vacuum—*zhenkong* 真空—in Chinese means "truly empty").[52]

I found a great deal of material on Jian Bozan in the *Diary of Deng Zhicheng*, so I'll mention a little more in passing. As early as February 12, 1949, Qi Sihe (1907–1980), Chair of the History Department, told Deng that "Our sociology department has appointed Jian Bozan, and from now on there will be a lot of trouble in the history department."[53] On April 19, 1950, Qi came to talk to Deng again and told him that "Jian Bozan is a troublemaker, and it would be best for you to be careful of him."[54] From this we can see that the old members of the history department were deeply suspicious of Jian and that Qi probably knew that politics must have been behind Jian's appointment at Yanjing University. On June 30, 1952, Deng recorded in his diary that his concubine (Banyun) gave Jian Bozan the nickname "bedbug" because Jian's "eyebrows and eyes were crowded together in one place" like a bedbug's.[55] From then on, the entries in Deng's diary often include the word "bedbug." At first, I did not understand what this meant, but when I finally read the passage on how this usage began it all became clear.

During the Cultural Revolution, Jian Bozan and his wife committed suicide together, which is a terrible tragedy, and I have absolutely no intention of speaking ill of him. I only want to point out that his appointment at Yanjing University was not the act of an individual, but rather he represented the Chinese Communist Party in their attempt to root out the so-called "historians of the bourgeois class." However, these "historians of the bourgeois class" were not fools and were long aware of what was happening. This demonstrates the immense value of the *Diary of Deng Zhicheng*. By carefully reading this diary, we can understand the terrible, imperious statements made by Jian Bozan during the Anti-Rightist Movement.[56] For example, he said, "As soon as we entered Beijing, those professors of the bourgeois class prepared a Hongmen Banquet for us."

Given all the important information provided by the *Diary of Deng Zhicheng*, I should also say a few words about Deng himself. Deng Zhicheng's (1887–1960) native place was Jiangning in Jiangsu, but he was born in Chengdu in Sichuan; from the age of eleven he lived for eighteen years in Kunming in Yunnan. In his early years he participated in anti-Manchu revolutionary activities and later opposed Yuan Shikai's imperial regime. On that account he formed a very close relationship with Chen Yi (Er-an, 1870–1939), and his diary contains many records of their activities in Beiping. When it came to politics, Deng was from the beginning opposed to the Northern Expedition led by Chiang Kai-shek and was extremely hostile to the Nationalist government in Nanjing.[57] Intellectually he scorned Hu Shi and the New Culture Movement that Hu advocated. After settling down in Beiping, he taught at Peking University, Beiping Normal University, and other schools. From 1930 on, he lectured in the history department of Yanjing University on Qin-Han, Wei-Jin Nanbeichao, and Ming-Qing history. Although he neither understood nor supported the Chinese Communist Party, when the defeat and fall of the Nationalist Party became obvious, his diary reveals that he was very pleased. He can be said to have been an old scholar of the culturally conservative faction but without the "anti-communist" consciousness of either the Nationalist Party or the liberals. Because of his political stance, his diary records many facts objectively.

I only saw Deng Zhicheng a couple of times while I was at Yanjing University. The *Diary of Deng Zhicheng* for December 19, 1949, records that "a dozen or so new students from the history department came this evening to eat *jiaozi*,"[58] and I was one of them. Furthermore, because his son Deng Ke and I were both transfer students entering in the second year and we both liked to play *Weiqi* [a board game usually given the Japanese name "*Go*" in English translations], I occasionally went to the Deng family home to play *Weiqi* and may have seen the old man then, but it's hard for me to be sure. In any case I do not remember talking to him then. Deng Zhicheng was famous for his love of swearing at people, and I will admit that my respect for him was unavoidably tinged with fear.

PART SIX: MY EXPERIENCES WITH THE NEW DEMOCRACY YOUTH CORPS

The last thing I would like to discuss in this chapter is my experience in the New Democracy Youth Corps. I never had any desire before to join a political organization. Once while we were chatting, my father told me that although he served as a Counselor in the Examination Yuan during the war, he repeatedly and diplomatically refused many invitations to join the Nationalist Party; and his attitude had a subtle influence on me. When I returned to Beiping from Shanghai and met Xiang Ziming again, I inadvertently grew distant; it was probably my unconscious urging me to avoid arousing any suspicion of playing up to someone in a position of power. To join the Chinese Communist Party or one of its Youth Corps under the new regime was something I had never dreamed of, and on that account I never attended the festivities at the ceremonial founding of the new People's Republic at Tiananmen on October 1, 1949. Quite unexpectedly, though, probably around the end of November, the New Democracy Youth Corps in the history department actively began working on me to "enroll in the Corps" (*rutuan* 入團). The first couple of times they asked, I used the excuse that I "was not qualified enough" so that I could decline diplomatically. I did not foresee that they would continue to pursue me with increasingly fierce efforts. Their arguments were the kind that could change the mind of a young person. Other than the promise of receiving the assistance of the collective and having the opportunity to show off one's abilities, enrolling in the Youth Corps was of no practical benefit and even called upon the individual to make great sacrifices.

After later self-analysis, I believe there were two main factors in my finally agreeing to apply for enrollment in the New Democracy Youth Corps. The first was a big weakness in my character: I cannot objectively turn down other people's requests because I often carefully consider the emotional aspects of the situation. I always believe that people have good intentions, and I should try hard not to embarrass them. This makes some people think that they can take advantage of an opportunity. The second factor was vanity. Although I did not really believe that entering the Party or the Youth Corps was an honor, when I saw how the Youth Corps was trying so hard to win me over and insisting that I had such great potential to "serve the people," a kind of intoxicating self-satisfaction swelled in my mind. I remember that after I was persuaded to join, I paced up and down in the dormitory hallway with my head down and deep in thought; fellow students acquainted with me all knew that I was very much preoccupied. My mind was engaging in what was then known as an "ideological thought struggle" (*sixiang douzheng* 思想鬥爭); in traditional Chinese terms, it was a case of "heaven and man waging war" (*tian ren jiaozhan* 天人交戰), but it was very hard to tell which side was "heaven" and which side was "man."

After I agreed to apply to enter the Youth Corps, extensive investigations began. This was something also completely unexpected because I thought that the organization already knew enough about me when they began to ask me to apply for membership; they had not mentioned that joining the Corps involved such complicated procedures. There were two parts to the investigations. The first part was to question the teachers and students who knew me about my shortcomings as observed from my words and actions. The second part would come after the initial investigations were completed; the Corps organization convened a large meeting of all the teachers and students in the department, and I had to appear and listen to everybody's questions and comments and then answer and address them one by one. I cannot recall the special name for this meeting, but at the time I felt that this was a meeting aimed at criticizing me. Luckily, I had only been at Yanjing University for a short time, and not very many flaws had been noted by the teachers and students; the most serious criticism they came up with was that I was somewhat arrogant about knowing a great deal intellectually, but this was a hurdle that could be easily overcome. Two or three months later, I received a notice in Hong Kong that my application had been accepted and that I could officially complete the enrollment procedures when I returned to the university.

I did not enroll in the New Democracy Youth Corps when I was at Yanjing University and therefore did not have the power as an organization member to bully and humiliate the masses [as some Chinese Communist Party cadres did]. During the period that I was applying to enroll in the Corps, however, I underwent a spiritual transformation (I came to recognize this as a result of my later self-analysis, but I was not aware of it at the time). This transformation manifested in two ways that were connected. First, I became infected with a kind of fanatical religious state of mind. Second, I contracted a "left-wing infantile disorder" (*zuoqing youzhi bing* 左傾幼稚病).[59] These two types of spiritual abnormality are mutually supportive; they can happen at any moment and in the Party's view, lead an individual to commit offences or crimes.

I am now going to relate a story that I have never told anyone before. In late December of 1949, when a fellow villager came to our house at Jiaodaokou North Warden's Office Lane to see cousins on my father's side, he was not there and there was no one else home, and so I received him. He was a Christian pastor who preached in Wuhu in Anhui where many Yü clan relatives also lived. He told me about the recent conditions in Anhui and, most importantly, about the cruel behavior of local (Chinese Communist Party) cadres who were committing crimes like extortion and even murder. He told me that the lives of the poor people had not only not improved but rather had become more difficult. Before he even finished speaking, my fanatical religious sentiments and "left-wing infantile disorder" flared up, and I loudly and sharply refuted his factual statements; in doing so, I relied on a boilerplate propaganda message I had just picked up. He was caught completely off guard, looked quite astonished, and left in a sorrowful state. At that moment it was as though I had drunk from the mythical Spring of Madness (*kuangquan* 狂泉) and had lost all self-control; my sense of humanity had been distorted so badly that very little of it remained.

In about ten days or so I went to Hong Kong and stayed at the home of a relative from Shanghai for two or three days, and there I heard reports that the situation in the south was even worse than what the pastor had reported. Although I still reluctantly disputed these reports, I nevertheless regretted treating that pastor in such a belligerent manner. As time went by, my feelings of shame and regret continued to grow stronger. It's been sixty years now, and every time I think of my encounter with that pastor I feel so ashamed. If this incident functioned as a lesson for me, it was to make me see that all kinds of evil are hidden in the deep recesses of every person's heart, and if they are ever let loose, they will definitely swallow up the individual's entire being. It is because of this experience that during the Cultural Revolution, I had a rather deep understanding of the Red Guard phenomenon.

NOTES

1. These two chapters are translated in Burton Watson, *Records of the Grand Historian of China*, vol. I (New York: Columbia University Press, 1961), 37–74 and 19–31 respectively. The quoted passage is on page 29, and Watson states this is in the colloquial language of the state of Chu.
2. Yü Ying-shih note: Yü Ying-shih, "Shuo Hongmen yan de zuoci," in Shen Zhijia, ed., *Shixue, shijia, yu shidai* (Guilin: Guangxi Shifan Daxue chubanshe, 2004), 70–77. Translator's note: English translation in Ying-shih Yü, *Chinese History and Culture*, Vol. 1: *Sixth Century B.C.E. to Seventeenth Century C.E.* (New York: Columbia University Press, 2016), 122–133.
3. Yu Pingbo was a scholar who studied the *Dream of the Red Chamber* and a writer; in the 1950s his excellent work was the target of politically motivated criticism, and he was persecuted during the Cultural Revolution. See Howard L. Boorman, *Biographical Dictionary of Republican China*, vol. 4 (New York: Columbia University Press, 1971), 67–70. Jiang Shaoyuan was a folklorist and scholar of comparative religions. For information on Jiang and his work, see *Folklores and Superstition (Chinese Edition)* (Beijing: Beijing Publishing Group Ltd, 2015). Fei Ming was a writer of essays and short fiction and a scholar of Chinese Buddhism. See Tang Yan, "Fei Ming 1901–1967," *The Routledge Encyclopedia of Modernism* (New York: Taylor and Francis, 2016).
4. Shen Qiwu, *Jindai sanwen chao* (Beiping: Renwen shudian, 1932). The younger brother of Lu Xun, Zhou Zuoren was a celebrated essayist. Imprisoned for his collaboration with the Wang Jingwei government, he was pardoned and released in 1949. His works are now widely read, and he is the subject of many studies in Chinese and English.
5. Zhou Zuoren, *Zhitang huixiang lu* (Taipei: Longwen, 1989).
6. Yanjing University was called Yenching University at that time; it was a Christian university in Beijing founded in 1919.
7. Yü Ying-shih note: See Deng Zhicheng, "Nanguan jishi," in Deng Rui, ed., *Deng Zhicheng riji*, vol. 8 (Beijing: Beijing Tushuguan, 2007). Deng Zhicheng was a professor of Chinese history at Beiping University, Beiping Normal University, and Yanjing University. Translators' note: See Li Leibo, "Deng Zhicheng (1887–1960) yu jindai Zhongguo shixue," Doctoral dissertation for Peking University, 2014.

8. Chen Qitian, *Shanxi piaozhuang* (Shanghai: Shangwu yinshuguan, 1937). See also *Shanxi piaozhuang kaolüe* (Taipei: Huashi, 1978) and (Beijing: Jingjiguanli, 2008).

9. Yü Ying-shih note: See Xiao Gongquan, *Wenxue jianwang lu* [Record of life-long study and rectification of the past] (Taipei: Zhuanji wenxue, 1972), 99.

10. Wang Senran was indeed a celebrated artist. See Wang Gong, *Zhongguo ming huajia quanji, di-er ji* (Shijiazhuang: Hebei jiaoyu, 2010).

11. Qian Mu's *Guoshi dagang* is chapter 27 and 28 of *Qian Binsi xian sheng quan ji* (Taipei: Lianjing, 1998).

12. Liang Shiqiu, *Ma ren de yishu* (Taipei: Yuandong tushu gongsi, 1994). Many other editions are available.

13. A new edition of the *Laozi*, or *Daodejing*, was one of many ancient texts unearthed at Mawangdui in Changsha, Hunan.

14. Wu Xuezhao, ed., *Wu Mi riji xubian* (Beijing: Sanlian shudian, [1998] 2006).

15. The Soviet army's killing of Zhang Shenfu as well as another ex-soldier in Harbin led to a large-scale anti-Soviet movement. The Chinese Communist Party branded it "counterrevolutionary," but other scholars saw it as "patriotic." It remains a controversial incident in postwar Chinese history. Based on recent information published by a prestigious magazine *Yanhuang Chunqiu*, although the KMT statement at the time implied that the Chinese Communist Party was responsible for the killing, the Chinese Communist Party most probably did it following the instructions of the USSR. See Zhu Yu 朱彧, Zhang Shenfu yuhai shijian zhenxiang kao" 張莘夫遇害事件真相考, *Yanhuang chunqiu* 炎黃春秋, February 27, 2015.

16. A recent edition of Ai Siqi's *Dazhong zhexue* was published by Zhongguo shehui (Beijing) in 2000.

17. Chu Anping was the editor of *Guancha* in the 1940s and later of the Chinese Communist Party's *Guangming Daily*. Considered a liberal, he was purged during the Anti-Rightist Campaign. He is believed to have committed suicide in 1966 during the Cultural Revolution. *Guancha congshu* (vols. 1–16) are available from the University of California at https:// books. google.ca /books/about/ 觀察叢書.html?id= KK9CAQAAIAAJ &redir _esc=y

18. In *Lunyu* 12.1, Confucius's favorite disciple Yan Yuan asks about benevolence (*ren* 仁). Lau, *Analects*, 112.

19. Fei Xiaotong was one of China's most celebrated sociologists and anthropologists whose works were instrumental in the modern study of rural questions in China. *Xiangtu Zhongguo* (Shanghai: Guancha, 1948) is translated as *From the Soil: The Foundations of Chinese Society* with an introduction and epilogue by Gary G. Hamilton and Wang Zheng (Berkeley: University of California Press, 1992). There is no translation of *Xiangtu chongjian* (Shanghai: Guancha, 1948). Wu Han was one of China's most important historians. He once served as mayor of Beijing and was arrested during the Cultural Revolution because his historical play *Hai Rui Ba guan* 海瑞罷官 [Hai Rui dismissed from office] was considered an attack on Mao Zedong. He died in prison. *Huangquan yu shenquan* 皇權與紳權(Hong Kong: Fenghuang, 1972). On Wu Han, see Clive Ansley, *The Heresy of Wu Han: His Play "Hai Rui's Dismissal" and its Role in China's Cultural Revolution* (Toronto: University of Toronto Press, 1971). For the Cultural Revolution, see Roderick MacFarquhar and Michael Schoenhals, *Mao's Last Revolution* (Cambridge, MA: Belknap Press of Harvard University Press, 2006).

20. Yü Ying-shih note with translators' additions: *Earthbound China*, revised English edition, prepared in collaboration with Paul Cooper and Margaret Park Redfield (Chicago: University of Chicago Press, 1972). There are many other editions. Fei Hsiao-Tung, "Peasantry and Gentry: An Interpretation of Chinese Social Structure and Its Changes," *American Journal of Sociology* 52, no. 1, (1946): 1–17.

21. Fei Xiaotong, *Towards a People's Anthropology* (Beijing: New World Press, 1981).

22. The heyday of the *Dagong bao* (Ta Kung Pao), one of the oldest Chinese newspapers, was 1926 to 1949 when it was known for its independent four editing principles of saying no to political parties, governments, companies, and persons. See L. Sophia Wang, "The Independent Press and Authoritarian Regimes: The Case of the *Dagong bao* in Republican China," *Pacific Affairs* 67, no. 2 (Summer, 1994): 216–241.

23. Qian Changzhao was one of the founders and organizers of ROC staterun industries. His *New Path* was shut down for criticizing Chiang Kaishek. Wu Jingchao was an expert on economics and demographics. Liu Dazhong was a professor of economics and economic advisor to the ROC. Jiang Shuojie (Sho-Chieh Tsiang) was an economist who lived in the United States. Both Liu and Jiang made important contributions to Taiwan's land and tax reforms.

24. Yü Ying-shih, *Minzhu geming lun* (Hong Kong: Ziyou, 1954; Taizhong: Jiusi chongyinben, 1979), and *Ziyou yu pingdeng zhi jian* (Jiulong: Ziyou, 1955).
25. Tan Fuying was a celebrated Beijing opera star. *Mount Dingjun* (literally, "mountain of decision for armies") is a play about a famous battle that took place there during the Three Kingdoms period (220–280).
26. Yang Zhensheng was a well-known writer and educator who taught at Peking University from 1946 to 1952.
27. An official English translation of "On the People's Democratic Dictatorship" is available at https://www.marxists.org/reference/archive/mao/selected-works/volume-4/mswv4_65.htm in their *Selected Works of Mao Tse-tung.*
28. "Zhongguo zhengju zhong" was originally published in *Guancha*, di 2 *juan*, di 2 *qi* (March 8, 1947). Complete text is available at https://web.archive.org /web/20160505175208/ http:// www.21ccom.net/ articles/ lsjd/ jwxd/article_ 2011092545930.html
29. Yü Ying-shih note: Hu Shi, *Hu Shi riji quanji*, arranged by Cao Boyan, vol. 8 (Taipei: Lianjing, 2004), 367.
30. The Huaihai Campaign began with the Chinese Communist army's attack on Nationalist headquarters in Xuzhou and ended with their complete victory on January 10, 1949. On the Chinese Civil War, see Diana Lary, *China's Civil War* (Cambridge: Cambridge University Press, 2015); and Odd Arne Westade, *Decisive Encounters: the Chinese Civil War, 1946–1950* (Stanford, CA: Stanford University Press, 2003).
31. Yü Ying-shih note: Fu Sinian, "Zhi Li Zongren shu," in *Fu Sinian quanji*, vol. 7 (Taipei: Lianjing, 1980), 2495.
32. Yuan Shikai was a powerful government and military official and reformer in the late Qing dynasty and early Republican era who tried to have himself declared emperor but died shortly after.
33. To this day "yellow ox" (*huangniu*) means a ticket scalper or to scalp tickets.
34. Yü Ying-shih note: Xiao Gongquan, *Wenxue jianwang lu* (Taipei: Zhuanji wenxue, 1972), 204.
35. Yin Haiguang was a philosopher, professor, and prominent liberal. He was one of the regular contributors to the *Free China Journal* in Taiwan and was persecuted for his critical views. On Yin's life and the publication of his complete works, see "Liberal thinker Yin Hai-guang lives on through his works," *Taiwan Today*, March 18, 2012.

36. Yü Ying-shih note: My stepmother, You Yaxian, married my father in 1940. She passed away in 2017 at the age of 106.
37. These are the third and fourth lines of Du Fu's celebrated "Eight Poems on Autumn" *Qiuxing bashou* no. 4.
38. The last two lines of *Shijing* #198.5 in James Legge's translation are "Their artful words, like organ-tongues, Show how unblushing are their faces." https://ctext.org/book-of-poetry/qiao-yan *Lunyu* 1.3, Lau, *Analects*, 59: "The Master said, 'It is rare indeed for a man with cunning words and an ingratiating face to be benevolent.'"
39. Yü Ying-shih note: Gu Jiegang, *Gu Jiegang riji*, vol. 7 (Taipei: Lianjing, 2007), 253.
40. Yanjing University merged with Peking University
41. An official English version of Mao's essay is available at https://www.marxists.org /reference/archive/mao/selected-works/volume-4/mswv4_67.htm
42. Qian Junrui was a well-known leftist intellectual who held many official academic positions in the PRC. He was imprisoned during the Cultural Revolution but was later rehabilitated and continued to hold official positions until his death.
43. Yü Ying-shih note: Yü Ying-shih, "Huiyi 1949 nian qiuji de Yanjing Daxue—Wu Ningkun xiansheng Guqin xu," in Wu Ningkun, *Guqin* (Taipei: Yunchen wenhua, 2008), 3–27.
44. Yang Lien-sheng, *Topics in Chinese History* (Cambridge, MA: Harvard University Press, 1950).
45. Fan Wenlan signed this book "Wubo" 武波, perhaps meaning "Martial Wave." In 1941, he wrote *Zhongguo tongshi* [General history of China] for Chinese Communist Party cadres.
46. Shao Dongfang is a noted scholar who has served as the director of the Stanford University East Asian Library and chief of the Asian Division of the Library of Congress.
47. Zeng Guofan was a general, statesman, and Confucian scholar who ruthlessly quashed the Taiping Rebellion (1850–1864) with the assistance of French and British forces and restored order to the Qing dynasty. Although it was an extraordinarily destructive event in Chinese history with perhaps 20 to 30 million deaths, the Chinese Communist Party under Mao Zedong considered the Taipings as precursors of their own communist revolution, and thus they were critical of Zeng Guofan. A good book on the Taiping war is Stephen R. Platt, *Autumn in the Heav-*

enly Kingdom: China, the West, and the Epic Story of the Taiping Civil War (New York: Alfred A. Knopf, 2012).

48. Plekhanov was an anti-Tsarist revolutionary and social-democratic Marxist theoretician of historical materialism. A complete English version of his 1895 work is available at https:// www.marxists.org /archive/ plekhanov/1895/monist/index.htm.

49. Bertrand Russell, *A History of Western Philosophy* (New York: Simon and Schuster; London: George Allen and Unwin, 1946 [1945]; revised ed., 1961). Russell is regarded as not Eurocentric because he did not title his book "A History of Philosophy"; by including "Western" in the title, he implied that Western philosophy did not constitute all philosophy.

50. Zhao Luorui (Lucy Zhao) was a Chinese poet and translator with a PhD from the University of Chicago. Her translation of Whitman's entire *Leaves of Grass* was well received. Her husband Chen Mengjia, one of the most noted authorities on oracle bones, committed suicide during the Cultural Revolution. See Peter Hessler, *Oracle Bones*, (New York: Harper Collins, 2006).

51. Wu Ningkun (1920–2019) was a prolific translator, interpreter, and retired English professor who suffered political persecution for twenty-two years until after the Cultural Revolution. Exonerated in 1979, he taught at the Institute of International Relations in Beijing until he moved to the United States in 1990. In addition to the two mentioned books, he also translated *The Great Gatsby*. See *Yi di lei* (Taipei: Yunchen, 2007), in English as *A Single Tear: A Family's Persecution, Love, and Endurance in Communist China* (London: Scepter, 1994), and *Guqin* (Taipei: Yunchen, [2008], 2009). For those unfamiliar with Wu, see his obituary in the *Washington Post*, August 18, 2019.

52. Jian Bozan was a historian, who was well-known for his Marxist interpretation of Chinese history. He was a professor of history and vice president of Peking University. *Gengzi xiao xia ji* [Record of avoiding the 1660 summer heat] was compiled by Sun Chengze 孫承澤 (1592–1676), and published by Bao Tingbo in 1761, about 150 years *before* the Boxer Rebellion.

53. Qi Sihe was a historian who received his doctorate from Harvard, taught at Yanjing University and Peking University, and published books on European history and historical methodology.

54. *Deng Zhicheng riji*, vol. 5.

55. *Deng Zhicheng riji*, vol. 6.

56. The Hongmen Banquet is mentioned earlier. The Anti-Rightist Campaign was a two-year (1957–1959) purge led by Mao Zedong and Deng Xiaoping (1904–1997) to root out Chinese Communist Party members who were critical of the Party's performance from 1949 to 1957 and branded as pro-capitalist. Some 500,000 to 700,000 people were persecuted. See the CD-ROM Database: Editorial Board of the Chinese Anti-Rightist Campaign, *Chinese Anti-Rightist Campaign (1957–) (CD-ROM)* (Hong Kong: Universities Service Center for Chinese Studies, the Chinese University of Hong Kong, 2010).
57. The Northern Expedition was a military campaign in 1926–1927 by the Nationalist Revolutionary Army led by Chiang Kai-shek to defeat various warlords and unify China. It ended with a split between the left and right Nationalist Party governments in Nanjing and Wuhan. See Donald A. Jordan, *The Northern Expedition: China's National Revolution of 1926–1928* (Honolulu: University Press of Hawaii, 1976).
58. *Deng Zhicheng riji*, vol. 5.
59. "'Left-Wing' Communism: An Infantile Disorder" is the title of a 1920 pamphlet by Vladimir Ilyich Lenin in which he criticized any communists or Marxists who did not agree with the Leninist Bolsheviks.

Chapter 4

Hong Kong and New Asia College

When I left Yanjing University in Beijing and transferred to New Asia College in Hong Kong, it was the most important turning point in my life; my entire life completely changed. It was, however, a random change within a random change, and at the time I was not at all conscious of it.

In chapter 3, I discussed sending off my father, stepmother, and younger brother in 1949 at the Yangshupu Pier in Shanghai so they could take a sailboat to Dinghai in the western section of the Zhoushan islands in Zhejiang and then transfer to Taiwan. At the time I felt it was like a life-and-death parting, and I was afraid that I would never see them again. Today I still remember very clearly when I was at a relative's house a few days later and received a notice they sent from Dinghai through the ship captain telling me that they had arrived safely; I could not stop myself from breaking down in tears. What was totally unexpected, however, was the letter I received at the end of November from my father telling me that they had already left Taipei and moved to live in Hong Kong and that he wanted me to come and visit them over the winter vacation.

Later, from talking to my father, I learned the reason why they did not stay in Taiwan. In the second half of 1949, Taiwan's situation was extremely chaotic and its international status was still undetermined. It was not until as late as January 5, 1950, that US President Harry Truman (1884–1972) officially declared, on the basis of the Cairo Conference and the Potsdam Declaration, that Taiwan would be returned to China.[1] He also said, however, that the United States would not interfere in the matter of which side Taiwan would belong in the Chinese civil war. On January 12 of the same year, the American Secretary of State Dean Acheson (1893–1971) announced in a foreign policy speech that the US defensive perimeter in East Asia did not include Taiwan. At that time, many of the refugees who had fled from Mainland China to Taiwan felt that their security was not guaranteed. As such, they felt that Hong Kong was not only a safer place for them but also could offer opportunities to emigrate to Southeast Asia or to Western countries.

Once I decided to go to Hong Kong and visit my relatives during the winter vacation, I was immediately faced with a difficult question: With Hong Kong being a British colony, would I be able to obtain a legal exit permit? I discussed this with several friends and relatives, and they all agreed that I should go to a sub-bureau of the Beijing police in charge of resident registration and apply for an exit permit, but there was another interesting complication. In their letter to me, my parents listed their address as Green Shandao, or Green Hill Road, in Kowloon, but had left off the place name "Hong Kong." Because of this, an older relative recommended that I should say on my application that I only wanted to go to Kowloon to visit my family, but I should not mention Hong Kong. He felt that if the sub-bureau policeman heard "Hong Kong," he would not dare decide on my case on his own and would seek permission from higher up. That could very well hold things up or ruin my chances. I followed my relative's advice, and I received permission right on the spot. I kept this document permitting me to travel from Beijing to Kowloon for many years as a rare reminder of the event, but later it was lost because we moved so many times.

I had to go through many hurdles to visit my family in Hong Kong; at the time my intention was only to be with my parents for a month during the winter break, and then I planned to return to Yanjing University to study after the visit; I had no intention at all of staying for a long time in Hong Kong. I still remember very clearly sitting on the ground in Kowloon on the last night of 1949 and waiting with many other people to cross the Luohu Bridge into Hong Kong the next day (January 1, 1950). I was so full of excitement at seeing my parents again and did not have any expectation of recovering my freedom [from Communist Party control in China]. However, just at the moment that I was crossing the Luohu Bridge, I had an extremely strange experience. My mind suddenly became very relaxed, and my whole body seemed to be in a free and easy state of unrestrained ease. This "unusual spiritual change" (*jingshen yibian* 精神異變) lasted probably less than a second, but the feeling was so profound that it is the strongest in my entire life. I never had such an experience again.

Why did I experience this "unusual spiritual stirring" (*jingshen yidong* 精神異動)? At the time I did not look for an answer, but many years later after going through repeated self-analyses, I finally came up with a relatively reasonable explanation. Between 1949 and 1950, at the level of my overt consciousness I accepted the guiding principles of the Chinese Communist Party (the coalition government based on the New Democracy), and so I did not feel oppressed in Mainland China.

On February 26, 1950, Gu Jiegang's friend Wang Shudi was about to leave for Hong Kong and he came over for a long talk and to say goodbye. Because of that, Gu could not sleep that night, and he wrote in his diary: "Since he is going to Hong Kong, he should surely be able to absorb the atmosphere of freedom."[2]

This was probably a common feeling among many people at that time, but I had absolutely no awareness of Hong Kong being a symbol of "freedom." Therefore my "unusual spiritual change" must have been something that came from my unconscious mind. From early on, *The*

Selected Writings of Hu Shi was one of my favorite books; so then even
before 1948 I must have unconsciously absorbed many of the values of the
"May Fourth" New Culture Movement, especially "science" and "democracy."[3] After the victory in the Anti-Japanese War of Resistance, I was
very much drawn to many popular journals of the day, like *The Observer*
(*Guancha*) and the *New Path* weekly. I also greatly enjoyed reading Hu
Shi's essays in *Independent Commentaries on Current Affairs* (*Duli shilun*)
from 1947 to 1948; these included "At the Present 'Two Worlds' Coming
Clearly into View" ("Yanqian 'liangge shijie' de minglanghua" 眼前兩
個世界的明朗化), "The Present Direction of World Culture" ("Yanqian
shijie wenhua de quxiang" 眼前世界文化的趨向), and "What is Liberalism?" ("Ziyou zhuyi shi shenme?" 自由主義是什麼).

Roughly speaking, my thinking at that time tended toward individual
freedom and democratic socialism (of the British and European kind).
As it happened while I was studying at Yanjing University, the Chinese
Communist Party was fiercely attacking the United States China White
Paper. The China White Paper was released on August 5, 1949. The
United States used it to make clear its position that it would be the
fault of the Nationalist Party if China fell into the communist camp
because the United States had already done its utmost to support them.[4]
The United States placed its final hopes for China on the "democratic
individualists," believing that these Chinese intellectuals, who accepted
the trends of thought that followed the eighteenth-century European
Enlightenment, might in the future lead China on the road to freedom
and democracy. The focus of the Chinese Communist Party attacks was
precisely these "democratic individualists." From their many descriptions
of "democratic individualists," I felt that I certainly seemed to be one
of them. This was something, however, that I definitely did not want
to admit consciously. Because of this I believe that subconsciously I
must have strongly repressed many of my original values and ideas, not
allowing them any opportunity to reveal themselves. This unconscious
restraint built up over several months, but as soon as I returned to a

society in which I was not restricted, this psychological pressure suddenly disappeared and I underwent my "unusual spiritual change."

When I left Beijing, I figured that this winter break visit with my family would last about a month, but after getting together with my parents and my younger brother in Hong Kong, I began to feel that I probably would not be able to leave as originally scheduled. First, for emotional reasons: I felt like the winter break would fly by and be over too soon. My parents hoped that I would stay a little longer, and I really could not bear to leave so quickly. Moreover, the possibility of being able to visit Hong Kong freely again after returning to Mainland China was extremely uncertain. Second, at that time my father had a very urgent task that he insisted I help him complete. When they left Shanghai the year before, my father had entrusted to a relative a great number of his books (including a set of the [4,000-plus volume] *Veritable Records of the Qing Dynasty*) and other cultural artifacts, paintings, and calligraphy he had collected for many years. We were pressed for time because the relative was about to move. I therefore accompanied my stepmother to Shanghai to complete this task, which took us about two weeks. In Shanghai I located several used bookstores and sold all of the books at a cheap price, but I carried some of the cultural artifacts, paintings, and calligraphy back to Hong Kong and delivered them to my father. By that time I had already come to a new decision: I would ask Yanjing University for one semester's leave and go back to school for the fall term.

My father was very happy that I wanted to stay for another six months. He immediately proposed something that never occurred to me. He told me that Professor Qian Mu had just established New Asia College on Guiling Street not far from our house. Since I was not going back to Yanjing University this semester, why not study Chinese history temporarily with Professor Qian? Professor Qian was an influential Chinese historian whom I had long revered, and so of course I cheerfully agreed. Naturally I understood that this was my father's way of trying to keep me in Hong Kong, but my determination to return (to Yanjing

University) was firm and had not yet wavered. At the end of July, I packed up my things and set off.

To this day, I still remember that the month or so before leaving Hong Kong—it was the period when I experienced the most intense conflict between my emotions and my reasoning. What was traditionally said to be "heaven and man waging war" probably referred to such a condition. My parents felt very bad, but they respected my decision; they did not want to give me further emotional pressure and therefore stopped urging me to stay. On an emotional level, I naturally did not want to leave my parents under these circumstances without any consideration. On a rational level, though, I could never accept the idea of this colony of Hong Kong as the place where I would live for a long period. At the time, I strongly believed that my native China was the only place where I would settle down and get on with my life goals, and the path that I most yearned for was that of academic research. New Asia College had a great scholar like Professor Qian, but after two or three months it ran into considerable economic difficulty, and it became questionable to both teachers and students whether it could go on. Moreover, the Hong Kong Ministry of Education only recognized one university in Hong Kong— Hong Kong University; legally New Asia College had only middle school qualifications, and its graduates could only teach in primary schools. All this reinforced the unshakable belief of my early years that my life could only be in my native China. Following this belief, I hardened my heart and found myself seated alone on a train headed for Guangzhou.

Then something completely unexpected happened. My train from Hong Kong to Guangzhou was originally timed to connect to a northbound Beijing train, and I was to change trains immediately in Guangzhou. The Hong Kong train had an unexpected breakdown at a small station called Shilong (Stone Dragon) shortly after crossing the border into China and had to stop for repairs. The repairs took four to five hours, and so I missed my connection to the Beijing-bound train. All I could do was wait there overnight and take a different train the next day. At first I was quite unhappy about this turn of events, but then during those few hours in Shilong, my thinking underwent a very great change that made me suspect that my decision to return to Beijing was a big mistake.

In the first place, I thought I was too selfish, thinking only of my own interests and not taking my father's situation into consideration. To me then, he was already old (around 52) and could not possibly find a suitable position in Hong Kong, and he often unwittingly revealed his anxiety about the future. Before I left Hong Kong, I did indeed have some impression of this, but I did not think too much of it. Sitting in the Shilong train station and thinking about the time I had just spent with my parents in Hong Kong, I could not help feeling shame and regret, and I began to weep. I finally realized that if I stayed in Hong Kong, perhaps I could help my family when they needed me, and my parents would definitely feel much more at ease. Secondly, my single-minded desire to return to China and work for the benefit of my own country was overly formalistic, without any concrete substance and in the end devolved into a kind of abstract empty talk. After all, my parents were also part of China and they were in urgent need of my care; if I left without caring for them, how could I speak of doing my utmost for China? Third and lastly, at this time the Korean War had been going on for over a month, and passage between Hong Kong and China was growing more difficult every day. After I returned to Beijing, the chances of visiting Hong Kong again were extremely slim. Parting from my parents and my younger brother this time would truly become a "life-and-death parting." Thinking about all this, I began to regret my decision to leave them.

My reflections during those few hours in Shilong ranged widely, but the three points were the most important and they remain etched in my memory. After going back and forth examining the situation, I finally came to one clear conclusion: there were a hundred reasons against my returning to Beijing and not one for it. Before the train repairs were completed, I had already made a new, resolute, and completely opposite decision. After arriving in Guangzhou, I would not continue north but return to Hong Kong instead. People may find it hard to believe this, but after I made this decision, the feeling of "heaven and man waging war" that had bedeviled me for several months suddenly vanished, and all I felt was a sense of serenity and peaceful tranquility. One negative thought did occur to me, and that was the fact that I had already joined the New Democracy Youth Corps to contribute to establishing a New Democracy in China and could not do so in Hong Kong. I soon came up with a way to deal with this dilemma: there were countless members in the New Democracy Youth Corps and their numbers were growing constantly; losing me would be insignificant. For me, I felt that my new decision was correct both emotionally and rationally, but to express it in the Chinese Communist Party's contemporary words, it was one hundred percent "petty bourgeois sentimentalism."

As soon as the train reached Guangzhou, I checked into a hotel and asked about ways to return to Hong Kong. At that time, the Hong Kong authorities were forbidding Mainland Chinese refugees from entering Hong Kong. My exit permit was still valid, but how to obtain permission to enter Hong Kong was a big problem. Luckily, someone pointed out to me that the "Yellow Ox Party" in the Guangzhou underworld worked together with the Hong Kong border police. All I had to do was pay them some money and I could enter Hong Kong. The next day, I did just that and went back into Hong Kong.

This was the moment that determined my entire destiny in life, and I'll never forget it.

PART ONE: TRANSFERRING TO NEW ASIA COLLEGE

As early as 1946 when my father was the Dean of Arts at Northeast Zhongzheng University in Shenyang, he invited Professor Qian Binsi (Qian Mu) to come and teach Chinese history. At that time, Professor Qian was determined not to teach in large cities where student strikes and campus upheavals were frequent (e.g., Beiping, Shanghai, Nanjing, and

Tianjin); he would rather go to some border area where the students did not cause too much trouble or disturbances, and so he indicated that he might come to Shenyang. I remember my father was very excited when he told me that "one of the finest historians of Chinese history, Professor Qian Mu, is coming here!" This was the first time I heard Professor Qian's name. We were, of course, very disappointed later when he ended up going to Kunming. However, the first year "General History of China" course at Northeast Zhongzheng University used Professor Qian's *A General History of China* (*Guoshi dagang* 國史大綱) as the textbook, and so the fall term of 1947 was the first time I encountered his writings.

Two years later at Yanjing University, in Professor Weng Dujian's "Methods of Historical Research" class, I had to write a paper in lieu of taking an exam. Because I had read some research earlier on pre-Qin thought by Liang Qichao, Hu Shi, and others, I found it very puzzling that after the Qin and Han period the Mohist School of thought had suddenly disappeared. So I proposed that I write on the subject; my paper's title was "An Investigation into the Decline of Mohist Studies." Professor Weng directed me to read Zhang Taiyan's *Essays on National Culture* (*Guogu lunheng* 國故論衡), Qian Mu's *A Chronological Survey of the Pre-Qin Philosophers* (*Xian Qin zhuzi xinian* 先秦諸子繫年), and other works.[5] This was how I came to read Professor Qian's most sophisticated and profound scholarly work. Given my level of education at that time, I found it extremely difficult to read *A Chronological Survey of the Pre-Qin Philosophers*, and I spent a great deal of time studying the book before I barely came to understand its general ideas. On that account, I had the utmost admiration for Professor Qian.

My father took me to call on Professor Qian and explain the purpose of our visit. Professor Qian told me that New Asia College had just been established and only had a freshman year, but I should be in the second semester of the sophomore year and would have to pass a special examination. He asked me to write on the spot two essays, one in Chinese and one in English, describing my past academic experiences and what my intellectual interests were at the time. Then he invited my father to go to his room for a chat and left me alone in the office to write the essays, which I completed in about an hour. When Professor Qian came back, he read the Chinese essay first and then the English one. Then he smiled at my father and told him, "your son has passed the examination and can enter the college tomorrow." I was quite surprised because I knew that Professor Qian was an autodidact and did not seem to have had a complete modern school education, so it had never occurred to me that he could be proficient in English.

During my first semester at New Asia College, I took Professor Qian's "Survey of Chinese Learning" course, and he used his earlier book *Outline of National Studies* (*Guoxue gailun* 國學概論). At that time because of the current political situation and his life in exile, Professor Qian's mood was not very balanced. With the college's finances also troubling him, he was often unable to concentrate fully on his lectures. At Peking University, Professor Qian was widely known for his especially lively lectures. In the 1940s, Professor Liu Cunren (Liu Ts'un-yan, 1917–2009) wrote an essay entitled "Peking University People" (Beida ren) that was widely circulated in academic circles; in it he described Professor Qian very vividly.[6] However, when I attended Professor Qian's lectures at that time, it seemed to me that he had an indignant and aggrieved air and could flare up at any time. I still remember one time when the newspapers printed a photo of US President Truman wearing a flowery Hawaiian shirt while receiving guests. Professor Qian pointed at the photo and loudly condemned President Truman for his complete lack of dignity; he pointed to a dog lying near the classroom door and said that "this dog is more presentable than Truman." I was very shocked—this was the first time I heard him vilify someone, and it was just too incongruous with the courteous, refined manner in which he usually treated people.

For the first semester, I continued to think that my time at New Asia College was only temporary and that during the summer break I would return to Yanjing University. For that reason, I did not pay much attention to the college and did not have any contact with Professor Qian outside the classroom. It was not until the autumn of 1950 after I decided to remain in Hong Kong indefinitely that I began to understand the nature of New Asia College and came to revere Professor Qian as my lifelong teacher. And that is what I would like to explain next.

New Asia College was founded in March 1950; its predecessor was the Asia Arts and Commerce College that had been established in the fall of 1949—the "new" in New Asia was used to designate it as the new version of that institution. Originally after May 1949 when the Nationalist government moved to Guangzhou, several academics such as Zhang Qiyun (1901–1985, historical geography), Cui Shuqin (1906–1957, political science), Xie Youwei (1905–1976, philosophy), and others who had relatively close relations with the Nationalist Party planned to found a university specializing in the humanities and social sciences. They registered with the Guangzhou Ministry of Education and the Hong Kong Bureau of Education and set it up with the name "Asia Arts and Commerce College." Cui and Xie went to Hong Kong to prepare to build the college. They registered Professor Qian as Dean of the college because he had the most clout for attracting supporters. Professor Qian tried repeatedly but unsuccessfully to decline this position, but he ended up taking it. A short time later, Cui and Xie left Hong Kong, so Professor Qian hired Professors Tang Junyi (1909–1978; philosophy) and Zhang Pijie (1905–1970; economics) to keep the college going. The three became the senior founders of New Asia College.[7]

The Asia Arts and Commerce College existed for less than a year, before it became New Asia College in 1950. This was because the people who set up the Asia Arts and Commerce College had all left. It was in financial straits from the very beginning and basically subsisted on the individual contributions from a small number of people. The college did not even have its own building and had to use the classrooms of a middle school to hold evening classes. In the spring of 1950, however, a Shanghai entrepreneur, Wang Yuefeng, who admired Professor Qian's determination to run a school in such difficult circumstances, put up the money to rent the third and fourth floors of a new building on Guilin Street in a slum in Kowloon to serve as the college's facilities. The three founders and some of the students could also reside in the rooms. The school's name was changed to New Asia College to mean "A New Asia Arts and Commerce College."

The Asia Arts and Commerce College did not leave behind any archives or records; there is only Professor Qian's essay entitled "Abstract of a Talk at the Opening Ceremony of the Asia Arts and Commerce College." In it, he put forth two important ideas: First, "In China's traditional education system, nothing can surpass the classical learning academy system (*shuyuan zhidu* 書院制度)"; and second, "The purpose of study must be very broad and far-reaching ... we must possess knowledge of Chinese culture, and at the same time we should understand the world's various different cultures. We should develop Chinese culture and also bring together the distinct and different cultures of China and the West."[8] New Asia College continued with these two important ideas and developed them further. Professor Qian's March 1950 New Asia College "Excerpts from the Concise Principles for Enrolling New Students" said that "this college was founded in the autumn of 1949 (the 38th year of the Republic). Its purpose is to follow the teaching spirit of the Song and Ming academies (*shuyuan* 書院) along with the tutorial system of Western European universities, to employ humanistic educational goals to bring together Chinese and Western cultures, and to work toward a happy and peaceful future for all humanity."[9]

Professor Qian traced the founding of New Asia College back to the fall of 1949, and this shows that in his mind the Asia Arts and Commerce College and New Asia College were one and the same. The aims of the latter were thus consistent with those of the former. Clearly, the two goals of paying equal attention to both Chinese and foreign cultures and understanding the cultures of the world have been the core of the spirit of the New Asia College from its foundation. The combination of the "teaching spirit of the Song and Ming academies" and "the tutorial system of Western European universities" embodies precisely the spirit of New Asia College.

I have briefly summarized my knowledge of the core nature of New Asia College. My understanding developed after the fall of 1950 when I had decided to complete my university studies at the New Asia College. My interest in the school was naturally now much greater than it had been during my first semester. In my later historical research, one of the most important methods I chose to investigate characteristics of Chinese culture was through a comparative study with Western history. This was obviously a result of the long-term influence of the pedagogical aims of New Asia College. In 1999, I summed up my overall understanding of my alma mater in an essay entitled "The Spirit of New Asia College and Chinese Culture" at an academic symposium on the golden anniversary of the college.[10]

The college spirit was of course passed on to me by its various professors, and so next I would like to discuss the relations between teachers and students at the New Asia College. Professor Qian Mu was my most important advisor, so next I will describe my experience of following his scholarship after the autumn of 1950.

On First Becoming Professor Qian Mu's Disciple

It was in the autumn of 1950 that I first began to interact with Professor Qian outside the classroom and he began guiding me intellectually. I believe that this should be considered the point at which I officially became Professor Qian's disciple. I still recall the first time I went to his small office to see him after class—it was because I wanted guidance on reading his book. Although I had read *A General History of China* long before, I still felt that it was too deep and not easy to comprehend quickly. This was because the work was written in the annals (*gangmu* 綱目) style and the outline (*gang*) parts were brief, concise critiques. What were the origins of these critiques? These can be found in the detailed parts (*mu*). Because the facts covered in the *mu* were often very complex, the author could only give the broad outlines and was unable to go into too many details due to space limitations. This was something that I was unable to grasp given my academic abilities at that time, and so I requested extra guidance from Professor Qian.

I would do a very intensive reading of *A General History of China*, from beginning to end, and then, as much as possible, write brief reports on each chapter and each section so that I could ask Professor Qian for comments, criticisms, and corrections. He very happily accepted my request, and I made my main assignment for that semester the writing of my notes on the complete book. I would first write and then discuss the material with Professor Qian (which mainly involved his explaining the background and context of the most important parts of the book); this work went on for many months. It goes without saying that Professor Qian's critical evaluations were of invaluable—they allowed me to enter the inner world of *A General History of China*. I have already given some examples of this in my September 1990 essay "Still Remembering the Wind Roiling the Waves Upon the Water" ("You ji feng chui shui shang lin" 猶記風吹水上鱗), lamenting the passing of Professor Qian, and so I won't repeat it here.[11]

What made the deepest impression on me at the time was not the actual contents of *A General History of China* but rather Professor Qian's general attitude toward the pursuit of knowledge. I can illustrate this with two examples. The first is what he said the first time he returned my notebook: "You should not write page after page until you completely fill up the notebook. You should start a new notebook and leave an empty page after each entry without writing a word. Why? Because other scholars have done research and analyses on the topics covered in my book (*A General History of China*), and their opinions are often different from or even opposite of mine. If you leave some empty pages, in the future you can record these different opinions for reference and comparison." (This is a paraphrase, but it does convey his meaning.)

This advice was completely unexpected. From it I came to understand that although he was confident that there was good reason or sufficient grounds for the arguments he made in his book and that these were argued properly and systematically, he did not disregard the research of others who held different views. I also realized that this was his way of solemnly warning me not to be tied down to only his views from the beginning and lose the capacity to learn and benefit from many other scholars. His painstaking efforts for my betterment were deeply moving.

The second example is that from Professor Qian's detailed instructions, I finally came to understand that *A General History of China* was not only completed by carefully selecting and outlining the subtle and essential points found in firsthand historical materials but also the new findings of first-rate historians of modern China such as Wang Guowei, Liang Qichao, Xia Zengyou (1863–1924), Chen Yinke (Chen Yinque), Gu Jiegang, among others.[12] In general, as he wrote *A General History of China*, Professor Qian not only included the new findings of recent scholars but also gave these further consideration and revised them as he deemed necessary before putting them in his book. As such, I have always believed that *A General History of China* combines the main accomplishments of new Chinese historiography from the late Qing to the 1930s. As Professor Qian wrote in "Note on the Completion of this Book": "I have often selected and learned from the writings of contemporary worthies, and the new findings of recent scholars have been often selected and adopted." This is an honest statement and not mere polite formality.

From his statement, we can see that Professor Qian had a generally open-minded attitude toward historical knowledge. *A General History of China* certainly fits what Sima Qian labeled "the views of one school" (*yi jia zhi yan* 一家之言), but it definitely does not present an overly subjective closed system as in "building a cart behind closed doors" (*bimen zaoju* 閉門造車) [without consulting other scholars]. This was a major characteristic of his research methodology in studying Chinese cultural and intellectual history, and he continued this in all his works, including *A Chronological*

Survey of the Pre-Qin Philosophers and *History of the Past Three Hundred Years of Chinese Scholarship* (*Zhongguo jin sanbai nian xueshushi* 中國近三百年學術史).[13] I feel that the greatest and most profound influence Professor Qian had on me was showing me how to recognize and understand the nature of "knowledge" or "learning" (*xuewen* 學問).

The greatest benefit I received from Professor Qian's private guidance and instruction was learning how to read and study the ancient sources of Chinese literature, history, and philosophy. He placed the emphasis on a thorough understanding of a text (*wenben* 文本) both internally and externally. By internally, he meant that we could not overlook "the meaning of any single word"; this was equivalent to the philology (*xungu* 訓詁) emphasized by Qing-dynasty scholars. By externally, he meant that we cannot simply understand a text in isolation; instead, we should compare its similarities and differences with other similar texts, and only then can we appreciate the true place of the text in its complete historical context.

Although Professor Qian believed in the Confucian value system, which was the equivalent to what the ancient Chinese called the Way (*Dao*) or the "tradition of Confucian moral principles" (*daotong* 道統), he did not inculcate this in me directly. To use the words of Han Yu's (768–824) "Discourse on Teachers" ("Shishuo" 師說), Professor Qian's teaching began with "imparting learning" (*shou ye* 授業) and "dispelling doubts" (*jie huo* 解惑), through which he also "transmitted the Way" (*chuan Dao* 傳道), but he avoided using the "preaching" style of most religious teachers when they "transmit" their "Way."[14] He seemed to believe that once I had the basic ability to read, study, and conduct research, I would find the "Way" (*Dao*) myself. In this, he was a disciple of Mencius, who said, "A gentleman steeps himself in the Way because he wishes to find it in himself" and "The Way is like a wide road. It is not at all difficult to find. The trouble with people is simply that they do not look for it. You go home and look for it, and there will be teachers enough for you."[15]

Professor Qian always encouraged me to seek a profound and holistic understanding of the Chinese cultural tradition in order to locate where its characteristic or definitive feature lies in the long, continuous civilization. In his mind that defining feature was really the "Way" (*Dao*), but I had to "steep myself in my studies in order to find it in myself" (*shen zao zi de* 深造自得); I could not just receive the "Way" directly that he had found for himself and use it as my own.

I studied at New Asia College for over two years, from March 1950 until I graduated in June 1952. That was when the college's financial situation was the worst, with no reliable sources of funds to cover its daily expenditures. Professor Qian had to run around soliciting even the smallest donations. In 1950 and at the end of 1951, he made two trips to Taiwan and stayed for a long time during each trip. On the second trip he was extremely unfortunate; while he was giving a lecture in Taipei in April 1952, the roof of the building caved in and he sustained a head injury. When he was released from the hospital, he had to remain in Taipei to recuperate and could not return to Hong Kong until August. He was unable to preside over my graduation ceremony on July 12, and I was very disappointed.

I have related all these incidents to show that before I graduated, I only had limited one-on-one instruction sessions with Professor Qian. However, after my graduation, especially during the 1953–1954 academic year, I had more opportunities to learn from him and in a more leisurely manner.

In the autumn of 1953, Professor Qian received the support of the Asia Foundation to establish a graduate school. The graduate school rented one floor of a building on Prince Edward Road in Kowloon. Professor Qian and three graduate students lived at the school, while I continued to live at home and came to the school daily to study. I met with Professor Qian almost every day that year. More importantly, this was when I began to study Chinese history under his direct supervision. The direction of my entire academic life can be said to have been made during this time, and so I would like to discuss the circumstances.

Professor Qian was my research supervisor, but he did not assign any research topic; he wanted me to discuss it with him after I settled on a topic. This was one way of how he practiced the Mencian principle of "steeping oneself in the Way."

At that time I was studying Marxist historiography, and my research interest was inclined toward the study of the economic history of Chinese society. In the mid-twentieth century, Chinese and Japanese historians were most enthusiastic about studying the Wei-Jin Nanbeichao (North-South Dynasties) periods (265–589) and had made many achievements. On that account, I became determined to trace the origin and development of the great families of that period and their connections with Confucianism and Daoism (the *mingjiao* 名教 or "Confucian ritual code of behavior" and *ziran* 自然, "spontaneity" or "the natural"). This was equivalent to making an experiential study of the relations between the "base" or "substructure" and the "superstructure."

Professor Qian approved my research concept and made an extremely important suggestion. He said that I should trace my research back to the Han dynasty (202 BCE–220 CE) before locating my point of origin. His suggestion led me to change my research approach. Originally, I had intended to begin with the *Records of the Three Kingdoms* (*Sanguo zhi* 三國志), but I ended up choosing the *History of the Later Han Dynasty* (*Hou Hanshu* 後漢書) as the starting point for my intensive reading of official history. There were two parts to what I call "intensive reading": the first was to do a thorough reading of the entire work from beginning to end, and the second was to arrange all the relevant material into records to use in future research investigations. I should elaborate on the second part. To accomplish my research objective, I collected every single mention of social, economic, political, and intellectual change—whether direct or indirect, great or small—in the *History of the Later Han Dynasty* and recorded them on cards with notations so that I could later organize them into various categories for future discussion. I copied out short passages from the text, but for longer passages I wrote summary abstracts. In the case of key vocabulary or terms and concise statements or aphorisms, however, I tried to conserve as much as possible on the note cards.

The graduate school at Prince Edward Road in Kowloon lasted only a year, and the following year (1954–1955) it was incorporated into the new school located on Grampian Road when the US Yale-in-China program's financial aid to New Asia College began. I continued to pursue my advanced studies at the New Asia graduate school for one more year. My intense reading went from the *History of the Later Han Dynasty* back to the *History of the Former Han Dynasty* (*Hanshu* 漢書) and then to the *Records of the Three Kingdoms*, and I accumulated more than a thousand note cards, which constituted the foundation for my Chinese history research. After nearly two years of making detailed notes from my intensive reading, in the spring and summer of 1955, I began writing a scholarly monograph. I originally titled it "The Social Background of Political Changes Between the Former and Later Han Dynasties" ("Liang Han zhiji zhengzhi bianqian de shehui beijing" 兩漢之際政治變遷的社會背景), but after completing the draft manuscript at Harvard University in January 1956, I settled on the title "The Establishment of the Eastern Han Regime and its Relations with the Great Land-owning Families" ("Dong Han zhengquan zhi jianli yu shizu daxing zhi guanxi" 東漢政權之建立與士族大姓之關係). This was my first scholarly monograph. The complete text came to around 60,000 characters; it was published in the *New Asia Journal* (*Xinya xuebao* 新亞學報).[16]

In 1959, the *New Asia Journal* published a special issue in honor of Professor Qian's sixty-fifth birthday, and I wrote another piece of 100,000 characters based on the primary historical materials in my note cards; this was entitled *The New Consciousness and New Thought Trends of the Scholar Class Between the Han and Jin Dynasties* (*Han-Jin zhiji shi zhi xin zijue yu xin sichao* 漢晉之際士之新自覺與新思潮).[17] In the fall of 1958, I wrote an English essay entitled "Sino-Foreign Economic Communication in the Han Dynasty" for Yang Lien-sheng's "Chinese Economic History Research" course, and this was also based on the research recorded on my note cards.

Only after that did I broaden my search to examine resources uncovered by Chinese and foreign archaeological excavations. The aim of my research was not to gather a multitude of facts and present them in a narrative fashion; rather, it was to investigate the structure of the economic system through the communications during the Han dynasty between the Chinese and foreign peoples (at that time called Man-Yi 蠻夷 or "barbarians"), in particular the so-called "tribute" system. It was only after conducting a multilayered analysis and synthesis of all the relevant accounts in the two Han histories that I was able to grasp an understanding of this. My note cards were very important in this research. Many years later, using this work as a foundation, I expanded my research into a book *Trade and Expansion in Han China: A Study in the Structure of Sino-Barbarian Economic Relations.*[18]

From what I have related concerning my early historical research, the reader can readily see that being under the direction of Professor Qian (from 1953 to 1955) for my intensive reading of the history of the Han dynasty has been a major influence on my academic life.

My relationship with Professor Qian was not limited to academic matters; there were many memorable heartwarming times in our teacher-student relationship. Generally speaking, Professor Qian was not only full of verve but also had a fine sense of humor. If one associated with him for some time, one would inevitably develop a long-lasting bond with him. This comes through very clearly in the letters he sent to his protégés. To discuss my own teacher-student bond with Professor Qian, I have to begin with my father's association with him.

My father had read the "national adversity edition" (*guonanban* 國難版) of *A General History of China* during the Anti-Japanese War of Resistance; it was printed on extremely coarse paper, and there were many detailed appreciative marginal comments (my father's copy was also the earliest version of the work that I read). This book was why my father was so intent on inviting Professor Qian to Shenyang Northeast Zhongzheng University in 1946, but unfortunately he was unsuccessful. After we moved to Hong Kong, my father and Professor Qian were often in contact, and their interactions became even more frequent when I entered New Asia College. In the fall of 1951, because New Asia College received some financial aid from Taipei, Professor Qian hired my father to teach a course on the general history of the West and later hired him again to serve as a full-time academic advisor at the graduate school at Prince Edward Road for the 1953–1954 academic year.[19] I remember very clearly that from 1951 to 1955 our families often got together; we would take the cable car to the top of Victoria Peak or have long conversations at a seaside tea house. There was one particularly memorable time when we spent the whole day walking by the ocean in Shek O (Shi Ao) and Professor Qian told us many anecdotes about several famous scholars of the time. He enthralled us with stories about their scholarship, character, and activities. Although Professor Qian included these stories of past events many years later in his *Random Recollections of Friends and Teachers* (*Shiyou zayi* 師友雜憶), it was not as vivid and lively as his oral descriptions.[20] Two lines in a poem I wrote in honor of Professor Qian's ninetieth birthday refer specifically to our excursions to Shek O:

> By the seaside looking back, separated from the past,
> I still remember the wind on the water roiling the waves.

These excursions continued until Professor Qian left to visit the United States. In the second half of June 1960, just before Professor Qian was about to leave Yale University, my father rented a small cabin in a scenic lakeside area in New Hampshire and invited Professor Qian and his wife to spend a week together with us. That was certainly an unforgettable vacation. More than twenty years later, Professor Qian wrote about this time, reminiscing:

My wife and I stayed in Cambridge for a week. We met many people and were very busy.[21] When we were about to leave [the United States], [Yu] Xiezhong insisted on inviting the two of us to come over again before we left New Haven to spend a week leisurely visiting with his family. We accepted his invitation and went to Cambridge again before leaving New Haven.

Xiezhong first rented a cabin in a scenic holiday spot and the six of us—he and his wife, his two sons Yingshi and Yinghua, and the two of us—went there together. I've forgotten the name of the place, but there was a lake surrounded by hills; the hills were not very high and the lake was not very big, but the scenery was beautiful and tranquil. Our two families went around the lake in a sailboat, walked leisurely around the meadows, and sat under the shade of the trees outside the cabin. The activities of those seven days still remain in my memory to this day. ...

Before Xiezhong and his wife left Hong Kong, my wife and I, together with them and their son Yinghua, had gone on a trip across the sea to Lantao Island, climbed the mountain until nightfall, stayed over in an ancient temple, and came back the next morning. Xiezhong remembered this excursion and so he invited us to come to this lake. It just happened that only our two families were there. My wife and I spent eight months in America, and those seven days were the most peaceful. Xiezhong has passed away, and now this lake truly resembles the "footprints of a goose in the snow" that remains only in our hearts.[22]

My father passed away in 1980, and Professor Qian wrote this reminiscence not long after that, expressing his deep sense of sorrow and loss. The friendship between Professor Qian and my father and our whole family was very strong, so it was quite natural that he was always concerned about my well-being—much more so than a teacher for a student—as if I were a member of his own family. Sometimes our one-on-one conversations gave me the profound sense that he was deeply concerned about my spiritual and general health, more than my academic endeavors. On May 28, 1960, when he was at Yale, he wrote me a very long letter about my studies and at the end of the letter he wrote the following:

> You intend to go far, but I hope you can try hard to remind yourself not to stay up late into the night and get up late in the morning. I am concerned for you, and so my advice will touch on everything that can possibly be said; I hope you will not take this the wrong way. I also think that your lifestyle resembles that of Liang Rengong [Liang Qichao]. When Rengong was in Japan, his daily life was quite irregular, he wrote late into the night, went to bed when the sun came up, and got up again at four or five in the afternoon.[23]

He was obviously worried that I would live like Liang Qichao and cut short my natural life span. When I read these lines, I was moved beyond words. I will discuss Professor Qian again later in this memoir.

Tang Junyi and the Rise of New Confucianism

Although Professor Qian was the main driving force behind New Asia College, the other two senior founders, Zhang Pijie (Tchang Pi-kai, 1905–1970) and Tang Junyi, have to be credited for their tremendous efforts and arduous labor. If it weren't for their working with Professor Qian, the college could not have carried on. From what I can remember during my five years in Hong Kong, Zhang Pijie was responsible for the college's practical affairs and held a position similar to a CEO, while Tang Junyi assumed full responsibility for educational administration matters, a position similar to a provost.

Professor Zhang's specialty was economics, which he had studied for several years in Germany, and so from the founding of New Asia College until his retirement he was the Head of the Department of Economics. I never attended his courses, such as "Problems in Chinese Economics" or "Land Economics," but I know that his views on the importance of traditional Chinese culture were the same as those of Professors Qian and Tang. He was also very concerned about the welfare of his students and looked out for them in every possible way, and I always had a very close relationship with him.

Professor Tang's influence on my thinking was second only to Professor Qian's. I took Professor Tang's course on the history of Western philosophy, but I never studied the history of Chinese philosophy with him. Perhaps that was because my interest was more inclined toward the history of scholarship and intellectual history; I can no longer remember why I did not attend his classes on Chinese philosophy. In any case, I was influenced by him not by attending his classes but rather through reading his steady stream of publications, which included monographs and journal articles. He also gave many scholarly lectures that I found both very enlightening and very challenging.

I should point out that as Professor Tang became known as a great master of New Confucianism, New Asia College also became known as a center of Confucianism. Professor Tang's reputation thus ascended with the rise of New Asia College. Professor Qian, in contrast, was already an eminent, nationally known history scholar when he moved to Hong Kong in 1949. Professor Qian's major publications—*A Chronology of the Pre-Qin Philosophers, History of the Past Three Hundred Years of Chinese Scholarship*, and *A General History of China*—had already been circulating for many years and were universally appreciated when New Asia College first began and thus it relied on Professor Qian's reputation to build itself up. At the time Professor Tang was only forty years old and, although he had made great strides academically with many publications on Chinese and Western philosophy, his reputation was not yet established as a leader of the school. His position as a great master of Confucianism for his generation was established on the foundation of New Asia College.

In 2008 I wrote an "appreciation" (*zan* 贊) for a bronze statue of Professor Tang in which I tried to present a succinct summary of his life and learning, as follows:

> Professor Tang Junyi, from Yibin city in Sichuan Province, received his early education at home and was initiated into learning through

the Confucian classics. As an adult, he studied in the north and south, away from home, and was taught by several great masters such as Ouyang Jian (1871–1943) and Xiong Shili (1885–1968) and thus became thoroughly versed in the realms of Confucianism and Buddhism.[24]

Professor Tang was sharp in his thought and able to make clear distinctions between various topics and issues. Because of his natural talents, when he first studied the views of Western philosophers, he immediately saw that they coincided with his own interests and were all naturally in sync, just as a magnet guides a compass and agate absorbs grass. After he mastered his learning, he spent more time on the study of German speculative and dialectic thought. [However,] all his life, he took rebuilding and restoring the Chinese humanistic spirit as his duty and tried to combine the old [traditional] learning with new [Western] knowledge into one [integrated] whole.

Layer by layer he built his own system of thought. This system is open, broad, and organized with a clear hierarchical order. It served as the initial foundation for any attempt at establishing a moral self; the spiritual value of Chinese culture was thus completely revealed therein; the mind and its nine realms also found their ultimate abode therein. This clearly proves that Professor Tang's learning was progressive over time.

In 1949, Professor Tang participated in the founding of New Asia College and established its first Department of Philosophy. From then on until he retired from being Chair Professor at the Chinese University [of Hong Kong], for twenty-five years he presided over the altar of Hong Kong philosophy. His large number of scholar disciples flourished greatly for an entire generation. When the wind and rain darkened the skies and the flowers withered and blew to the ground, it was due to Professor Tang's contributions that, through his efforts, the philosophy of our sacred land was able to continue its intellectual life in this coastal area.

Professor Tang never forgot the proper way and good rule in his teaching. He experienced the changes of his time and was very concerned for this present age. He made great efforts to return to the roots or the basics in his learning in order to open up new possibilities and perspectives. While doing so, he upheld and advocated Confucius's teaching for the world. This is the reason why New Confucianism began to rise outside of China. The aim and scope of the New Confucianism was laid out in the cultural manifesto composed by Professor Tang. This manifesto has for several decades been circulating and spreading inside and outside China with the undulations of the fate of the world.

Professor Tang strove to illuminate the [Confucian Moral] Way and to save the world. He continued the works of previous worthies and philosophers, and his humaneness was so sincere that it should serve as a model for later generations. Looking at his portrait, we will always remember him and never forget his teaching.

Professor Tang's book *The Spiritual Value of Chinese Culture* (*Zhongguo wenhua zhi jingshen jiazhi* 中國文化之精神價值) was published in 1951. Nearly everyone in the Taiwan, Hong Kong, and overseas Chinese intellectual circles had a copy. It was reprinted repeatedly and had a broader influence than Liang Shuming's 1921 work *Eastern and Western Cultures and Their Philosophies*.[25] It can be said that from the 1950s on, whenever scholars inside or outside China discussed issues concerning Chinese and Western culture, no matter their position, they all had to take into account the observations and analyses in Professor Tang's book. Furthermore, starting in 1949, Professor Tang also wrote and published many long journal articles that both interpreted and propagated the spirit of the humanities, and these had an even more far-reaching and profound influence. His essays were not only full of passionate patriotism and original thought but also often constructed in the German dialectical style that had an overwhelming impact on their readers. These essays were mainly published in Hong Kong journals such as *The Democratic Review* (*Minzhu pinglun* 民主評論), *Life* (*Rensheng* 人生), and *Motherland Weekly* (*Zuguo zhoukan* 祖國周刊) that were sold in Taiwan, Southeast Asia, Japan, and the United States.[26] Professor Tang's reputation rose steadily with these publications. From the 1950s through the 1970s, with his richly creative spirit, Professor Tang was unquestionably one of the leaders of overseas Chinese humanities circles.

There is much more behind the assertion in the "appreciation" that the objectives and the scope of New Confucianism were established by Professor Tang's cultural manifesto. The manifesto refers to "A Manifesto for a Re-Appraisal of Sinology and Reconstruction of Chinese Culture" ("Wei Zhongguo wenhua jinggao shijie renshi xuanyan" 為 中國文化敬告世界人士宣言).[27] The original proposal seems to have come from Zhang Junmai (Carsun Chang, 1886–1969), but it was very quickly supported by Tang Junyi, Mou Zongsan (1909–1995), and Xu Fuguan (1902/03–1982). The four of them signed it and published it in *The Democratic Review*,[28] but Professor Tang wrote the draft—its title was later changed to "A Manifesto of Chinese Culture and the World" ("Zhongguo wenhua yu shijie" 中國文化與世界), and this manifesto was included in his collected works. If we read closely *The Spiritual Value of Chinese Culture* by Professor Tang, we will see immediately that one by one the main points of the manifesto were already elaborated there. This is, of course, not to say that the manifesto came from Professor Tang's ideas alone. The cultural views of the four signatories were originally very close, and Professor Mou Zongsan's and Professor Tang's lines of thinking were even in complete agreement. (It was only in later life that they developed some disagreements, but that is not relevant here.) What I want to emphasize here is that Professor Tang's willingness to take the initiative and write the manifesto indicates that he wanted to unite like-minded comrades and establish a brand-new intellectual camp. This was "New Confucianism," which has been circulated both inside and outside of China. This new school of thought gradually gained traction only after the publication of the manifesto.

On May 6, 1959, Professor Qian sent me a letter in which he wrote:

> Last year when Zhang Junmai, Tang Junyi, and the others signed the "Manifesto of Chinese Culture," they invited me to sign, but I refused. I wrote a letter to Zhang that was published in the Hong

Kong journal *Rebirth* (*Zaisheng*). I have never liked such actions [because] I fear they will give rise to unnecessary barriers in the academic world.

Professor Qian's views on [Chinese] culture were not very different from those of Zhang Junmai, Tang Junyi, and the rest, and his refusal to sign the manifesto was not due to intellectual differences but rather the wish to avoid causing factional disputes. When the four signatories were not moved after he expressed his misgivings, he knew that they had already planned to raise a new banner to appeal to the masses and expand their influence. When Professor Tang resolutely took up the heavy responsibility of writing the manifesto, his attitude was obviously even more positive [than before].

Finally, I would like to point out that Professor Tang played the most crucial role in the process of New Confucianism becoming a formal school of thought. Here is an example testifying to this: Overseas, New Confucianism had three representatives—Tang Junyi, Mou Zongsan, and Xu Fuguan—who were all disciples of Xiong Shili. Tang Junyi and Mou Zongsan were both professional philosophers who spent their whole lives in the academy, and Xu Fuguan occupied a position "between academics and politics"; it was only in his middle years that he moved from politics into academic circles. On this account they were jokingly referred to in academic circles as the "two sages" (Tang Junyi and Mou Zongsan) and one "worthy" (Xu Fuguan). At first the three of them lived in different places. Tang Junyi went to New Asia College in Hong Kong, while Mou Zongsan and Xu Fuguan went to teach at Donghai University in Taiwan. Although their opinions overlapped, they were unable consult frequently with one another about their ideas and approaches to the moral way (*Dao*). A few years later, Professor Tang used his considerable influence in academic circles at New Asia College and in Hong Kong to bring Mou Zongsan from Donghai to the Department of Chinese at Hong Kong University and then later to help him get appointed to the Department of Philosophy of the Chinese University of Hong Kong (New Asia College).

Xu Fuguan retired from Donghai and also moved to Hong Kong, and Professor Tang found him a position at the New Asia College Research Institute. The two "sages" and one "worthy" were then altogether in one place, and "New Confucianism" had finally established its base in New Asia College.

From the end of the 1960s to 1978 when Professor Tang passed away, "New Confucianism" at New Asia College was at its height and drew the attention of intellectual circles around the world. I remember clearly when my Harvard colleague Professor Benjamin I. Schwartz (1916–1999) came to Hong Kong in the middle of May 1975 to visit New Asia College after lecturing at Oxford University. He specifically wanted to speak with the various members of the New Confucianism school. It was arranged for him to engage in an afternoon of discussions with Tang Junyi, Mou Zongsan, Xu Fuguan, and their disciples at the New Asia College Research Institute. I was unable to participate in this discussion session because I had to attend to other university affairs, but the next day Professor Schwartz very enthusiastically told me that we should be very proud that New Asia College has such "a unique and highly original school of thought." Professor Schwartz was never one to offer praise to be polite; his commendation was completely sincere and made a profound impression on me.

This brief narrative of Professor Tang's contributions to the rise and development of New Confucianism comes from my own personal observations, and I am confident that although it may not be an exact account, it cannot be far off. Fortunately, Tang Junyi, Mou Zongsan, and Xu Fuguan all left behind copious diaries and letter collections, so future researchers can certainly study these and I need not say much more here.

During the five years I studied at New Asia College, I frequently heard about and became generally conversant with Professor Tang's comparisons and generalizations about the spiritual value of Chinese and Western cultures. Although I could not completely follow his line of thinking, every time I read one of his works it would compel me to re-explore and reconsider many issues. Professor Tang's influence on me in both learning and thought was thus both profound and lasting.

Part Two: Seeking Knowledge Off Campus

After I began studying with Professor Qian and chose traditional Chinese history as my research focus, there was no more room for hesitation. Given that this was to be my area of specialty, I would have to go through a long period of preparation and extensive reading and could not expect quick results. My most pressing problem during my time at New Asia College was not how to do well in my area of specialty but rather how to overcome the challenges of the Marxist materialist conception of history, or historical materialism.

At Yanjing University, I took a course "Major Issues in Politics" for a semester, and it was pure ideological indoctrination. At that time, the *History of the Communist Party of the Soviet Union—Bolsheviks Short Course* published in the USSR in 1938 was put forth as a "Marxist classic." The fourth chapter on "Dialectical Materialism and Historical Materialism" came from Joseph Stalin (1878–1953) himself and was all the more asserted to be the supreme "truth."[29] With Marx's theory that the material base or foundation (economic production and the relations of production) determines the superstructure (social structure, thought, ideology, and so on), Stalin put forth the well-known five-stage theory of social development, which proposed that the history of a place or a people must necessarily go through five stages; namely, primitive communism, slavery, feudalism, capitalism, and socialism (finally ending with communism). Stalin declared this to be a scientific "law" [of historical development], and because it is determined by the material base or foundation it cannot be changed by the will of any individual. The official academics of the Chinese Communist Party completely accepted this five-stage theory of social development from the very beginning. The writings of Guo Moruo, Fan Wenlan, Hou Wailu (1903–1987), Jian Bozan, and others as well as their later debates on the periodization of Chinese history all attest to this. Their disagreements were only about the earlier or later appearance of the five stages.

Because I had read Georgi Plekhanov's *The Development of the Monist View of History* in Professor Weng Dujian's class, I felt that the "five-stage theory of social development" seemed too simplistic. The most obvious problem was that Marx had pointed out that ancient Eastern societies like China, India, and some Islamic areas had a sort of "Asiatic mode of production" that was different from ancient Western countries like Greece and Rome. In his five-stage theory, however, Stalin did not account for this. The Yanjing University course on "Major Issues in Politics" thus could not convince me of the validity of historical materialism, but I still did not have the ability to make any judgments about this large issue; the best I could do was to set it aside and not comment on it.

After I entered New Asia College and decided to specialize in Chinese history, I very quickly realized that I had to gain a clear-cut understanding of the materialist conception of history. The reason was very simple. As noted earlier, the five-stage theory of social development had already captured Mainland China's historians. If I could not state clearly why I did not accept this theory, it would be very difficult for me to move ahead with my research. My writings would be summarily rejected by mainstream historians, who would write them off with a single word —"idealist" (*weixin* 唯心).

I did not have the necessary academic expertise at that time to face the challenge squarely; so after thinking about the issue for a while, I believed that the only way to handle this predicament was to conduct the following sequence of research tasks.

First, I had to obtain a general understanding of the most recent scholarship on European history, especially for the period from the Renaissance on. Only then would I be able to assess whether theories of Marx and Engels from a hundred years ago had been modified and, if so, to what degree. I focused especially on the long development of capitalism. Would it inevitably be transformed into "socialism" by means of a "proletarian revolution?" From the deaths of Marx (1883) and Engels (1895) to the 1950s, Western capitalist society experienced extremely complex changes in its composition and structure. I wanted to understand how Western historians in general recounted the history of this period spanning approximately seventy years. My first step was to read as much as I could the most recent comprehensive expositions and specialized discussions by Western historians on the problem with which I was concerned.

The second task was related to the fact that Marx and Engels both matured as scholars in the general environment of nineteenth-century intellectual thought. Thus, their major theories, including dialectical materialism, historical materialism, and "scientific socialism," developed in intimate interaction with various contemporary currents of thought and styles of study. The most salient of these—such as Hegel's philosophy, the British political economy (especially that of Adam Smith [1723–1790] and David Ricardo [1772–1823]), French utopian thought, and the anthropological ideas in *Ancient Society* by Lewis H. Morgan (1818–1881)—together made up the foundation of Marx's and Engels's conceptional standpoint. I was deeply aware that only by obtaining a broad understanding of Western scholarly thinking in the middle of the twentieth century would I be able to judge the modern status and significance of Marxism. As such, I had to read the relevant writings of contemporary social science and currents of political and cultural thought.

After establishing my reading project, the next problem was where to find the books I needed. At that time New Asia College did not have a library, and the Hong Kong University library did not loan out books. After much asking around, I found out that the United States Information Service had a public reading room and that the British Council had a small library. More importantly, books could be checked out from their collections, which meant that I could finally study for my research project. There were not many books in the two establishments, but they were sufficient for my purposes as a young person just beginning his research.

Having been guided by my father, especially in European history for the period from the Renaissance on, I was able to locate quickly the relevant modern works in the field and began reading these, taking many notes. My later publications, *The Development of the Democratic System* (*Minzhu zhidu de fazhan* 民主制度的發展, 1953) and *The New Trends of Modern Civilization* (*Jindai wenming de xin qushi* 近代文明的新趨勢, 1954), were based on this research and can be considered a summary of my reading notes but are not really worth considering as treatises.[30]

In the second part of my research, I went through the translations, reviews, and arguments in various contemporary journals from Hong Kong and Taiwan to select the most popular Western works to read in order to broaden my horizons. This was a method of "making greater progress by studying from many teachers" (*guangyi duoshi* 廣益多師). The process of determining what to read and how to locate such works was very complicated, and it is difficult to explain this in detail, but what I would like to emphasize is that it had the effect of determining my way of thinking and my scholarly research. Let me explain a little more with three points.

First, I finally gained an understanding of the contribution and status of Marxism in modern historiography. Marx and Engels examined historical change from the perspectives of the mode of production and relations of production, and they opened up a new avenue for historical research that influenced the rise of innovative research in socioeconomic history in the twentieth century. As an overall system, however, the Marxist conception of historical materialism could only occupy the position of one of many among the various historical theories. As far as Stalin's dogmatic five-stage theory of social development was concerned, it inevitably came to be ridiculed.

Second, as noted earlier, before 1948, I related to the "democracy" and "science" concepts that had developed since the May Fourth New Culture Movement, even though at the time I only knew of them but not the reasons for them. On that account while I was at Yanjing University, I could not argue against the Chinese Communist Party's all-out attack on "democratic individualism"; in the end I was even moved by the popular contemporary "new democracy." It was only after my systematic reading of specialist research on mid-twentieth-century political and social thought that the universal values of democracy, freedom, and human rights became my most deeply held lifelong convictions. At the same time, I also came to further understand that to reform society and realize these values, it was necessary to avoid the extremist idea of both the left and the right that each side could accomplish the whole task with one stroke; instead, it was necessary to have a gradual step-by-step process.

At the time, the two books which had the greatest influence on me were *The Open Society and its Enemies* by the major philosopher Karl Popper and *The Vital Center: The Politics of Freedom* by the American historian Arthur Schlesinger, Jr.[31] Published in 1945, *The Open Society and its Enemies* had long been considered a classic, and I often saw it quoted in the writings of important contemporary scholars. *The Vital Center* came to my attention because of my father. From 1926 to 1927 when my father was studying in the Harvard Graduate School, his advisor in American History was Arthur M. Schlesinger, Sr., and they continued to communicate by letter after my father returned home. He had just learned from an American friend that Arthur M. Schlesinger, Jr. (1917–2007) had followed in his father's footsteps and had also become a famous historian; father and son then had taught together in the history department at Harvard. My father asked me to look up Schlesinger, Jr.'s works when I had the time. A clerk at the United States Information Service told me that the book that made Schlesinger, Jr. famous was *The Age of Jackson*, but *The Vital Center* was then receiving much attention in the intellectual world and gaining great influence.[32] If it were not for the recommendations by my father and the clerk, I probably never would have discovered this book.

Third, by studying cultural anthropology, I came to have a new understanding of the relationship between Chinese culture and the universal values discussed earlier. After the May Fourth Movement, these universal values were being affirmed in China, but many intellectuals had begun to doubt their own cultural tradition. At first their suspicions were raised only about the Confucian ritual code of ethical behavior (*mingjiao*), but after a while they started a rather complete antitraditional movement and believed that the failure to implement "democracy" and "science" smoothly in China was primarily due to the obstruction by Chinese cultural tradition dating back thousands of years. This view was widely accepted, and Yin Haiguang was promulgating it in Taiwan in his *Free China Bimonthly* (*Ziyou Zhongguo* 自由中國). These beliefs puzzled me a great deal.

As I wrote in chapter 1, due to the Anti-Japanese War of Resistance I remained in my old home in Anhui for a full nine years (1937–1946) where I lived in a society based on clan rules (*zongfa* 宗法) and received a traditional private-school education. As such, before I was sixteen years old the basic values of life that I adopted came primarily from traditional Chinese culture. It was not until 1946 when I moved from the countryside to the city that I encountered the May Fourth new culture and thought. When I read about democracy, freedom, human rights, and other such values in *The Selected Writings of Hu Shi*, I felt that they were reasonable and fair and never thought of contradicting them. So even though the anti-traditionalists, like Yin Haiguang, quoted chapter and verse from the classics and argued with seemingly impeccable logic and clarity, in my heart of hearts I was still unconvinced, but I was unable to refute them theoretically. It was not until I studied cultural anthropology that I finally freed myself from these conundrums.

The two works which were most beneficial to me at the time were *Patterns of Culture* by Ruth Benedict (1887–1948) and *Configurations of Culture Growth* by Arthur L. Kroeber (1876–1960).[33] Both scholars emphasized the integral or holistic nature of culture and believed that the culture of every human group (*minzu* 民族) constituted a unique system or pattern of its own. We only had to compare different cultures, as Arnold J. Toynbee (1889–1975) did in *A Study of History*, for this point to become clear.[34] Benedict was widely known for her study of Japan; her sharp, vivid analysis and synthesis of the integral patterns of Japanese culture greatly influenced the academic world. Kroeber was especially appreciative of her theory of the integral nature of cultural patterns. He went further and argued that anthropological research should not stop at the current state of a culture but should also explore its historical origins because the pattern or integral nature of a culture has been built up gradually over time. Therefore, the longer the history of a people's (*minzu*) culture, the more profound its integration.

From reading these two books and other studies, I was no longer as pessimistic as before concerning the future of the universal values of democracy, freedom, and human rights in China. Since a people's (*minzu*) culture is an integral system that has developed over time, it cannot be completely swept away to clear the path for the establishment of a new culture. If ignorant individuals rashly tried to sweep away Chinese culture (as in "destroy the old and establish the new" advocated by the Cultural Revolution), the result would only be to distort and ruin tradition, making it worse while being unable to eliminate it. Due to the integration of a cultural tradition, a culture's reception of values and ideas from the outside and its final harmonization with them to become another integral whole is bound to experience various difficulties and cannot be achieved in one leap.[35] This is because cultural communication is a process that "pulls on one hair and moves the entire body"—the introduction of Buddhism to China is a perfect example of this.[36] The implementation of democracy, freedom, and human rights not only requires a transformation of thought and belief but also involves changes in social structure. The difficulties this will meet are much greater than those encountered with the arrival of Buddhism, which has also reinforced my belief in the acceptance of modern universal values in China.

The key factor which led to the ultimate integration of Buddhism into Chinese culture was its reception by Daoist thought, which was followed by a long period of "matching the meaning" (*geyi* 格義) of Buddhist terms to Chinese thought. Enlightened by the example of Buddhism, we discover that Chinese culture contains many elements sufficient for the introduction and reception of a system of democracy (similar to what Hu Shi called the "historical foundations for a democratic China"). Therefore, from the scholar-officials of the late Qing (like Wang Tao, Guo Songtao, Yan Fu, Kang Youwei, and so on) to the intellectual leaders after the May Fourth, they all wholeheartedly endorsed the democratic systems of Europe and America.[37] Even many of those intellectual youth who supported the politics of the Chinese Communist Party in the 1940s did so because the CCP used the idea of "New Democracy" to attract them. In sum, the elements in Chinese culture that would be accepting of a democratic system far outnumber those that would reject it; this is a conclusion in which I had already come to believe firmly at that time. I presented an expanded account of this view in two works —*Between Freedom and Equality* (*Ziyou yu pingdeng zhijian*) and *Essays on Civilization* (*Wenming lunheng*).[38] My practical knowledge then was superficial, but the general direction of my intellectual leanings was established based on this conclusion.

This is why I believe that my extracurricular studies also had a lifelong influence on the direction of my thinking and scholarship.

PART THREE: POLITICAL AND CULTURAL DEVELOPMENT OF A LIBERAL INTELLECTUAL

During my entire five years in Hong Kong, from 1950 to 1955, I did not have any opportunities to associate with the industrial and commercial segments of the British colony because I lived only in the small world of exiled intellectuals, which had distinct characteristics that are worth discussing. It was a community of liberal Chinese intellectuals (*ziyou pai* 自由派) who came together and were active in a mostly free society. The

British employed a rather thorough rule of law (*fazhi* 法治) in their Hong Kong colony; as long as they did not break the law, everyone enjoyed freedom of speech, association, publication, and other such civil liberties. The exiled intellectuals collectively affirmed that Hong Kong does not have democracy, but it has freedom. That was truly the situation then. During this period, Hong Kong offered liberal Chinese intellectuals an unprecedented opportunity to uphold their own spiritual and intellectual values without any fear of untoward consequences. Even more importantly, there were tens of thousands of liberal intellectuals living in Hong Kong at that time, and, although they differed in backgrounds, they were united in their insistence that China should follow the path of freedom and democracy. This was an extremely important intellectual community that possessed immeasurable potential. As such, I feel it necessary to discuss briefly the spiritual and intellectual activities of this community.

At that time this group was generally dubbed "China's Third Force" (*Zhongguo disan shili* 中國第三勢力) by both Chinese and Americans, but it should not be confused with the "Third Force" that was proposed by Indian prime minister Jawaharlal Nehru, who advocated that the nations that were independent of both the United States and the Soviet Union should establish an "International Third Force" that would be beyond the control of the two superpowers. "China's Third Force" was an attempt, outside of the "dictatorial" regimes of the Chinese Nationalist and Communist parties, to set up a spiritual force advocating the universal values of democracy, freedom, and human rights as its ultimate goals. In Hong Kong, though, this "Third Force" was not organized as a comprehensive political party; it was just a group of intellectuals who came from many different backgrounds—there were members of the Nationalist Party, the China Democratic Socialist Party, and the China Youth Party; and there were many more who were unaffiliated with any party. Regardless of their background, they were united as a group. Let me give a few examples to illustrate this.

At the beginning of November 1949, a number of high- and mid-level officers of the Nationalist Party who had escaped from Guangzhou to Hong Kong made the following declaration:

> In the present political situation, it is believed both inside and outside of China that the Chinese Communist Party dictatorship is unendurable and definitely cannot succeed. The Nationalist Party and the Nationalist government have already given up hope, and everyone longs for the emergence of a new political force that supports freedom and democracy.[39]

This statement is identical to the political views of the Third Force Movement. At that time these members of the Nationalist Party who supported liberalism regarded Gu Mengyu (1889–1972) as their spiritual leader; although they did not form a "new force" (*xin shili* 新勢力), they were still generally known as the "Third Force."[40] Gu's influence quickly spread outside the Nationalist Party, and he soon became one of the leaders of the Third Force Movement [not part of the Nationalist Party]. At that time, Gu worked with a very forceful activist named Li Weichen, who was a good organizer, but he later withdrew. I never met him.

Another example also reveals the dynamics of the Third Force Movement in Hong Kong. The following entry appears in *The Diary of Hu Shi* for May 7, 1952:

> At eight o'clock this morning Zhang Junmai [Carsun Chang] came to breakfast, and we talked for an hour and a half. He wanted to discuss the question of the Third Force Movement. I told him that at this time there are only the forces of the Communist International and the anti-Communist forces; there is absolutely no possibility of any third force. The Third Force Movement in Hong Kong can only beg a little "chicken feed" from the "little demons" in the [US] State Department. These "little demons" have no power at all; they cannot do anything, and they cannot influence government policies![41]

He had mistaken the Third Force Movement of Hong Kong for a branch of Nehru's "Third Force" and did not realize it was indeed an authentic anti-communist group. Because Hu Shi believed that anti-communism had to be backed by military force, he always defended Chiang Kai-shek and the Nationalist regime, and he could not accept the Hong Kong Third Force's complete rejection [of Chiang Kai-shek and the KMT]. His disparagement of the Third Force Movement probably stemmed from his deeply rooted prejudice. His prediction that the Third Force Movement could not "do anything" and would not "influence government policies" was, however, unfortunately correct. I have quoted this diary entry not to discuss Hu Shi's views but to emphasize Zhang Junmai's efforts and contributions in the major campaign to establish the Third Force Movement.

From early on Zhang Junmai (Carsun Chang) was influenced by Liang Qichao and, as such, thought very highly of Chinese culture and thought. However, he also believed in Western-style constitutional democracy, especially admiring the democratic socialism of the British Fabian Society, and thus he named the party he founded the "China Democratic Socialist Party" (*Zhongguo minzhu shehui dang* 中國民主社會黨 or *minshedang* 民社黨). Even more noteworthy is that after the victory in the Anti-Japanese War of Resistance in 1945 and during the period the Nationalist, Communist, and various other parties were discussing peaceful unification, Zhang Junmai did the principal work on drafting a constitution. He exhausted every possible way to prevent the constitution from being overtaken by Nationalist Party ideology while at the same time making it acceptable to them. For example, the Nationalist Party insisted that the "Three People's Principles" (*sanmin zhuyi* 三民主義)—"nationalism," "people's power," and "people's livelihood" (*minzu* 民族 *minquan* 民權, *minsheng* 民生)—had to be written into the constitution as the foundational principles of the state (or nation, *guo* 國). Zhang Junmai very cleverly replaced the "Three People's Principles" with [government] "by the people" (*minzhi* 民治), "of the people" (*minyou* 民有), and "for the people" (*minxiang* 民享). In order to ensure the cooperation of other parties, and because Sun Yat-sen had voiced his support for the phrase from Abraham Lincoln's famous Gettysburg Address, "government of the people, by the people, for the people," the Nationalist Party silently acquiesced in the stratagem of "exchanging the post for a pillar." Thus, the Constitution of the Republic of China that the National Assembly passed on December 25, 1946, was for the most part based on Zhang Junmai's original draft, and it is still in use in Taiwan even though it has been partially amended.[42]

After 1949, Zhang Junmai was fully aware that in the face of the new situation of the Chinese Communist Party's totalitarian rule in Mainland China, he could no longer rely on the China Democratic Socialist Party alone to push for the realization of freedom and democracy in China. This was why he finally transcended the narrow ideas of party politics and decided to try to unite anti-communist intellectuals into a single Third Force Movement. Not only did he try to persuade Hu Shi to join the movement, but he also earnestly invited Professor Qian Shibin [Qian Mu], who had never been involved in politics before. Professor Qian's *Random Recollections of Friends and Teachers* has the following recollection:

> I met my old friend Zhang Junmai again in Hong Kong. ... he wanted to gather together the China Democratic Socialist Party and the China Youth parties and other people exiled in Hong Kong and found a new party, and he encouraged me to join. I told him, "You have been engaged in political work for many years and made fine contributions to the nation, and I have never been opposed to it. Nevertheless, today when the situation has changed greatly, you want to establish a new party outside of the Nationalist Party and the Chinese Communist Party; this can certainly not be done all at once. My humble suggestion is that you should invite a number of people together and carry out a detailed discussion about how to build from the ground up a long-term great plan to save the nation and save the people. First draft a new political program and then invite your comrades to set up a new party on the basis of that program. ... If you want to first

set up such a meeting, I would also be willing to take a seat in the back row and contribute what little I can."

A day later I unexpectedly met Zhang again in a teahouse, and he told me he was planning to visit India and that he had passed on my opinions to a few friends and expected to be discussing that big plan with them soon. Then I said, "What I said to you earlier was only a basic plan for establishing a new party. Although we have not been very close, I know somewhat about your personal character and so I recklessly made some offhand suggestions. But this is not a project about which one can simply ask a stranger how it is done. Even if people who are unfamiliar with me will not ridicule me for being pedantic or ignorant, where can I start from [to advise you]? Let us wait for the time being until you return from India and then we can talk." Later on in Hong Kong I heard that the formation of a Third Party was being planned and that the United States was giving it monetary support. I was asked many times to participate in their meetings, but I never dared to attend.[43]

What Professor Qian wrote of as a "new party" or a "Third Party" simply referred to the Third Force Movement. Due to his trust in Zhang Junmai, Professor Qian affirmed that the goal of the Third Force Movement was to find "a long-term great plan to save the nation and save the people." On that basis he was willing to attend a meeting chaired by Zhang and present his opinions. He could not, however, discuss the formation of a new political party with a group of political figures hitherto unknown to him, and so in the end he and the Third Force Movement took different paths.

The passage quoted earlier from Professor Qian's memoirs is a record of Zhang Junmai and the Third Force Movement, with the same historical source value as *The Diary of Hu Shi*.

Without any doubt, Zhang Junmai was one of the most active and most influential leaders in the Third Force Movement. In his generation, there were also many well-known political personages, like Zuo Shunsheng (1893–1969) and Li Huang (1895–1991) of the China Youth Party, who also actively played leadership roles in the Third Force Movement.[44]

There were also many more high-ranking cadres of the China Youth Party over the age of forty who were exiled in Hong Kong than there were cadres of the China Democratic Socialist Party. They published newspapers and books and made great contributions to the propagation and popularization of the Third Force Movement (which will be discussed more later). In addition to the Democratic Socialist Party and the China Youth Party, Zhang Guotao (1897–1979) who had separated from the Chinese Communist Party and even Chiang Kai-shek's former superior Xu Chongzhi (1887–1965) also participated in the organizational activities of the Third Force Movement.[45]

I was a young student at the time and by disposition uninterested in political organizations, so I never once participated in any of the meetings of the Third Force. I also never once met any of the Third Force Movement leaders like Gu Mengyu, Zhang Junmai, and others. I did, however, relate to the Third Force Movement in terms of political thought because I deeply believed that China had to establish a transparent and tolerant democratic system before it could follow the path of modernization. As for who promoted or who led the movement, that was a problem involving others and was of secondary importance. I did not know any of the leaders and did not feel it was necessary to follow them. My interests were thought and culture, and I ended up writing and editing. This was also the general path taken by the community of exiled intellectuals in Hong Kong.

PART FOUR: HONG KONG POPULAR ANTI-COMMUNIST PUBLICATIONS

After 1949 there were very many popular anti-communist publications in Hong Kong, but they all held different positions. In general, they reflected the mainstream thought currents of overseas Chinese in the second half of the twentieth century. What I mean by "overseas" includes Hong Kong, Taiwan, Southeast Asia, and the United States. I can present only a brief introduction here based on my own direct personal experience.

Not long after I first arrived in Hong Kong and after I transferred to New Asia College, I was drawn to two fortnightly publications: *The Democratic Review* (*Minzhu pinglun*) published in Hong Kong and the *Free China Bimonthly* (*Ziyou Zhongguo*) published in Taiwan. I was most interested in the *Free China Bimonthly* because Hu Shi was its publisher, and its goal was to push forcefully for the realization of freedom and democracy in China. I also had great respect for *The Democratic Review* because the editor and principal writers were the professors who founded New Asia College: Professor Zhang Pijie was the chief editor, and Professors Qian Mu and Tang Junyi served as advisors. The basic standpoint of *The Democratic Review* was to protect Chinese culture with Confucianism as its core. That was why they had to oppose the Chinese Communist Party. As everyone knows, the Chinese Communist Party had always regarded modern Confucianism as a "remnant of feudalism" whose "reactionary nature" was even worse than "bourgeois thought" and had to be completely eradicated.[46]

I have written an analysis of the backgrounds, similarities, differences, and interactions between these two publications in an essay entitled "The New Confucian Orientation of *The Democratic Review*" ("*Minzhu pinglun* Xin Ruxue de jingshen quxiang" 民主評論新儒學的精神去向).[47] What I would like to emphasize here is that the *Free China Bimonthly* and *The Democratic Review* represented Chinese periodicals of the highest level culturally. Almost every exiled intellectual in Hong Kong had copies, and I, for one, never missed an issue. What is noteworthy is that the pursuit of the ideals of freedom and democracy (*Free China Bimonthly*) and the exploration of the contemporary significance of Confucianism (*Comments on Democracy*) eventually gave rise to two important major trends of thought for several decades to come as they unceasingly and innovatively pushed out the old thought and brought in the new. Furthermore, after the 1980s these two trends of thought were transmitted to Mainland China, and their repercussions are still felt today. These two major journals both published some of my essays on "equality" (*pingdeng* 平等) and "liberty" (or freedom *ziyou* 自由), and the editors were very encouraging. That was the extent of my relationship with them, and now I would like to introduce several journals to which I was closely related. Directly or indirectly, these journals influenced the development of my scholarship and thought.

Life and *Freedom Front*

The first journal is *Life* (*Rensheng* 人生) founded by Mr. Wang Dao (Wang Guanzhi, ? –1971) completely as an individual effort. He was a Fujian native, who joined the Nationalist Party early during the Northern Expedition era of 1926–1928 and continued to work for the party while in the military. He was devoted to learning in the Chinese humanities and undertook a great amount of self-study whenever he could. During the 1948–1949 period of great changes, he left his Nationalist Party post and took a position with the overseas Chinese news world in the Philippines. In the end, unable to bear the systematic ravaging of Chinese traditional culture taking place in Mainland China, he returned to Hong Kong and used his own meager funds to publish the journal *Life*. In the second year, his funds dried up, but Professor Qian Mu and another senior colleague wrote a joint letter to the Asia Foundation recommending the journal and obtained some funds to continue its publication. Professor Qian Mu described how Wang Dao worked on *Life*:

> Guanzhi used these meager extra funds with the utmost energy and zeal. Besides necessarily writing something himself for each number, all the duties of editing, proofing, collating, printing, and distributing were taken on by himself and his wife. When he had some funds left over, many exiled intellectuals in Hong Kong were invited to join in the work and thus received help and relief. All of Guanzhi's energy and activity were focused on *Life*. He had no social interactions, no amusements, and no rest. They saved on food and clothing and lived a most frugal and spartan life.[48]

This description mirrors exactly what I saw, without the slightest exaggeration.

Wang Dao had only one goal in publishing *Life*: to protect and maintain Chinese traditional culture with Confucianism as its core. As soon as he arrived in Hong Kong, he established a relationship with New Asia College and respectfully looked up to Professors Qian and Tang as his teachers, even though he was about the same age as Professor Tang. Essays by Professors Qian and Tang appeared in nearly every issue of *Life*, and so I regarded *Life* as a New Asia College publication. Given these connections, from the beginning Wang Dao regarded me as his younger schoolmate; he encouraged me to write essays and, after a short time, made me one of his editorial committee members to participate in the selection and rejection of manuscript submissions. During this time, *Life* published a number of my essays, mostly cultural critiques. The one that attracted the most attention was my 1958 "After Reading Chen Yinque's *On Twice Destined in Marriage*" ("Chen Yinque Xianshen Lun *Zaisheng Yuan shuhou*" 陳寅恪先生《論再生緣》書後). [49]

Life was very similar to *The Democratic Review*, except that it leaned toward the more popular and general and thus complemented the *Democratic Review* with its strategically focused topics. *Life* was widely circulated because of its popular, generalist nature. On the tenth anniversary of *Life*, Professor Qian wrote in his commemorative essay:

> Year by year its readership increased, manuscript submissions increased, and news items and topics discussed also increased. It reached as far as Taiwan, Japan, the Philippines, Singapore, and various places in Southeast Asia, and even the United States and Europe. In any area where Chinese language and people who could read Chinese were located, except for our motherland, the Chinese mainland, *Life* can be found almost anywhere. [50]

The situation at that time was just as Professor Qian described; I received letters from Taiwan, Singapore, and other places where people wanted to discuss matters with me. In 1955 after I went to the United States, I also met several *Life* readers who offered some criticisms of my essays; this wide readership was beyond my expectations.

In February 1971, *Life* published its twenty-year anniversary issue, and a few days later Wang Dao passed away. The anniversary issue became the final issue as both *Life* and its founder expired. This is the most extremely moving story in the publishing history of Hong Kong's exiled intellectuals.

The next publication I would like to discuss is the *Freedom Front* (*Ziyou zhenxian* 自由陣線).[51] One of the representative journals of the Hong Kong's Third Force Movement, it was published by the Freedom Publishing House. The founder of the Freedom Publishing House was Mr. Xie Chengping, a second-generation leader of the Chinese Youth Party. He was a political scientist who studied international politics at Columbia University. In April 1947, when the Chinese Youth Party joined the Nationalist Party, Zuo Shunsheng entered the Cabinet as Minister of Agriculture, and Xie Chengping served as his Deputy Chief for Government Affairs. After 1949 when Xie Chengping went into exile in Hong Kong, he was trusted by the Americans because his wife was a Chinese American. On that account, he received strong support from a US government organization to promote the development of the Third Force Movement in Hong Kong.

In the 1950s the Freedom Publishing House published a number of books, which included ones on the development of the concepts of freedom and democracy as well as the harm done by the Chinese Communist Party regime to traditional Chinese culture and the new thought trends since the May Fourth Movement. This publishing focus served two functions: First, through these books the ideals pursued by the Third Force Movement and its operations were constantly publicized. And second, the publisher's remuneration provided the exiled intellectuals in Hong Kong with the bare minimum they needed to continue their struggle. My first two books—*The New Trends of Modern Civilization* (*Jindai wenming de xin qushi*, 1953) and *On the Democratic Revolution* (*Minzhu geming lun*, 1954)—were published by the Freedom Publishing House.[52]

As an organization, the *Freedom Front* was very influential and had greater sway than its publications. Its goals were similar to the *Free China Bimonthly* published in Taiwan, but its emphasis was more on popular understanding and therefore less academic in nature. When I began submitting articles for publication, I established a relationship with the *Freedom Front*, and then Mr. Zhang Bao-en (the chief editor) and I gradually got to know each other.[53] From the northeast and about twenty years older than I, Mr. Zhang embraced nationalism and joined the Chinese Youth Party because of his hatred of the Japanese for invading China. Sincere and responsible, he was dedicated to doing a good job at the *Freedom Front*. It was probably around the fall or winter of 1951 that he officially invited me to join the editorial department and take charge of a youth column; a little later he added a special column for scientific knowledge. Not wishing to hinder my studies at New Asia College, he only required that I work at the publishing office three nights a week. On the fourth night, I went to the print shop to read the proofs of each issue, which usually took from around nine o'clock to midnight. The editorial office was in Kowloon and all of us editors lived there, but the print shop was across the water in Hong Kong. There were no ferries at midnight, and so we had to return on a small motorboat, which we all regarded as an amusing way to cross the water and no trouble at all. I often wrote some short opinion pieces for the youth column, none of which exceeded a thousand characters. *On the Road to Thought* (*Dao siwei zhi lu* 到思維之路) was a collection of these short essays.[54]

I worked at the *Freedom Front* for two years and gave up my editorial duties in the autumn of 1953 when I joined Professor Qian Mu's research group.[55] This was because after receiving the assistance of the Asia Foundation, researchers at New Asia College were paid a stipend for living expenses, which meant that they had to work full time and could not be employed elsewhere. I had a very pleasant time at the *Freedom Front* working as an editor for two years. My frequent interaction with authors and readers took me out of my bookish world and gave me an opportunity to engage with the intellectual and cultural circles of society.

That my vision has not been limited to the world inside the walls of academe was perhaps due to my experience during those two years.

Four or five years after I left Hong Kong, both the Freedom Publishing House and the *Freedom Front* ceased operations because their assistance from the Americans ended. At the end of the 1960s, Mr. Xie Chengping immigrated to the United States and took a teaching position at a university on the West Coast. I spoke to him on the phone, but eventually we lost contact.

The Youlian Publishing Group and its Founders

The last journal I would like to discuss is *Motherland Weekly* (*Zuguo zhoukan*), an even more important publication. Since *Motherland Weekly* was part of the Youlian Publishing Group, I need to elaborate on the group first to present the publication in its proper context.

Youlian 友聯 (literally Friends and Allies or Friends United) was a syndicate formed by a group of young friends involved in political and cultural affairs. The name was taken from the idea of friends united as allies. The group members were in their mid-twenties to early thirties; most of them had graduated from university before 1949. United in their pursuit of a liberal democratic social order, they were the most prominent new power rising in the Third Force Movement. Initially, there were around twenty people involved in launching the Youlian Group, but only around ten of them were principal members.

The first one who comes to mind is Xu Dongbin. He was three years older than I and born in Beiping, but his ancestral home seems to have been Hubei. He first entered the Department of Foreign Languages at National Southwest Associated University but later withdrew. After the Anti-Japanese War of Resistance, he transferred to the Western languages department at Peking University; in 1949 he went into exile in Hong Kong. He had been trained as a translator and interpreter during the war and translated for the American Air Force, so he was very fluent in both written and spoken English. Given the connections between the Youlian

Group and American aid organizations (like the Asia Foundation), he was given important responsibilities. A learned scholar with a very rich knowledge of Chinese and Western history and international relations, he wrote a number of essays using different pen names. In his later years —using the pen name "one who pours the tea" (*guancha jia* 灌茶家), a homophone for "observer" 觀察家—he wrote, for a long period, highly acclaimed articles for several major Hong Kong newspapers, analyzing important changes on Mainland China.

Xu Dongbin was extremely conscientious in his work, always making the utmost effort for every job, including the important positions of general editor and director of the Youlian Publishing Group, as well as general editor of *Motherland Weekly* and head of the Youlian Research Institute—he performed brilliantly in all these positions. He also worked for the Youlian Publishing Group for a very long time, from 1951 when it began to 1989 when he immigrated to the United States for health reasons. I had the opportunity to meet him again later when I made a short visit to Stanford University in 1993 and went to see him at his home in San Francisco where we had a long chat. Sadly, he passed away just two years later.

The next person I would like to highlight is Mr. Hu Xinping. About eight or ten years my senior, he was from northeast China and had studied in Japan. He had two most important pen names: Hu Yue 胡越 and Sima Changfeng 司馬長風. He had studied the works of Marx and Engels; and whenever he criticized Marxism-Leninism and the Chinese Communist Party, he used the pen name Hu Yue. He also had a great love for literature; and whenever he wrote about literature, he signed off as Sima Changfeng. If my memory is not mistaken, he may have been the first general editor of *Motherland Weekly* (the first issue was published in January 1953), while also being responsible for editorial work at the Youlian Publishing Group. From the time I was in Hong Kong to the start of my residence in the United States, and he enthusiastically cajoled me into writing many essays that were published in *Motherland Weekly*.

That the Youlian Publishing Group had many intimate relationships with the academic intellectual circles of that era was very much due to his dedication. Hu Xinping and I also cultivated a friendship because we both loved to play *Weiqi* and would have many long, enjoyable conversations over the game.

In discussing the founding of the Youlian Group, another important individual who should be mentioned is Ms. Qiu Ran. Like Xu Dongbin, she was also a student in the Western languages department of Peking University, either in the same year or one below. Her Chinese- and English-language skills were very good, and she had an elegant demeanor and a warm personality. Even rarer was her fervent dedication to the pursuit of the ideals of democracy. Her father, Qiu Chun (Qiu Da-nian, 1897–1966), was not only greatly renowned in academic circles but also a pioneer of liberalism and of the same generation as Hu Shi. In a diary entry for March 8, 1931, Hu Shi wrote:

> Mr. Qiu was a student of John Dewey (1859–1952) and his doctoral dissertation was entitled "Educational Theories of the Utilitarian School." We found a congenial agreement in our discussions of the intellectual history of England.[56]

At the time, Qiu Chun was a professor at Beiping Normal University, but in April of the same year he was "expelled" from the Nationalist Party because he joined the Chinese Youth Party.[57] A few years later, probably due to Hu Shi's enthusiastic support, he was finally hired by the education department of Peking University. In 1948 his health prevented him from going to Hong Kong, but I understand that without any concern for his own safety he encouraged his daughter to strive for freedom and democracy.

Qiu Ran was not only a dynamic activist in cultural and political arenas, but she was also an excellent creative writer. Under the pen name of "Swallow's Return" (Yan Guilai 燕歸來), she wrote quite a few prose essays and poems that were quite well-known for a time (one of her other pen names was "Swallow Clouds" [Yan Yun 燕雲]). Being such a talented person in so many areas, she commanded the attention of society, especially the cultural and political communities of Hong Kong in the 1950s. The Youlian Publishing Group considered her a core member, and to further the development of their enterprise, she, like Xu Dongbin, maintained close connections with the relevant American organizations and personages.

After I left Hong Kong, I had the opportunity to have a long and very pleasant conversation with her. It was probably around 1970 when she visited the United States at the invitation of the US State Department. She came to Harvard to see me, and we had a long conversation at my home. She had become a Catholic while in Hong Kong, and after reaching middle age (around the end of the 1970s) she went to Germany and entered a convent. Religious faith became her final refuge, and this was something I had never expected.

There were many talented people in the Youlian Group, and they are not limited to the three individuals I have mentioned. Due to space constraints, I am unable to list them all in detail. There are, however, still a few more individuals that I should note.

The first is Mr. Xu Guansan (1924–2011). He was from Anhui and five years my senior. He graduated in 1947 from Northeast Zhongzheng University (located in Sichuan Province, Santai County during the Anti-Japanese War of Resistance) where Xie Chengping was his teacher.[58] In 1949 he went to Taipei, where he served as secretary to Fu Sinian, then president of Taiwan University. When Fu Sinian gave a lecture on "What Kind of a Country is the Soviet Union After All?" ("Sulian jiujing shi yige shenmo guojia?" 蘇聯究竟是一個什麼國家?), that year Xu transcribed and published it in the *Free China Bimonthly*[59]; this was just one reason why Fu Sinian was appreciative of him. In 1950, at the request of Xie Chengping, Xu Guansan went to Hong Kong to manage the editorial work at the Freedom Publishing House. As a result of this opportunity, he became one of the founders of the Youlian Group. Within the Youlian

Publishing Group, his academic achievements and writing skills were higher than the other members. For example, the book *On the Democratic Way of Life* (*Tan minzhu shenghuo fangshi* 談民主生活方式) that he wrote under the pen name Yu Pingfan 于平凡 (Ordinary Yu) expounded vividly the complicated subject of Dewey's arguments on democracy in a very accessible manner and had a great influence on young students.[60] I was one of those influenced by him at that time. However, his clout made Xu Guansan inordinately prideful, and this with his extremely unyielding personality meant that he did not get along easily with others. On this account it was not long before he left the Youlian Publishing Group and went solo on his future endeavors.

I mention Xu Guansan in particular because I must emphasize that the Youlian Publishing Group was able to develop into the most successful group in Hong Kong's Third Force Movement primarily because its members could cooperate over a long period with mutual respect. Xu Guansan was the only exception, which was why he and the group parted ways.

The next person who should be mentioned is Mr. Chen Zhuosheng. He came from Peking University and was resolutely anti-communist while in school. He went to Hong Kong and joined the editorial department of the *Freedom Front* for a while. In the Youlian Publishing Group, he was involved in the overall planning and operations with the objective of developing the Youlian Publishing Group into a modern company. It was for that reason that all the various departments of the Youlian Publishing Group were unified into the Youlian Cultural Enterprise Limited Corporation. Chen Zhuosheng was not the only one of the Youlian founders who was shrewd in business. Xi Huizhang, my classmate at New Asia College (one year below me), also had outstanding business enterprise skills. He worked for the Youlian Publishing Group for a long time and made important contributions in the areas of investment and management. This business acumen set Youlian apart from the other political and cultural groups which also received American support and was a key factor in their success.

The Scope and Influence of the Youlian Publishing Group

The Youlian Publishing Group had a large-scale all-encompassing plan from its inception. In addition to a publishing house and *Motherland Weekly*, it also had the *Chinese Student Weekly* (*Zhongguo xuesheng Zhoubao* 中國學生周報), the *Children's Playground* (*Ertong* leyuan 兒童樂園) bimonthly, the *College Life* (*Daxue shenghuo* 大學生活) monthly, and the Youlian Research Institute, thereby catering to readers of many age groups. The Youlian Research Institute collected newspapers, journals, and other publications from various parts of Mainland China; and after several decades, it had the largest collection outside of China. At the end of the 1990s, the collection was transferred to the Chinese University of Hong Kong.

Compared to other Third Force Movement groups, the Youlian Publishing Group had two distinct characteristics: First, its influence and impact went beyond Hong Kong and reached overseas Chinese communities in places as far as Southeast Asia, Europe, and America. In Singapore and Malaya (now Malaysia), for example, they set up branch offices and put out publications primarily aimed at middle-school readers; at the same time, they obtained the right to compile textbooks for Chinese-language schools in Singapore and Malaya. Second, they functioned to educate and enlighten generations of young people from middle school to university level. Youlian used their publications, which were in highly accessible language, to transmit and spread the humanistic values that were most important to Chinese tradition, such as humanity (*ren* 仁), righteousness (*yi* 義), propriety (*li* 禮), wisdom (*zhi* 智), honesty (*xin* 信), together with the universal values of democracy, freedom, and human rights. They continued these efforts constantly over a long period, and their impact was immeasurable.

At this point, I should say something about the *Chinese Student Weekly* (*Zhongguo xuesheng zhoubao*), where I did work for a while.

In June 1952, after I graduated from New Asia College, my friends in the Youlian Publishing Group invited me to join them in establishing the *Chinese Student Weekly* and to be its general editor. I was very sympathetic to the ideals of Youlian at the time, so I accepted their offer without any hesitation. I worked there only for a little more than three months before I resigned and returned to my part-time position at the *Freedom Front.* It was not because I did not value this student publication, but rather because I had already set my mind on academic research. I was also not good at handling complicated personnel matters and editorial work. At the same time Professor Qian Mu told me that the New Asia College Research Institute they were building was almost ready and would soon be opened officially, and so I should be prepared. Under these circumstances, I knew that I could not stay in my editorial post for very long, so it would be best for me to leave earlier for Youlian to find a suitable long-term candidate. Time soon showed that the *Chinese Student Weekly*'s cultural achievements were outstanding.

The *Chinese Student Weekly* began publication in July 1952 and ceased in July 1974; in those twenty-two years it published a total of 1,128 issues.[61] For twenty-two years the issues continuously expanded in length, with increasingly richer content; its coverage expanded to cover the arts, drama, film, music, painting, and it published many articles by students. It quickly became a bestseller among young students. I remember that when it began publication, the *Chinese Student Weekly* only sold a few hundred copies. According to an editor who had been there for seven years, by their first year, sales had already increased to more than twenty thousand, which included more than ten thousand subscriptions and retail sales in Hong Kong, as well as distribution of around ten thousand to overseas Chinese communities in Taiwan, Southeast Asia, Europe, and the United States. This editor wrote:

> The *Chinese Student Weekly* is really not political but rather a cultural publication. Looking at its performance for twenty-two years, it has functioned gradually and imperceptibly to influence a generation of young people over a long period of time in terms of their intellectual and cultural life."[62]

I believe that this statement is both objective and accurate. On this account I will venture to go a step further and infer that the seeds of the young students of Hong Kong's current pursuit of the universal values of democracy, freedom, and human rights that gave rise to the umbrella movement [of the fall and winter 2014] and astonished the world were perhaps sown from the earliest dissemination of the *Chinese Student Weekly*.

My preceding discussion of the Youlian Publishing Group is rather long, but this is necessary for an objective presentation of the cultural and intellectual situation of Hong Kong in those days. The scope of the Youlian Cultural Enterprise Limited was large, its operations were diverse, and it carried on its businesses for almost thirty years, and so its overall achievement and influence were greater than similar groups. My personal understanding of Youlian is somewhat deeper, not only because most of the founders were my friends and of the same generation but also because the employees in its various departments were fellow graduates from New Asia College. Thus, what I witnessed was relatively more intimate. Having detailed Youlian's background, let me now offer a brief description of the Youlian Publishing House and *Motherland Weekly*.

The books published by the Youlian Publishing House and the articles in *Motherland Weekly* were aimed at intellectuals in general. In both academic quality and breadth of coverage, they surpassed all other publishers. There were two main reasons: First, they solicited contributions from Chinese authors all around the world and their editorial review process was extremely stringent; and second, Youlian ran its own book and periodical distribution company so their marketing was very professional. Youlian published many good books, which I have read, albeit a long time ago. There are two books that still stand out in my mind. The first was *Naked Earth* (*Chidi zhi lian* 赤地之戀) by Zhang Ailing (1920–1995), published in 1956. By chance I had read her *Rice Sprout Song* (*Yangge* 秧歌) before I left Hong Kong, and I was very interested in her description of the behavior of middle- and lower-ranking Chinese Communist Party cadres in the countryside.[63] In 1955 when I heard that Youlian was going to publish her new book, I asked Xu Dongbin to reserve a copy for me. When the book came out the next year, he sent me a copy by air mail and the book left a deep impression on me.

The second book was *On Twice Destined in Marriage* by Chen Yinque, which I had recommended to Youlian. In 1958 I read the manuscript version of this book that had made its way to Harvard from the Academia Sinica Institute of History and Philology. I was very moved by this work and hoped that it could be circulated widely, but the Chinese Communist Party forbade its official publication. I sent the manuscript to Hu Xinping and asked him to take it to the Youlian Publishing House so they could consider publishing it. Youlian very quickly decided to publish it and wrote me a letter saying that although this manuscript faced the two difficulties of being hard to sell and having copyright problems, it was of such great value that it was worth taking the risk to publish it. This decision fully reflects the fundamental nature of the Youlian Publishing House.

After its publication, *On Twice Destined in Marriage* caused quite a sensation for a while. There were fierce reactions in official circles in Mainland China, which I did not expect at the beginning of my research career.[64]

The Unique Impact of *Motherland Weekly*

Motherland Weekly began publishing in January 1953; about a decade later it changed to a monthly publication and continued until the mid-1970s. *Motherland Weekly* was one of the Third Force Movement's periodicals, advocating anti-communism as well as the pursuit of democracy, freedom, and human rights. At the same time, *Motherland Weekly* gave equal importance to the traditional Chinese humanistic spirit. Due to the intimate relationship between the Youlian Publishing Group and New Asia College, Professors Qian Mu and Tang Junyi were *Motherland Weekly* authors from its inception; their two like-minded friends, Mou Zongsan and Xu Fuguan, also regularly published important essays in the journal. It is my understanding that many friends of the Youlian Publishing Group actively affirmed the idea that there exists a great deal of overlapping consensus in spiritual values between the traditional Chinese humanistic tradition and modern Western culture, and that the differences between the two should not be prejudicially exaggerated as a kind of cultural conflict. In this light, *Motherland Weekly* can be said to have combined the merits of *Free China Bimonthly* and *The Democratic Review,* and being more open than both, it attracted many more authors and readers who held different points of view.

Motherland Weekly was the Hong Kong publication for which I wrote the longest. After I went to the United States in 1955, I wrote very few Chinese articles, but due to the ceaseless urging of Hu Xinping I continued to write some essays for *Motherland Weekly.* Most of them were reviews of the latest Western studies of literature, history, and philosophy. The last essay I wrote for the *Motherland Weekly*—"Humanistic Thought in the Western Classical Age" ("Xifang gudian shidai zhi renwen sixiang" 西方古典時代之人文思想)—was in 1960.

Although *Motherland Weekly* was a democratic anti-communist publication, its early opinions were not too radical and so for a while it received permission from the Nationalist Party to be sold legally in Taiwan. The scope of its influence was wider than that of other similar publications. Because it could not avoid criticizing Taiwan politics, it became subject to inspections and confiscations from public security agencies, and consequently its subscribers often did not receive their issues. By 1959, relations between the two sides completely broke down, and the Nationalist Party canceled *Motherland Weekly*'s license for its publication distribution in

Taiwan. An influential Taiwanese newspaper, *Public Opinion* (*Gonglun bao* 公論報), strongly protested this in its October 26, 1959 edition. In an editorial entitled "Our Opinions on Hearing that the Hong Kong Journal *Motherland Weekly* Has Been Banned from Sale in Our Domestic Market," besides denouncing the Nationalist Party's "high-pressure tactics, that only cause pain to its supporters and joy among its enemies," the article asserts that:

> For a resolutely anti-communist publication like *Motherland Weekly* full of weighty arguments to be banned from sale in our domestic market is actually no loss to that journal itself ... but the loss to the reputation of the government is truly incalculable.[65]

These words show us how much *Motherland Weekly* was appreciated in Taiwan; its influence was beyond question. Why, then, did the Nationalist Party shut down *Motherland Weekly*'s circulation in Taiwan and had it banned? The key to this was the question of Chiang Kai-shek serving as president for a third term.

According to the Constitution of the Republic of China promulgated on January 1, 1947, the president serves a six-year term and can be reelected for one more term, making a total of twelve years. Mr. Chiang [Kai-shek] was elected as the first president in 1948 and was then reelected in 1954; his second term was up in 1960, and he could not campaign for a third term. The Nationalist Party however, insisted that the third president had to be Chiang Kai-shek and no one else, and Chiang himself, bearing the responsibility to "oppose the communists and restore the nation" (*fangong fuguo* 反共復國), felt he had to continue to lead the country. The Nationalist Party authorities then put forth all sorts of proposed bills in an attempt to prove that this did not violate the constitution.

With the support and at the initiation of Hu Shi and *Free China Bimonthly*, however, the democratic figures of Taiwan rose up and protested with one voice. They asserted that they were not opposed to

Chiang's leadership but rather striving to maintain the integrity of the Constitution. From 1959 to March 1960, Taiwan's media circles were completely immersed in this dispute about Chiang's third presidential term. Overseas democratic party elements and liberal figures from Hong Kong, Southeast Asia, Japan, and the United States also actively chimed in on this controversy. It goes without saying that they were all on the side of Hu Shi and *Free China Bimonthly* and opposed to Chiang's "destroying the Constitution to serve another term." These overseas personages included Chinese Social Democracy Party leader Zhang Junmai (one of the drafters of the Constitution), Chinese Youth Party leaders Zuo Shunsheng and Li Huang, philosophy professor Xie Fuya (1892–1991), among others. Several members of the Youlian Publishing Group, such as Hu Yue, Shi Changzhi, Li Dasheng, and Xiao Huikai, who held responsibilities for various Youlian departments, also signed up as participants in this movement to defend the Constitution; and *Motherland Weekly* continued to play a central role in overseas public opinion.

The last joint declaration, "A Warning to Those Who Are Plotting to Destroy the Constitution" ("Women dui huixian cedongzhe de jinggao" 我們對毀憲策動者的警告), by Zuo Shunsheng, Zhang Junmai, and seventy others was first published in *Motherland Weekly* on February 17, 1960.[66] That was why the Nationalist Party banned the circulation of *Motherland Weekly* in Taiwan. On November 10, 1959, after the weekly journal had been banned in Taiwan, Hu Shi wrote a letter to the Youlian Publishing Group; I quote from it here to conclude my discussion of [importance of *Motherland Weekly* and the high standards of] the Youlian Publishing Group:

> To the members of the Youlian Publishing Group: Having heard that *Motherland Weekly* is not permitted to be sold in Taiwan, I am very unhappy and very disappointed.
>
> I recently read Mr. Xiao Ping's *Those Who Pursue a Fantasy* (*Juiqiu huanxiang de renmen* 追求幻想的人們) and I think it is very well written. I want to buy four or five copies to send to my

friends. Could your publishing company please send me five copies? Moreover, Mr. Wang Guangti once gave me a copy of his *Biography of a Wild Horse* (*Yema zhuan* 野馬傳), and I took it abroad with me and read it there. I liked it very much and left it there for my friends to read and pass around. Could I also ask you to please send me five copies? Please tell me the prices for these two books and I will find a way to send you the money.[67]

Conclusion

Finally, I would like to relate a short story about my participation in the founding of a publishing company and journal. In 1954 my friends Xu Zhiping (1924–1981) and Liu Wei were commissioned by the United States Information Service to have a large number of American masterpieces in the humanities translated into Chinese and published. They decided to take advantage of the opportunity to establish a publishing company, which would also publish high-quality, influential Chinese writings, including their own works. They kept inviting me to join them, and because of our friendship I did not feel it right to refuse. I told them that I would only participate in vetting manuscripts and editorial forms of written work and that I would not get involved in business operations and external negotiation duties.

Xu Zhiping and Liu Wei had been editors for *Freedom Front*, and they had worked with me for many years and became trusted friends. Xu Zhiping was a good creative writer. Under the pen name of Xu Su, he wrote a novel entitled *Stars, Moon, and Sun* (*Xingxing, yueliang, taiyang* 星星, 月亮, 太陽), which was a bestseller in Hong Kong, Southeast Asia, and Taiwan.[68] A short time later it was made into a movie. Liu Wei graduated from the economics department of Tsinghua University, but his interests extended to many areas in the social sciences. In his writings he frequently used modern concepts to explain and interpret classical Chinese wisdom, and for that reason he and I had quite a few intellectual interactions. This period of cooperation lasted only a short time because

I left Hong Kong in October 1955. Nevertheless, one year of working together on this new undertaking was a very pleasant one!

Our publishing company was called Gaoyuan 高原, meaning high plateau, but because we were publishing translated works for the United States Information Service, we needed an English name and so we called it Highland Press. I gave my two books, *Essays on Civilization* and *On the Road to Thought*, to Gaoyuan to publish without taking any royalties as a show of support.

We also published an occasional journal focused on discussions of thought and culture. It was only occasional because we did not have the wherewithal to publish a periodical regularly. For the journal's name, I chose *Hailan* 海瀾, meaning ripples on the sea, as the name of the journal; and although it was taken from the sound of the English highland, it had another profound connotation. Mencius said "...it is difficult for water to come up to the expectations of someone who has seen the Sea ... [but] there is a way to judge water. Watch for its ripples. ..."[69] For *Gaoyuan* (Highland) to turn into *Hailan* (Ripples on the Sea) very neatly encompassed Confucius's thoughts that "the benevolent find joy in mountains" and "the wise find joy in water."[70]

I no longer remember how many issues of *Hailan* were published nor how many articles I wrote for it, but there is one incident that remains in my memory.

Sometime around December 1955, the English historian Arnold J. Toynbee came to Harvard to give a lecture, and this had been announced in the papers in October. I was very interested in Toynbee, and I wrote a letter telling Xu Zhiping and Liu Wei about the event. They wrote back immediately, urging me to write a report about it to attract more readers for *Hailan* because someone in Hong Kong had just published a book introducing Toynbee's historical theory, and it had attracted wide attention.

The first six volumes of Toynbee's *A Study of History* were published between 1934 and 1939, but because of the Second World War, the final four volumes were only completed in 1954. As a result, 1955 was the time when Toynbee's reputation was at its height, especially in the United States.[71] On the day of his lecture, the crowd was so huge that no classroom could accommodate them; finally the lecture had to be held in the Sanders Theatre Memorial Hall on Quincy Street. I not only listened to his lecture but also waited in a long line for his autograph, the first time in my life I ever did such a thing. My report and Toynbee's signature were both printed in *Hailan*. Unfortunately, with so many house moves, I don't know where this journal went. It was a noteworthy piece of writing, and I very much regret losing it.

This may be said to be the epilogue to my early years of cultural activities in Hong Kong.

NOTES

1. In the Cairo Conference of November 1943 and the Potsdam Conference of November 1945, the allied powers presented their conception of the postwar world. Chiang Kai-shek participated only in the Cairo Conference. The Potsdam Declaration set out the terms of Japan's "unconditional surrender." See United States Department of State *Foreign Relations of the United States: Diplomatic Papers: The Conference of Berlin (The Potsdam Conference), 1945*, vol. II (Washington, DC: U.S. Government Printing Office, 1945).

2. Wang Shudi was the author of a well-known book on the history of World War II and several other books on Chen Duxiu, Li Dazhao, and others (see WorldCat).

3. Since the 1921 edition published by Beida chubanbu (Beiping), there have been many subsequent editions of Hu Shi's selected writings; for example, *Hu Shi wencun, ba juan* (Taipei: Yuandong, 1985).

4. This "White Paper" was officially called *United States Relations with China with Special Reference to the Period 1944–1949* (Washington, DC: U.S. Government Printing Office, 1949).

5. Zhang Taiyan, *Guogu lunheng* (Shanghai: Gushu liutong chu, 1924); with many later editions. Qian Mu, *Xian Qin zhuzi xinian* (Shanghai: Shangwu yinshuguan, 1935); with many later editions.

6. Liu Ts'un-yan was a graduate of Peking University and the University of London. He taught Chinese literature and thought (especially Daoism) in many universities in America and other countries. The essay mentioned here is probably "Beida he Beida ren: Han Huayuan de lengjing" [Peking University and its people: The cool-headedness of Han Huayuan]. See Chen Pingyuan and Xia Xiaohong, eds., *Beida jiushi* [Old happenings at Peking University] (Beijing daxue, 2009), 309.

7. All of these founders or important members of New Asia College had illustrious careers and made other important contributions. Zhang Qiyun (Chang Chi-yun) was a graduate of Nanjing Higher Normal School (later Nanjing University) in history and geography; he was the Minister of Education in the ROC (Taiwan) and served as chief editor of *Zhongwen da cidian*. Cui Shuqin received his doctorate in political science from Harvard in 1934 and taught in Peking University and National Taiwan University. See https://www.pccu.edu.tw/intl/page/english/about_02.

html. Xie Youwei received an MA in philosophy from Harvard and taught in the Whampoa Military Academy in Guangzhou and at Taiwan Normal University. Tang Junyi was one of the most celebrated and influential twentieth-century Chinese philosophers. He founded the school of New Confucianism (Xin Rujia) and was a Chair Professor in the philosophy department of the Chinese University of Hong Kong. See Thomas Fröhlich, *Tang Junyi: Confucian Philosophy and the Challenge of Modernity* (Leiden and Boston: Brill, 2017). Zhang Pijie received his doctorate in economics from the University of Freiburg, served as chair of the New Asia College Department of Economics, and handled the college's finances.

8. Yü Ying-shih note: Qian Mu, *Qian Binsi xiansheng quanji* (Taipei: Lian-jing, 1998), vol. 50, Xinya Yiduo 新亞遺鐸, 1–2.

9. Ibid., 3.

10. Yü Ying-shih note: This essay is in my *Huiyou ji, zengding ben* [Collection of essays on friendship through writing, supplemental edition] (Taipei: Sanmin shuju, 2010), vol. 1, 136–152.

11. Yü Ying-shih, *You ji feng chui shui shang lin: Qian Mu yu xiandai zhong-guo xueshu* [Still remembering the wind roiling the waves upon the water: Qian Mu and modern Chinese scholarly thought] (Taipei: Sanmin shuju, 1991), 1–15.

12. Xia Zengyou was a late Qing to early Republic historian of China who wrote a well-known history of ancient Chinese.

13. Qian Mu, *Zhongguo jin sanbai nian xueshushi* [History of the past three hundred years of Chinese scholarship], 2 vols. (Shanghai: Shangwu yin-shu guan, 1937, reissued 1997; with many other editions.)

14. For an English translation of Han Yu's celebrated "Discourse on Teach-ers" (*Shishuo*), see William Theodore De Bary and Irene Bloom, eds., *Sources of the Chinese Tradition from Earliest Times to 1600*, 2nd ed., vol. 1 (New York: Columbia University Press, 1999), 582–583. It begins, "Stu-dents of ancient times all had their teachers, for it is only through the teacher that the Way is transmitted (*chuan Dao*), learning imparted (*shou ye*), and doubts dispelled (*jie huo*)."

15. Quotations are from *Mengzi* 4B.14 and 6B.2. (Lau, *Mencius*, 130 and 172.)

16. Yü Ying-shih, "Dong Han zhengquan zhi jianli yu shizu daxing zhi guanxi" [The establishment of the Eastern Han regime and its relations with the great land-owning families], *Xinya xuebao* [New Asia journal] 1, no. 2 (1956). See also Yü Ying-shih, *Dong Han zhengquan zhi jianli yu shizu daxing zhi guanxi: Lüe lun Liang Han zhi ji zhengzhi bianqian*

de shehui beijing [The establishment of the Eastern Han regime and its relation to the great families: A brief discussion of the political changes and social background between the two Han dynasties] in his *Zhong-guo zhishi jieceng shilun (Gudai pian)* [On ancient Chinese intellectuals: Ancient volume] (Taipei: Lianjing, 1980), 109–203.

17. Yü Ying-shih, *Han-Jin zhiji shi zhi xin zijue yu xin sichao* [The scholars' new awareness and new thought tides between the Han and Jin dynasties] (Hong Kong: Xin Ya Shuyuan, 1959).

18. Yü Ying-shih, *Trade and Expansion in Han China: A Study in the Structure of Sino-Barbarian Economic Relations* (Berkeley: University of California Press, 1967).

19. See the *Xinya Yiduo*, 18–48.

20. See Qian Mu, *Bashi yi shuangqin, Shi you za yi, (hekan)* 八十憶雙親, 師友雜憶, 合刊 [Reminiscences on my parents at the age of eighty, Miscellaneous reminiscences of teachers and friends (joint publication)] (Taipei: Dongda tushu gongsi, 1986). An English translation of "Reminiscences on my parents at the age of eighty" is in Jerry Dennerline, *Qian Mu and the World of Seven Mansions* (New Haven, CT: Yale University Press, 1989), 115–149.

21. Yü Ying-shih note: This refers to April 1960 when Professor Qian came and lectured at Harvard.

22. Yü Ying-shih note: Qian Mu, *Shiyou zayi* 師友雜憶 [Random recollections of friends and teachers] in *Qian Binsi xiansheng quanji* [Complete works of Mr. Qian Binsi], vol.51, 346–347.

23. Yü Ying-shih note: Qian Mu, *Sushulou yu shen* [Further notes from the sushu studio], in *Qian Binsi xiansheng quanji* [Complete works of Mr. Qian Binsi], 53 ce, 430. Translators' note: Qian Mu always refers to Yü Ying-shih as *di* 弟 meaning "younger brother" and always leaves a deferential space before the character.

24. A native of Jiangxi, Ouyang Jian was a pioneer in the modern Chinese study of Buddhism. His student, Xiong Shili was a major Chinese philosopher who worked to revive Confucianism and wrote a well-known critique of the Consciousness Only school of Buddhism entitled *Xin Weishi Lun* [A new treatise on Vijñaptimātra]. He continued to teach at Peking University after 1949 and was persecuted during the Cultural Revolution. See John Makeham, ed., *New Confucianism: A Critical Examination* (New York: Palgrave Macmillan, 2003); and Jana Rošker, *Searching for the Way: Theory of Knowledge in Pre-modern and Modern China* (Hong Kong: Chinese University Press, 2008).

25. Tang Junyi, *Zhongguo wenhua zhi jingshen jiazhi* [The spiritual value of Chinese culture] (Taipei: Zhengzhong shuju, 1959; Taipei: Taiwan xuesheng shuju, 1991). Liang Shuming is discussed in Chapter 1.

26. *Minzhu pinglun*, [Democratic review] (Hong Kong: Minzhu pinglun she, 1949–); *Zuguo zhoukan* [Motherland weekly] (Jiulong: Zuguo zhoukan she, 1953–1964); *Rensheng* (Hong Kong: Rensheng zazhishe, 1951–). *Minzhu pinglun* is available online at http://lib.mh.sinica.edu.tw/wSite/ sp?xdUrl=/wSite/Search/browseDo.jsp&queryDtd=15&queryWord= 民主評論%20 The%20Democratic%20 Review&ct Node=146&mp =HistM&idPath=103_104_117_146&moreClked=N&hereSeq=1

27. The text of *Wei Zhongguo wenhua jinggao shijie renshi xuanyan* [A manifesto for a re-appraisal of sinology and reconstruction of Chinese culture] is in *The Development of Neo-Confucian Thought*, vol. 2, by Carsun Chang (Zhang Junmai) (New York: Bookman Associates, 1962). A reprint of the Chinese original is available in Feng Zusheng, ed., *Dangdai Xin Rujia* (Beijing: Shenghuo, Dushu, Xinzhi Sanlian Shudian, 1989), 1–52.

28. Zhang Junmai, Tang Junyi, Mou Zongsan, and Xu Fuguan, "Wei Zhongguo wenhua jinggao shijie renshi xuanyan" [A manifesto for a reappraisal of sinology and reconstruction of Chinese culture], *The Democratic Review* 9, no. 1, (1958).

29. Commission of the Central Committee of the C.P.S.U. (B.), ed., *History of the Communist Party of the Soviet Union (Bolsheviks) Short Course* (New York: International Publishers, 1939). Joseph Stalin (September 1938), "Dialectical and Historical Materialism," https:// www.marxists.org/ reference/ archive/ stalin/works/1938/09.htm.

30. *Minzhu zhidu de fazhan* [The development of democratic systems] (Hong Kong: Yazhou, 1954) and *Jindai wenming de xin qushi* [New trends in modern civilization] (Hong Kong: Ziyou, 1953). These two books were republished together as *Xifang minzhu zhidu yu jindai wenming* [Western democratic systems and modern civilization] (Taizhong: Hanxin, 1984).

31. Karl Popper, *The Open Society and its Enemies* (London: G. Routledge & Sons, Ltd., 1945); and Arthur Schlesinger, Jr., *The Vital Center: The Politics of Freedom* (Boston: Houghton Mifflin, 1949).

32. Arthur Schlesinger, Jr., *The Age of Jackson* (Boston: Little, Brown, 1945).

33. Ruth Benedict, *Patterns of Culture* (Boston: Houghton Mifflin, 1934); and Arthur L. Kroeber, *Configurations of Culture Growth* (Berkeley: University of California Press, 1944).

34. Arnold J. Toynbee, *A Study of History* (London: Oxford University Press, 1934–1961).
35. To "destroy the old and establish the new" (*pojiu lixin* 破舊立新) was one of the main slogans of the Chinese Cultural Revolution.
36. "Pulls on one hair and moves the entire body" is an expression alluding to a well-know poem by Gong Zizhen (1792–1841) of the Qing dynasty.
37. Yü Ying-shih note: For a detailed study of this period, see my chapter "The Idea of Democracy and the Twilight of Elite Culture in Modern China," in *Justice and Democracy: Cross-Cultural Perspectives*, eds. Ronald Bontekoe and Mariétta Tigranovna Stepaniants (Honolulu: University of Hawaii Press, 1997), 199–215. Reprinted in Ying-shih Yü, *Chinese History and Culture*, Vol. 2: *Seventeenth Through Twentieth Century* (2016), 234–251.
38. *Ziyou yu pingdeng zhijian* [Between freedom and equality] (Jiulong: Ziyou, 1955). *Wenming lunheng* [Essays on civilization] (Taipei: Jiusi chuban youxian gongsi, 1979.
39. Yü Ying-shih note: see *Chen Kewen riji* [Diary of Chen Kewen], 1937–1952, vol. 2 (Taipei: Zhongyang yanjiuyuan jindaishi yanjiusuo, 2012), 1277.
40. Gu Mengyu received a degree in economics and politics from Berlin University and joined Sun Yat-sen's Tongmenghui in 1910. He held many positions in the Nationalist government, broke with Wang Jingwei over working with the Japanese, and continued to work with Chiang Kai-shek until he moved to Hong Kong in 1949. After living in Berkeley, California, he moved to Taiwan for the rest of his life. See Huang Kewu, "Gu Mengyu yu Xianggang di san shili de xingshuai" [Ku Mengyu and the rise and fall of the Hong Kong third force], http://www.cuhk.edu. hk/ics/21c/media/articles/c162-201706007.pdf.
41. Yü Ying-shih note: *Hu Shi riji quanji* (Taipei: Lianjing, 2004), vol. 8, p. 9.
42. An English version of the Constitution of the Republic of China can be found at https://en.wikisource.org/wiki/Constitution_of_the_Republic_ of_China_(1947).
43. Yü Ying-shih note: *Shiyou zayi* [*Random recollections of friends and teachers*] in *Qian Binsi xiansheng quanji* [Complete works of Mr. Qian Binsi], vol. 51 (Taipei: Lianjing, 1998), 296–297.
44. Zuo Shunsheng was a political activist and a historian and cofounder of the Chinese Youth Party. Li Huang was educated in France where he was also a cofounder of the China Youth Party. During the Anti-Japanese War of Resistance, the China Youth Party joined the China Democratic

League (*Zhongguo minzhu tongmeng* or *minmeng*) as part of the Third Force Movement. "Third Force" is translated as the "Third Way" in some other English sources. For Zuo and Li, see Edmund S. Feng, *In Search of Chinese Democracy: Civil Opposition in Nationalist China, 1929–1949* (Cambridge, UK: Cambridge University Press, 2000).

45. Zhang Guotao was a founding leader of the Chinese Communist Party and a challenger to Mao Zedong's leadership. He left the party in 1938. His memoirs are a major source of the party's history. Xu Chongzhi had a long military and political career during which he was both a friend and an enemy of Chiang Kai-shek; he ended his days in Hong Kong. See "Chang Kuo-t'ao," in *Biographic Dictionary of Chinese Communism 1921–1965*, vol. I, ed. Donald W. Klein (Cambridge, MA: Harvard University Press, 1971), 38–43.

46. We translate *fengjian canyu* 封建殘餘 as a "remnant of feudalism" because that is what the Chinese Communist Party would call it in English; *fengjian* is not, however, the same as feudalism in Europe.

47. Yü Ying-shih note: See my long preface to Peng Guoxiang, *Zhizhe de xianshi guanhuai: Mou Zongsan de zhengzhi yu shehui sixiang* 彭國翔, 智者的現世關懷 ： 牟宗三的政治與社會思想 [A wise man's contemporary concerns: Mou Zongsan's political and social thought] (Taipei: Lianjing, 2016).

48. Yü Ying-shih note: Qian Mu, *Shiyou zayi, fulu* [Appendix to random recollections of friends and teachers 10 "Wang Guanzhi Aici" [Lament for Wang Guanzhi] in *Qian Binsi xiansheng quanji* [Complete works of Mr. Qian Binsi], vol. 51, 453.

49. Yü Ying-shih's review is available at https://book.douban.com/review/72 12228/. "Zaisheng yuan" [Twice destined in marriage] is a long poem by a Qing-dynasty woman poet, Chen Duansheng (1751–1796?), which tells the story of a woman disguised as a man who rose to be prime minister and then was reunited with her fiancé. Chen Yinque was "probably the first one to point out that Chen Duansheng advocated freedom and independence for women ... [and he also] praised the work for its elegant language, its tightly and finely knit structure, and its clear lines of thought." *The Indiana Companion to Traditional Chinese Literature* (Bloomington: Indiana University Press, 1986), 236. See Chen Yinque (Yinke), *Lun Zaisheng Yuan* [On twice destined in marriage] (Hong Kong, Jiulong: Youlian, 1959).

50. Yü Ying-shih note: Qian Mu, "Yi wen hui you, yi you fu ren—wei Rensheng zazhi chuangkan shinian zuo," 以文會友, 以友輔仁—為人生雜

誌創刊十年作 [Making friends through writing, relying on friends for humanity, written for the tenth anniversary of *Life*], *Zhongguo wenhua congtan, Quanjiben*, vol. 44, 346.

51. See *Disan shili yundong: Ziyou zhenxian jituan de xingshuai* [The third force movement: Rise and fall of the freedom front], http://news.ifeng.com/ gundong/ detail_2013 _09/04/29296357_0.shtml. For Xie Chengping, see also Cheng Zhengmao, *Wuling niandai Xianggang di san shili yundong shiliao soumi*, 50 [Collected materials on the Hong Kong third force movement of the 1950s] (Taipei: Xiuwei zixun keji gufen youxian gong si, 2011).

52. *Minzhu geming lun* [On the democratic revolution] (Hong Kong: Ziyou, 1954). *Jindai wenming de xin qushi* noted earlier.

53. Zhang Bao-en was a well-known editor associated with the Hong Kong Third Force Movement. See Cheng Zhengmao, *Wuling niandai Xianggang di san shili yundong shiliao soumi* [Collected materials on the Hong Kong third force movement of the nineteen fifties] (Taipei: Xiuwei chubanshe, 2011.

54. *Dao siwei zhi lu* [On the road to thought] (Hong Kong: Gaoyuan, 1954), reprinted by Hanxin of Taizhong in 1984.

55. Yü Ying-shih note: See the section "On First Becoming Professor Qian Mu's Disciple."

56. Yü Ying-shih note: *Hu Shi riji quanji* [Hu Shi's complete diary], vol. 6, p. 522.

57. Yü Ying-shih note: Ibid., p. 538.

58. Xu Guansan was a well-known historian who taught at National Taiwan University, Hong Kong University, and the Chinese University of Hong Kong. He authored many books on historiography and the "new history." See https://baike.baidu.com/item/许冠三/4967937?fr=aladdin.

59. Fu Sinian, "Sulian jiujing shi yige shenmo guojia?" 蘇聯究竟是一個什麼國家? [What kind of a country is the Soviet Union after all?], lecture transcription, *Free China Bimonthly* 1, issue 3 (December 20, 1949).

60. *Tan minzhu shenghuo fangshi* [On the democratic lifestyle] (Hong Kong: Pingfan, 1951).

61. For the essays in *Zhongguo xuesheng zhoubao* [Chinese student weekly], see http:// hklitpub.lib. cuhk.edu. hk/journals/zgxszb/.

62. Yü Ying-shih note with full title added: See Luoka, "Lengzhan shidai de Zhongguo xuesheng zhoubao de wenhua jiaose yu xin dianying wenhua de yansheng," [Role of the Chinese student weekly during the Cold War era and new film culture], 2009. Translators note: This article is in

Lengzhan yu Xianggang dianying [The cold war and Hong Kong film], eds. Huang Ailing and Li Peide (Ai-ling Wong and Pui-tak Lee) (Hong Kong: Hong Kong dianying ziliao guan, 2009), 111–116.

63. Zhang Ailing (Eileen Chang) was of course one of the most celebrated writers of modern China. For English translations, see Eileen Chang, *The Rice-Sprout Song: A Novel of Modern China* (Berkeley: University of California Press, 1998) and Eileen Chang, *Naked Earth* (New York: New York Review of Books, 2015).

64. Yü Ying-shih note: For the details, see my 2010 essay "Chen Yinque yanjiu de fansi he zhanwang" [Reflections and prospects of research on Chen Yinque], in *Chen Yinque wannian shiwen shizheng* [Explication and interpretation of the later poetry and prose of Chen Yinque], new edition (Taipei: Dongda tushu gongsi, 2011).

65. Yü Ying-shih note: *Hu Shi riji quanji* for October 26, 1959, vol. 9, pp. 437–438.

66. Yü Ying-shih note: For more details, see two reports in Taipei's *Public Opinion* for February 13 and 21 in *Hu Shi riji quanji*, vol. 9, pp. 589–592 and 614–618.

67. Yü Ying-shih note: See *Hu Shi quanji* [Complete works of Hu Shi] (Hefei: Anhui jiaoyu, 2003), vol. 26, page 331. Translators' note: Sima Sangdun (Wang Guangti), *Yema zhuan* [Biography of a wild horse] (Xianggang: Youlian, 1959). Xiao Ping, *Zhuiqiu huanxiang de renmen* [People pursuing fantasy] (Jiulong: Youlian, 1959).

68. *Xingxing, Yueliang, Taiyang* [Stars, moon, sun] (Hong Kong: Gaoyuan, 1958).

69. Quotation is from *Mengzi*, 7A.24, Lau, *Mencius*, 187.

70. *Lunyu* VI.23, Lau, *Analects*, 84: "The Master said, 'the wise find joy in water; the benevolent find joy in mountains'" (*Zhizhe le shui, renzhe le shan*, 知者樂水，仁者樂山).

71. Yü Ying-shih note: For more on this, see William H. McNeill, *Arnold Toynbee, A Life* (Oxford University Press, 1989), chapter IX, "Fame and Fortune, 1946–1955," 205–234.

CHAPTER 5

HARVARD UNIVERSITY YEARS

In Hong Kong in the 1950s, our family was living in very poor circumstances, and I did not have the slightest notion of going abroad to study.
Yet in 1955 I went to Harvard University in the United States to further
my studies, which was truly beyond all expectations. Professor Qian Mu
wrote the following brief description about this:

> The Harvard-Yenching Institute first wrote in 1954 inviting New
> Asia College to send a young teacher under thirty-five years old
> to visit Harvard. I asked Hong Kong University about this and
> learned they had not been approached, and so I realized that only
> New Asia College had received such an invitation. Because New
> Asia College had no eligible young teachers, and at the time only
> one of the older teachers had ever studied in America, I asked
> him if he would accept this invitation and he agreed. However,
> Harvard refused because that would not be in agreement with
> their conditions. The next year Harvard asked us again, and so
> Yü Ying-shih, of the first New Asia College graduating class who
> had remained as a graduate student, was sent to Harvard with
> the title of Teaching Assistant. When the first year ended, he
> also received another year's extension. He then asked that he be
> allowed to enter Harvard as a PhD student and remain there to

teach after graduation. He was the first person whom New Asia College sent to study abroad.[1]

This note is mostly accurate, but there are some inevitable discrepancies in the details. Allow me to take this opportunity to supplement this account from my memory.

I clearly remember that in late January 1955, Mr. Wu Zhenxiong was sent by Professor Qian to the Graduate Institute to look for me. Wu had studied at Yale and was then teaching at the New Asia College, and he was also concurrently the college's English Secretary. He brought all the documents from the Harvard-Yenching Institute to New Asia College for me to read and decide if I wanted to be recommended for a year of advanced study at Harvard. It turned out that beginning in 1954 the Harvard-Yenching Institute had established a new program— the Harvard-Yenching Institute Scholars Program—which was an annual invitation by the Harvard-Yenching Institute extended to scholars in the humanities and social sciences from China, Japan, and Korea to visit Harvard for a year. They would be able to attend classes and conduct research but were under no obligation to take examinations, and they could apply for another year's extension at the end of the year. However, there were age requirements set for these visiting scholars, who had to be over thirty and under forty years old. The primary goal of this program was to upgrade the teaching and research capabilities of middle-aged scholars. At that time the Harvard-Yenching Institute planned to recruit eleven or twelve visiting scholars, mostly from Japan, with one or two from South Korea, while Hong Kong and Taiwan would each have one representative. (Originally only National Taiwan University received an invitation, but later the Institute of History and Philology of the Academia Sinica and Taiwan Normal University were also invited. Of course, being nominated did not guarantee being accepted.)

Mr. Wu Zhenxiong told me that there were no successful applicants for the previous year because the candidates did not meet the age requirements and that the situation had not changed this year—the senior scholars were too old, and the junior scholars were too young. The college had decided to nominate Professor Tang Junyi and me anyway and see if the Harvard-Yenching Institute would choose one of us. That year Professor Tang was forty-six and I was twenty-five; he was too old, and I was too young. Nevertheless, I eventually agreed to give it a try and even drafted a long advanced-study plan, even though I had no expectations of going to Harvard. I had two very strong reasons. First, in the Harvard-Yenching Institute's documentation, a "visiting scholar" referred to someone who had had a certain level of accomplishments in academic research, and so they should be at least more than thirty years old. At the time I was a young student who had graduated not too long ago and had just begun my graduate research. Second, Professor Tang Junyi was an eminently successful philosopher, but I had not even published a single piece of original scholarly work. How could I be placed in the same category with Professor Tang? I regarded my nomination as an honor as well as a form of encouragement but did not give it any further thought.

Two months later, I received a wholly unexpected official letter from the director of the Harvard-Yenching Institute, Serge Elisséeff (1889–1975), inviting me to come to Harvard in the fall. The letter also stated that I could come to Harvard two months early and arrive in early July so that I could familiarize myself with Harvard and improve my English-language writing and speaking skills. Of course, this letter pleased me beyond all expectations, but it also left me confused as to why I was selected. It was not until after I was at Harvard for a few months that I finally learned that the core focus of the Harvard-Yenching Institute Scholars Program was on young scholars, and its goal was to cultivate their potential for scholarship and intellectual thought so they could develop these fully. Therefore, my age being below the requirement and my scholarship not being advanced actually were the principal reasons why I was chosen for the program. I also believe that the Harvard-Yenching Institute made an exception and selected me because they had already rejected the nominations of New Asia College the year before and because they were supportive of New Asia College and sympathetic about its situation.

The description by Professor Qian Mu just cited mentions the nomination of "an older person" but does not give his name, so I will elaborate on this. This "older person" was Mr. Chen Bozhuang (P. C. Chun, 1892–1960). Using a government stipend, Professor Chen studied in the United States in 1910, the same year as Hu Shi and Zhao Yuanren (Y. R. Chao, 1892–1982). Professor Chen's specialty was chemical engineering, but after he returned to China he became involved in various areas of economics and transportation. After the victory in the Anti-Japanese War of Resistance, he took up the post of Chief of the Beijing and Shanghai Railroad Bureau, and at the beginning of 1949 he escaped southward to settle in Hong Kong. From then on, his interests shifted to the philosophy of John Dewey and the social sciences. He offered a course in Sociology at New Asia College and founded a very important journal, *Modern Academic Quarterly* (*Xiandai xueshu jikan* 現代學術季刊), that specialized in research on and translations of the latest intellectual trends in Western humanities and social studies. He also immersed himself in the study of Talcott Parsons's new book *The Social System*.[2] I had frequent discussions with him, and the *Modern Academic Quarterly* greatly expanded my intellectual horizons. Because Professor Chen Bozhuang edited the *Modern Academic Quarterly*, he very much wanted to visit the United States so that he could discuss the translation and introduction of the latest intellectual trends with the appropriate academics. This was the main reason that he agreed to New Asia College's nomination; however, his proposal was not in accord with the Harvard-Yenching Institute's goal and he was over the age limit, so he was unable to realize his wish to visit the United States again at the time.

In his letter to Yang Liansheng dated June 1, 1954, Hu Shi confirms this:

> I heard that one person New Asia College nominated was Mr. Chen Bozhuang (P. C. Chun). He passed the examination to study abroad in 1910 at the same time as Mr. Yuanren and myself. He handled

several major enterprises at home and was a very respectable official. He has recently been studying [John] Dewey's school of thought and reading innumerable books on philosophy, and so he wanted to go abroad and meet some people that he could directly discuss it with. He is the same age as Yuanren, and so I'm afraid he cannot qualify.[3]

Professor Yang was involved in the program, and it appears that Professor Hu discussed Chen Bozhuang's case with him, possibly in the hopes of persuading him to consider Chen. Professor Chen's wish to visit the United States was finally realized in 1959–1960 when the Ford Foundation decided to support his proposal to edit a book series of translations of new intellectual trends. In the beginning of 1960, I had two months of pleasant meetings with him and agreed to edit a volume of translated essays on the philosophy of history for his book series. Unfortunately, he passed away soon after returning to Hong Kong. He was part of the older generation in Hong Kong who had a positive influence on me, and so I wanted to include a part of his life story here.

Starting at the end of March 1955, I actively began preparations to take care of the legal procedures for going to the United States, but unexpectedly I encountered enormous resistance and was almost unable to embark on my journey. It turned out that at the time the Nationalist government in Taiwan and the United States State Department had an agreement that Chinese from Hong Kong and Macao had to use a Republic of China passport to enter the United States. Under this agreement, I had to apply to the Ministry of Education and the Ministry of Foreign Affairs in Taiwan for a passport to go abroad. However, the underground security personnel sent from Taiwan had, without any investigation and without ever interviewing me, secretly submitted a report saying that I was a member of the anti–Nationalist Party Third Force Movement and would express unfavorable opinions of Taiwan after I went to the United States. With that my application was set aside, and neither the Ministry of Education nor the Ministry of Foreign Affairs dared to react. After Professor Qian Mu became aware of the situation, he wrote an official letter to the Executive Yuan in Taipei, but it was of no use because I could not get security clearance. My application dragged on for six months; I was unable to go to the United States in July, and even after Harvard's classes began in September I still had yet to receive any response from Taipei. It was an indubitable certainty that I would not be granted a passport.

The most laughable thing was that although I had published many essays in Third Force Movement periodicals, I had not written a single word about the Nationalist Party. My essays were mainly written from a historical point of view and advocated freedom and democracy, as discussed earlier.

Knowledge of my predicament spread widely in Hong Kong until even the Asia Society representative in Hong Kong, James Ivy, learned about it. Ivy had great respect for Professor Qian; it was Ivy's decision that resulted in the Asia Foundation providing the capital for the establishment of the New Asia Institute of Advanced Chinese Studies. Ivy asked Professor Qian to have me discuss the matter with him. After he came to understand my situation, he wrote a letter to Everett Drumright (1906–1993), the American Consul General in Hong Kong (later Ambassador to the Republic of China [Taiwan]). Ivy pointed out that my going to Harvard to study was a once-in-a-lifetime opportunity for a young scholar and should not be lost because of a technicality. In his response letter, Drumright suggested another legal channel for me to enter the United States. I could find a lawyer in Hong Kong before whom I could swear an oath that I was a "stateless person." The lawyer could then prepare an official document with his signature, which would substitute for a passport, and the United States Embassy could legally affix a visa to that document.

This "stateless person" status caused many great difficulties. Every year I had to apply for an extension at the Office of Immigration. There did not seem to be many people with this special status, and the immigration officers would always question me in great detail every time. They would also warn me repeatedly not to leave the country; for if I left the country, my visa would be invalid. This situation continued for several years and only ended when I finally obtained permanent resident status.

PART ONE: ON FIRST VISITING HARVARD

During my first year at Harvard, my official status was that of "Harvard-Yenching Institute Visiting Scholar," and so this section is "On First Visiting Harvard."

Due to the passport problems mentioned earlier, I did not leave Hong Kong until October 3, and by that time classes had already begun at Harvard. To ensure that I was taken care of, James Ivy arranged for the Asia Foundation general headquarters in San Francisco to send someone to meet me when my plane arrived. Ivy also arranged for me to stay an extra day in San Francisco to see the West Coast. After I went through customs, an Asia Foundation representative, Mr. Robert Sheeks (his Chinese name was Xu Lebo), was waiting for me and holding a sign with my name. After dinner that evening he took me to my hotel, and the next day he drove me to the University of California (UC) in Berkeley. He said that the purpose of the visit was so that I could see this famous West Coast campus and later compare it to Harvard's campus in the East Coast. While at the UC campus, I visited the East Asian Library where it just happened that the librarian was Mr. Fang Zhaoying (1908–1985), who was an early alumnus of Yanjing University and had studied with Professor Hong Ye (William Hung) and my father. He was very cordial and kindly brought out some rare books for me to look at; in particular, I remember there was, among them, a Guanhuatang edition of the novel *Water Margin* (*Shuihu zhuan* 水滸傳).[4] In the afternoon of October 5, Robert Sheeks took me to the airport from where I flew nonstop to Boston. I was extremely grateful to Mr. Sheeks, but unfortunately never had the opportunity to see him again. In 1964 he held the post of Co-Chairman of the Pacific Science Board of the American Academy of Sciences and presided over Sino-American scientific cooperation in Taiwan; eventually he joined the State Department where he was in charge of China-related affairs.

Reception by Harvard-Yenching Institute

Robert Sheeks had phoned the Harvard-Yenching Institute the day before to tell them my flight number and arrival time. He told me that they would send someone to meet me and that I need not worry. The person who came to meet me was Mr. John Pelzel (1914–1999), the Deputy Director of the Harvard-Yenching Institute. He was a professor of anthropology and well-known for his studies of the changes in Japanese society after industrialization.[5] In the 1960s, he officially took over the position of Director of the Harvard-Yenching Institute (serving from 1964 to 1975). All the members of the Harvard-Yenching Institute were professors doing research on China and Japan and holding concurrent posts; with the exception of a secretary in charge of sending and receiving documents, there were no other special staff members. On the drive to Harvard, Professor Pelzel gave me detailed instructions on how to find a place to live, how to select courses at Harvard, and how to use the different libraries. He repeatedly emphasized that I was free to act on my own initiative in conducting my research and in selecting my courses; I did not need to seek consent from the Harvard-Yenching Institute. He asked if I was acquainted with Professor Lien-Sheng Yang, and I could only answer truthfully that this was the first time I had heard Professor Yang's name. His reaction seemed to be one of surprise, but he did not say anything; I just saw it in his expression. At that time in Western Sinological circles, especially in America, there was virtually no one who did not know of Professor Yang. My ignorance and lack of experience was probably unimaginable to him.

Early one evening in the middle of October, the Harvard-Yenching Institute held a gathering for the visiting scholars. In addition to the two groups of scholars from 1954 and 1955 (about twenty people), all the professors who participated in the vetting process also attended. Director Serge Elisséeff gave a talk explaining the nature of the institute's program and related a most interesting incident. One of the Harvard-Yenching applicants did not know that "Yenching" was Romanized Chinese; he thought it was the progressive tense of a verb "Yench." He could not locate this word in the dictionary, and so he asked, "What does it mean to come to Harvard for Yenching?" This story had the whole room roaring with laughter.

At the end of the meeting, there was a dinner with about five or six tables. Seated at my table on my left and right were two professors. One was Professor Francis Cleaves (1911–1995), an expert on Mongolian language and the Yuan dynasty. He had lived for many years in Beijing (called "Beiping" at the time) and spoke the Beijing dialect extremely fluently.[6] The other was Professor Morton White (1917–2016) who had just become the Head of the Department of Philosophy.[7] At the time, Professor Cleaves engaged in daily discussions with Professor Hong Ye about the Yuan dynasty and Mongolian history. When he learned that Professor Hong was my father's teacher, any barriers between us came down and we felt free to be candid in our discussions. The subject of our conversation quickly came to Chen Yuan (also known as Yuan-an Laoren, 1880–1971). I thought very highly of Professor Chen's scholarship, but Professor Cleaves had read "Chen Yuan's Open Letter to Hu Shi" and was extremely angry about it.[8] He said that Chen was learned but an opportunist who lacked virtue. I could not find any reason to defend Chen.

My conversations with Professor Morton White had an unexpected influence on the direction of my studies. I asked him about the orientation of the Department of Philosophy at Harvard and if there were any recent Chinese graduate students from the department. When answering my second question, he told me that after World War II there was one Chinese student who came to Harvard to study mathematical logic with astonishing success. Although this former student was still an assistant professor in the Department of Philosophy, he was already a leader in his field. He was referring to Wang Hao (1921–1995).[9] I had read about him in an essay by Yin Haiguang while I was in Hong Kong. However, I did not get to meet him at the time because he had gone to England, and it would be many years before I would meet him. I also asked Professor White what courses he was offering. He said that in addition to "Analytic

Philosophy" and "American Philosophy," he had recently been preparing to offer a new course that would deal specifically with issues in the philosophy of history. He immediately added that he was not going to use metaphysics as applied to the understanding of world history in the manner of Hegel, Marx, Oswald Spengler (1880–1936), or more recently, Toynbee. Instead, he planned to utilize the most recently developed analytic philosophy, especially linguistic philosophy, to examine the nature and function of historical knowledge. I had been dealing with Marx's historical materialism for many years and had recently been drawn to Toynbee's theory of civilization, so as soon as I heard what Professor White said I was extremely pleased and immediately expressed my sincere wish to study under him, which I will discuss later.

It was also at this big gathering that I first met two visiting scholars from Taiwan—Mr. Dong Tonghe (Tung Tung-ho, 1911–1963) and Mr. Xing Muhuan (Hsing Mo-huan, 1915–1999).

Dong Tonghe: Fellow "Sophomore" at Harvard

In 1954, on the recommendation of National Taiwan University, Mr. Dong Tonghe had come to Harvard; 1955 was his second and last year. He laughingly referred to himself as a "sophomore" and called Xing Muhuan and me "freshmen." He was a top student from Tsinghua University and specialized in Chinese linguistics, especially phonetics, following the research path of major scholars Zhao Yuanren and Li Fanggui (Li Fang-kuei, 1902–1987).[10] He participated in the Harvard-Yenching Institute Scholars Program at the slightly advanced age of forty, the program's maximum age, but this was probably because of his first-rate scholarly accomplishments. He spent over ten years in the linguistics section (directed by Zhao Yuanren) at the Academia Sinica Institute of History and Philology. His *Table of Ancient Chinese Phonetics* [draft] (*Shanggu yinyunbiao gao* 上古音韻表稿) had long since become a classic.[11] He also wrote a *History of Chinese Phonetics* (*Zhongguo yuyinshi* 中國語音史), which explained a difficult subject in accessible language that could be appreciated by both scholars and general readers.[12] He was straightforward, modest, and amiable; and he looked out for me as his junior schoolmate. That year we both lived on Shepard Street in Cambridge, and so we were in frequent contact. In the summer of 1962 he was hired to teach at Indiana University, and he visited Harvard while en route to the US immigration department to make arrangements. I was very happy to see him again and invited him to lunch where we had a long three-hour conversation. I never imagined that after he went back to Taiwan for a health checkup, he would discover that he was in the last stages of lung cancer and passed away soon after.

Xing Muhuan: Like an Old Friend at First Meeting

Xing Muhuan was Professor of Economics in the Faculty of Commerce at National Taiwan University. From 1945 to 1947, recommended by the National Resources Commission, he was in the United States for advanced studies; this was his second time in America. The day after the Harvard-Yenching Institute dinner, we arranged to meet for another dinner to become better acquainted. We were in the same class and had Chinese backgrounds, although he was from Taiwan and I was from Hong Kong; thus it was all the more a good idea to get together and exchange views. From the onset of our conversation, we both felt very comfortable with each other, "like old friends at first meeting." This was one of the rarest occurrences of my life. Thinking back on it, it was no coincidence but due to a variety of reasons.

First, he was from Huangmei County in Hubei, not very far from Qianshan County in Anhui, so our dialects were closely similar; for example, the countryside Huangmei opera (local opera of Anhui) that I loved most originated from his home county. So we felt more or less like fellow townsmen.

Second, although his specialty was economics, a field derived from the West, he had conscientiously studied ancient Chinese, classical poetry, and calligraphy before the age of sixteen because he was educated in private schools. He loved poetry and composed many poems that were so good that they were compiled for posterity. After his death, his friends edited a volume entitled *Selected Poems by Academician Xing Muhuan* (*Xing Muhuan yuanshi shici xuanji* 邢慕寰院士詩詞選集), which was distributed in 2000 as a complimentary edition by the Culture and Educational Foundation of the International Commercial Bank of China in Taipei. I remember that day at our dinner, he wrote out a seven-character per line quatrain (*qiyan jueju* 七言絕句) to describe his impressions of the first time he flew in an airplane. This is on page 11 of his *Selected Poems*. The title is "Noticed in Flight," and the poem reads as follows:

> With no sight of Huainan's chickens and dogs,
> I only feel Heaven's stairway is smooth.
> A myriad peaks and mountains compete before my eyes,
> Looking back, each one engenders white clouds.

The words "Heaven's stairway" and "white clouds" express the distinctive feelings of one climbing up to Heaven (flying into the sky) for the first time. This poem was written in 1945, the first time he came to America; that he could still easily write it down to show me ten years later demonstrates how proud he was of it. Before the age of sixteen, I, like Muhuan, was educated in the same type of private school where my teacher first taught me how to write poetry. Our educational backgrounds were thus very similar.[13]

Third, in studying economics Muhuan was initially inclined toward the planned economy; he did not accept the Soviet Union's violent dictatorship and instead embraced the nonviolent socialist model of the British Fabian Society. From 1945 to 1946 he spent two years as a graduate student in the economics department at the University of Chicago, which at the time was considered the headquarters of the American school of liberal economics. He was greatly influenced by Friedrich A. Hayek (1899–1992) and finally came to understand that any planned economy subject to government intervention would necessarily lead to *The Road to Serfdom* (the title of Hayek's 1944 classic). In 1946 he wrote a quatrain, "Studying in Chicago" specifically to record his awakening:

In the past I admired and followed the Fabians,
Only because [other] contemporary views were too partisan.
After a year's silent study outside [Hayek's] gate,
I began to understand Yang Zhu's early farsightedness.

The poem borrows from the phrase "Yang Zhu's teachings are for oneself" (i.e., for individual freedom) to express his return to the school of liberal economics.[14] Muhuan's liberalism also extended from the realm of economics into the political. During our conversation we touched upon the impact of *Free China Bimonthly* (*Ziyou Zhongguo*) in Taiwan, and, although he did not write contemporary opinion pieces, his sympathy was obviously with *Free China Bimonthly*. In the beginning I had misgivings about him: What if he was a closed-minded member of the Nationalist Party or someone who accepted the Nationalist Party's "one-party dictatorship"? How, then, was I supposed to get along with him? By the end of this dinner, though, any such concerns had disappeared.

Fourth, as an academic, Muhuan had many virtues which led people to have a deep respect for him. Due to space constraints, I will discuss just three. First, there was his pursuit of truth. He studied economics all his life, with an emphasis on theory, constantly deepening his understanding, perfecting what was already outstanding—he embodied the Western spirit of seeking "knowledge for the sake of knowledge." Second, his diligence was not driven by motivation to improve his station in life. Seeing the backward state of economics in Taiwan, he did not begrudge the immense expense and effort to foster future generations of talent. While at the Economic Research Institute of the Academia Sinica, "he decided to personally train and establish junior researchers in the fundamentals of economic theory and the tools for analyzing economic resources."[15]

In 1963, the Song-dynasty history specialist Liu Zijian (James T. C. Liu; 1919–1993) just happened to be in Taipei and by chance sat in on one of Muhuan's classes. He later told me that when Muhuan directed the junior scholars' reading, he did not let a word or sentence get by without making certain that they thoroughly understood the material. Professor Liu said that he admired Muhuan greatly.[16] Muhuan exemplified the Confucian traditions of "teaching without growing weary" and "obtaining the best talents in All Under Heaven and teaching them."[17]

Third, Muhuan made both direct and indirect contributions to Taiwan's economic development. His direct contributions included calculating and preparing the national income and participating in tax reform among other important matters, and indirectly his impact was made through his policy suggestions—all of which achieved considerable success. Clearly, he embraced the Chinese "scholar-officials' (*shi*) fundamental value of "putting one's learning to practical use."[18] He was steadfast in his position as a professional economist and was never swayed by power or money in his search for "practical utility"; throughout his entire life he was never beholden to anyone in the bureaucratic or commercial worlds. Although I knew that I had no chance of matching him in virtues, I nevertheless yearned to follow in his direction!

Our value systems were thus very similar, and it was only natural that my view would be in accord with Muhuan's. If I wanted to add another element, it would be that our temperaments were quite congenial—as Westerners say, our so-called "chemistry" was most compatible. Given all this, I do not believe that the feeling of us being "like old friends at first meeting" was accidental.

During the first semester, we lived in different places, but we frequently ate together in a Chinese restaurant in Cambridge. In the spring of 1956, we decided to move in together and we could cook our own simple Chinese food. Muhuan said that he already had experience cooking for himself the first time he was in America. In June, when our leases expired, we moved into a small apartment I had located on Harvard Street and became roommates. Harvard Street was a convenient location, just a ten-minute walk from the campus. I was a complete amateur when it came to cooking, and so except for shopping for groceries together at the market, our division of labor was as follows: he was solely in charge of cooking while I was responsible for washing the dishes and straightening up the kitchen and dining room. As the year went by, this division of labor proved to be very successful. Muhuan was an excellent cook; not only could he effortlessly prepare everyday dishes, but when necessary he could also come up with elegant delicacies for guests. Two such occasions were in 1956, when we entertained his friend Zhou Hongjing (1902–1957), formerly Principal of Central University as well as Secretary-General of the Academia Sinica; and in the spring of 1957, when my former teacher Professor Tang Junyi came to visit. From the beginning to the end of the meal, both honored guests kept praising Muhuan's cooking.[19]

The three-month summer holiday was the happiest time of my life; it was also the most productive for studying. Every day after dinner, weather permitting, Muhuan and I would take a walk by the Charles River for about an hour; then we would return home, go to our separate rooms, and continue the day's reading until midnight. Muhuan studied economic theory, while I caught up on my reading of classic works of Western history and thought. This was because I was going to be a graduate student in the next academic year and felt that my knowledge of Western literature, history, and philosophy was superficial; so I had to bone up on this.

"To keep the bow strung for a while and unstrung for a while was the Way of King Wen and King Wu," and so we did not have our heads buried in books all the time.[20] When we felt tired, we would go into the kitchen to drink tea and chat, sharing information about our backgrounds and experiences. Besides our reading for scholarship, Muhuan and I also read for recreation; at the time Muhuan was reading *Lust for Life*, a biographical novel on Vincent Van Gogh by the American writer Irving Stone. It had just been made into a movie, and the paperback was a bestseller. Muhuan liked this book very much; he would read a little and then enthusiastically tell me about it. Later on, I read it too. For my part, I was always very fond of detective novels and read a thick volume of the *Complete Sherlock Holmes* during that summer break.

All in all, that summer our lives were carefree and easy, our moods peaceful, and we thoroughly enjoyed the pleasures of reading.

When classes began in September, Muhuan and I became extremely busy. My studies and writing were very arduous because I was taking three courses in Western history and philosophy, in addition to John King Fairbank's seminar on research topics in Qing-dynasty history, which will be discussed later. Muhuan's primary interest was economic theory, and he often told me that he had a set of theoretical conceptions that could only be easily developed in the research environment of the United States where there were so many talented people. As such, in his last year as a visiting scholar at Harvard, he had to make the most of his opportunities and redouble his efforts. I do not know how many courses he was taking, but in our random chats he told me that he was studying mainly with two professors that year: one was Wassily Leontief (1905–1999) of Harvard, and the other was Paul Samuelson (1915–2009) of the Massachusetts Institute of Technology (MIT), and they were quite different.[21] Samuelson was a major scholar who founded the study of scientific and mathematical economics; Muhuan attended his lectures twice a week primarily to acquire new knowledge. He attended Leontief's seminar on "The Structure of American Economy" and made a close connection to it with his own research. Muhuan was not just auditing this class but also participating, making oral presentations, and writing papers. Leontief was born in Russia and first studied in Germany. In 1928 he accepted a one-year position as an advisor in China's Ministry of Transport, and he was very cordial to the Chinese students. Muhuan had a good relationship with Leontief, and they were very driven in their research. I remember once when he was preparing for an oral report, he drew up a very large and complicated table, but due to time constraints, in the end I had to help him copy out the final draft on a big piece of cardboard. Leontief obviously enjoyed his presentation very much because he later published the outline of Muhuan's main points in a journal that he edited.

Our year of rooming together was full of fine memories; there were never moments of unhappiness or misunderstanding. I believe that such friendships are not easy to come by. In June 1957 he returned to Taiwan, and it was a whole decade later before we met again.

Over the years, Muhuan sent me several poems—the one I treasure most is a pentasyllabic ancient-style poem of one hundred characters that he gave me in 1975. He wrote it out in exquisite calligraphy. That year our family left Hong Kong to return to America, and so Muhuan composed this poem to send us off and wrote us all into it. After I returned to the United States, we moved three times, but no matter where we lived this poem was always hung on our living room wall. I have reproduced it here along with Muhuan's note to show its importance to me and my family:

> How lonely was this world, and
> You were the only one who knew me.
> Sharing completely our inner thoughts,
> Our views complemented like gold on stone.
> Long separated, you wandered through my dreams,
> Reunited, I cherished your sincere feelings.
> Remembering the intoxicating late autumn maple leaves
>   of Cambridge,
> And the clear bright snowy nights on Pei Mountain.[22]
> You soon had an appointment in the East Forest,
> So we gathered together again by the South Sea shore.[23]
> Our fates were bent like the daisy's stems,
> But we chose as our intimates Iris and Orchid.[24]
> Your marriage of mutual respect is filled with sweet fragrance,
> And your phoenix daughters are young and beautiful.
> Listening to the wind and rain in the approaching dawn,
> We forgot our sorrows discussing ancient and modern.
> Mo Gang was refined and gentle,
> And Mo Chuan was serene and calm.[25]
> Overwhelmed with emotion, I wanted to return home,
> The cold bright moon already filled the vast sky.

Elder Brother Ying-shih and I have been friends for twenty years but have been separated more than we have been together. These last two years we unexpectedly met again in Hong Kong and had many long talks. Elder Sister Shuping has also treated me like a best friend. Today we are parting again, and so I wrote this for you to keep as a fond remembrance.

—Muhuan, *yimao* 1975.

LOOKING BACK ON A YEAR OF "VISITING SCHOLAR" WORK

Finally, I would like to recap what I did during my year as a visiting scholar. Because I arrived late, as noted earlier, it was not until the end of October that I finally found a place to stay and my life in Cambridge could be considered settled. During the first semester, I audited only a few courses, starting them while they were already midway through. With the exception of slightly improving my English-language listening skills, I could not say that I gained any new knowledge. Another even more important reason that prevented me from fully applying myself to the pursuit of new learning was that I had to complete a paper for the New Asia College Research Institute.

In an earlier section "On First Becoming Professor Qian Mu's Disciple," I mentioned that between the spring and summer of 1955 I had started writing the essay "The Social Background of Political Changes Between the Western and Eastern Han Dynasties" ("Liang Han zhiji zhengzhi bianqian de shehui beijing") which was my report for New Asia College Research Institute. I had completed only half of it and did not have time to complete it before leaving Hong Kong. Professor Qian urged me to finish it when I arrived in America so that it could be published in the second issue of the *New Asia Journal* (*Xinya xuebao*). The deadline for submissions for that issue had been set at February 1956, and Professor Qian hoped that my essay could be published without delay so that it, being a publication by one of its students, would reflect the achievements of New Asia College Research Institute and validate the support of the

Harvard-Yenching Institute. Once I was settled in, I took advantage of Harvard's rich library collection and rewrote this essay. The entire draft was completed at the end of January 1956; it had more than fifty thousand characters, and I changed the title to "The Founding of the Eastern Han Regime and its Relationship with the Great Families" ("Dong Han zhengquan zhi jianli yu shizu daxing zhi guanxi"). In an unexpected turn of events, this essay led to my first opportunity to learn from Professor Yang Liansheng, which sparked my first encounter with Japanese and Western Sinology.

Seeking Advice from Professor Yang Liansheng

In the two- or three-month process of rewriting my essay, the friends whom I saw more often were already aware of my research topic. Among them were Liu Zijian and Zhang Jinghu (Chang Jen-hu, a.k.a. J. H. Chang, 1927–2019) who told me that Professor Yang Liansheng had published a famous paper when he was at Tsinghua University and that the focus of his paper was very close to my research topic, so they urged me to seek his guidance.[26] Liu Zijian had always admired Professor Yang and often sought to learn from him. Zhang Jinghu was a climatologist and was attending Harvard as a postdoctoral student. He and Professor Yang were both fond of *Weiqi* and mahjong, and they were close friends. Zhang Jinghu was Zhang Xiaofeng's (Zhang Qiyun, a.k.a. Chang Ch'i-yun, 1901–1985) son, so he was familiar with Professor Yang's accomplishments in historical research.[27] Given their encouragement, I decided that I would ask Professor Yang to read my completed manuscript and provide his feedback.

As noted earlier, before I came to the United States, I had never heard of the celebrated Professor Yang Liansheng. It was probably not long after the Harvard-Yenching Institute dinner (mentioned earlier) that I had dinner with Dong Tonghe and Muhuan, and Mr. Dong suggested that we visit Professor Yang after dinner one day. They had been classmates at Tsinghua University and knew each other very well, so Mr. Dong did not need to make an appointment or phone ahead first. This was the first time that I met Professor Yang Liansheng (he did not attend the Harvard-Yenching Institute dinner). We talked for two or three hours in Professor Yang's dining room, discussing history, language, literature, the social sciences, and other such subjects. Not only was Professor Yang a sophisticated conversationalist but his words expressed the wide scope of his knowledge and the depth of his experience. I still remember when we were discussing contemporary Chinese poets, he recommended Professor Xiao Gongquan and showed me one of his poems which Xiao himself had written out in calligraphy. He said that among the Tsinghua University professors with a talent for poetry, the first was Wang Guowei and the second was Xiao Gongquan; he praised them as "the continuation of beauty from Wang to Xiao."

That night when I returned to my lodgings, I immediately wrote a letter to Professor Qian, telling him about the meeting and expressing my admiration for Professor Yang. I asked Professor Qian whether he was acquainted with him, and he wrote back that "Mr. Yang has done research on economic history for many years, and if you [literally, my younger brother] are able to interact with him regularly, it will certainly be of great benefit." (This letter is not included in Sushulou yu shen. shuzha 素書樓餘瀋. 書札, but the original should still be in the Sushulou [Sushu Studio].) This made me hope even more fervently that Professor Yang would review my manuscript.

On the afternoon of the second day after I had completed my manu-script, Professor Yang invited me to meet him in his office. He first lent me a copy of the Qinghua xuebao issue containing his essay "Great Families of the Eastern Han" and smilingly said "Let's first read each other's essays."[28] He read my essay very quickly and corrected missing or incorrect characters and unsatisfactory passages, but afterwards he told me that the main points of my essay were different from his and that there were very few areas of overlap with his essay; my essay could be published as a separate work. With that, I finally settled down after several days of worrying. Professor Yang recommended two recent books for me to consult: *The Restoration of the Han Dynasty* by Swedish scholar Hans Bielenstein (1920–2015) and *Kandai shakai keizaishi kenkyû* 漢代社會經濟史研究 (Research on Han dynasty society and economics) by Japanese scholar Kiyoyoshi Utsunomiya.[29] I took them home right away and read them carefully; only then did I realize the level of research on China that scholars of other countries had already achieved. With that, the prejudices I had harbored before due to my ignorance concerning overseas Sinology were eliminated.

Professor Yang's persistent intellectual pursuits greatly influenced me. He believed that Bielenstein's theory that the Wang Mang (45 BCE–23 CE) regime (Xin dynasty, 9–23) collapsed due to a change in the course of the Yellow River was one-sided, not supported by any strong evidence, and in conflict with the main ideas of my essay. On that account, he especially wanted me to discuss it. The "Afterword" to my essay, entitled "Doubts About Bielenstein's Theory that the 'Wang Mang Regime Collapsed Due to a Change in the Course of the Yellow River,'" was written under his direction, but to avoid causing friction for Professor Yang, I could not openly state this at the time. From then on, I paid continuous attention to the works of European and American Sinologists but did not allow myself to accept easily any novel or questionable theories. The following passage by Xiao Gongquan most clearly expresses Professor Yang Liansheng's attitude toward Western Sinology:

> As I see it, "hypotheses" that are set up without broad reading and a clear and comprehensive view of all the facts are only prejudices or misconceptions without objective foundations. ... In recent years, some European and American "scholars" being in too much of a hurry to "make a unique reputation" could not help taking this dangerous road. Professor Yang Liansheng implicitly pointed out this trend at the 1960 Sino-American Conference on Intellectual Co-operation. He said the strong point of American "historians" is that they are richly imaginative, but if their imagination is not tempered by appropriate restraint they could "mistake some clouds in the sky for forests on the horizon."[30]

Later, Professor Yang told me that he took the phrase "some clouds in the sky" from Fu Sinian's mocking of the thoughtless remarks by Owen Lattimore (1900–1989) about the history of the border regions of China.[31] In his later years when Professor Xiao Gongquan taught at an American university, he shared this sentiment about "some American 'scholars' studying Chinese history" and, in support of Professor Yang's view, cited the famous comment of the Ming dynasty Neo-Confucian scholar Wang Yangming (1472–1529):

> When scholars today examine the Way, their views are as narrow as observing Heaven through a stove pipe. When they see a part of it, they immediately become self-satisfied and full of themselves and they proudly hold on unquestionably to their opinions without any doubts.[32]

Professors Yang and Xiao made these observations fifty years ago, but they are not out of date; if anything, they are even more applicable today. That is because the classical Chinese-language training of the young Chinese scholars from China, Taiwan, Hong Kong, and Southeast Asia today is not at all what it used to be, and they are no longer able to judge the merits or the (in)accuracy of the "unique ideas" of such "scholars." Not only are they incapable of reading with a critical eye, they swarm after such questionable ideas and add momentum to them. The reason I have quoted Professors Yang and Xiao here is that I hope they might serve as a warning; even if they have no effect, at least I have followed my conscience [by sounding the alert.].[33]

Auditing Three Classes

Most of my time during my first semester as a visiting scholar was mainly focused on the aforementioned essay and related matters. It was not until the second semester (February to June) that I was able to devote my full attention to sitting in on courses and reading the assigned material. During that semester, I audited three courses: "Social Systems" by Talcott Parsons (1902–1979) in the Department of Social Relations, "History of Modern European Thought" by Crane Brinton (1898–1968), in the Department of History, and "Renaissance and Reformation" by Myron P. Gilmore (1910–1978), in the Department of History. What follows is a brief background explanation of why I selected these courses.[34]

Talcott Parsons's "Social Systems"

As mentioned earlier, I gained a slight understanding of Talcott Parsons's 1951 book *The Social System* through Professor Chen Bozhuang and his *Modern Academic Quarterly*. After I came to Harvard, I discovered that Parsons's new theories were at the peak of their popularity in the world of American social sciences and that his influence and impact extended far beyond the sphere of social studies. Given that I was at Harvard while he was teaching his "social systems" course, I naturally wanted to attend it so that I could get a clear understanding of his ideas from his lectures. Parsons constantly revised and developed the content of his lectures, and they corresponded with his written texts, supplementing them but with very few repetitions or similarities. In class he discussed not only theory but also cited the mutual "verification" between "facts" and "theory" that emerged from different ways of life. ("Verification" or "verify" were words he used frequently.) He also analyzed the Chinese social system, and his reference books included *Earthbound China* (*Xiangtu Zhongguo* 鄉土中國) by Fei Xiaotong; that was when I learned that Fei's later publications *From the Soil* (*Xiangtu Zhongguo* and *Rural Recovery* (*Xiangtu chongjian* 鄉土重建) in the *Observer Collection* (*Guancha congshu*) were originally written in English.[35]

In the process of attending his classes, I finally came to grasp the intellectual origins of Parsons's theories. I had read many contemporary scholars' reviews of his work and, with much effort, Parsons's celebrated 1937 book *The Structure of Social Action*. In this large tome of 800 pages, he traces his own strongly proposed "theory of social action" back to a group of late nineteenth- and early twentieth-century European social scientists, the most important among them being England's Alfred Marshall (1842–1924), Italy's Vilfredo Pareto (1848–1923), France's Émile

Durkheim (1858–1917), and Germany's Max Weber (1864–1920). Parsons held Max Weber in especially high regard, and he can be said to be Weber's American successor. Weber's ideas were transmitted across the United States and became a noted school of thought, and no one made a greater contribution than Parsons, whose 1930 English translation of Weber's *The Protestant Ethic and the Spirit of Capitalism* was circulated throughout the world.

In attending Parsons's course, my interest in his theory of modern society gradually diminished, but I became increasingly fascinated in Max Weber's multifaceted observations concerning historical societies. I was especially interested in Weber's comparisons and analyses of traditional and modern society, which I will discuss later.

The popularity of Parsons's ideas reached its high point in the 1950s, but in the early 1960s due to the violent changes in American society, people began questioning his theories. This was especially the case after the anti-Vietnam War movement when radical currents of Marxist thought became prominent, and Parsons's model of modern society based on the United States came to be seen by a younger generation of sociologists and students as representative of "backward" or even "reactionary" thinking. According to some studies I read by chance recently, it does, however, seem that after his death Parsons's theories received some positive assessments, but the glories of the 1950s were long gone. In the United States the rise and decline of clusters of new theories and new points of view in the humanities and social sciences are occurrences that happen every five to seven years, so this is not at all surprising. However, Parsons's was the first case I encountered firsthand, so it left an indelible mark on me.

I had no personal relationship with Parsons, but there is one interesting story I can tell that may provide a laugh for readers. In the fall of 1973, I left Harvard and returned to New Asia College to assume administrative duties and fulfill my promise to work for my alma mater for two years. I do not remember if it was in the fall of 1973 or the spring of 1974 that

Parsons went to Japan to lecture and visited Hong Kong on the way. My colleagues (including my friend Jin Yaoji) at New Asia College invited him to come and give a lecture.[36] When Parsons heard that the president of New Asia College was a Harvard professor who was on leave, he indicated he would be willing to visit. All this happened very suddenly, so I was extremely flustered when I greeted him. Our short conversation was very pleasant. I asked him out of curiosity if the sociologists of Hong Kong had invited him to visit Hong Kong. He said they had not and that he had arranged the trip himself through a Japanese travel agency and only notified one or two acquaintances upon his arrival. I asked, "Were some friends there to greet you when you got off the plane?" He just laughed and answered: "There were only two tailors there to greet me; they wanted to make me a suit." When I heard that, I could not help laughing out loud.

Crane Brinton's "Modern European Intellectual History"

I audited Crane Brinton's "Modern European Intellectual History" primarily because I had read his celebrated 1950 book *Ideas and Men*. The book was a bestseller at the time; it presented difficult subjects in an accessible manner that could be of use to both scholars and general readers. The book discusses the differences and the relationships between the systematic "formal thought" of the upper strata of society—like Western "philosophy" and the Chinese "study of the classics" (*jingxue* 經學) or "study of the various philosophers" (*zixue* 子學)—and the "popular thought" that circulated among the lower strata of society. Brinton points out that research on intellectual history had always unduly emphasized the scope of "formal thought" while "popular thought" was yet to receive the same consideration. Perhaps this was because it is embedded in the lifestyles of ordinary people and is sometimes even hard to separate completely from their behavior. He further emphasized, however, that the overall task of an "intellectual historian" (his term) is to assemble everything, from the abstract concepts of philosophy to concrete behavior, and make it cohere "as an intelligible whole." Thus, in terms of the nature of his own work, on one level, he was a historical philosopher or philo-sophical historian who dealt with metaphysics, and, on another level, he was a social historian who wanted to explore the outline of people's thought from studying their everyday life. His mission, then, was to link these two endeavors.[37] If we borrow Wang Yangming's famous terms, we can say that *Ideas and Men* represented a kind of intellectual history that embodied the "unity of knowledge and action."

I was very interested in Brinton's observations because there were people in traditional Chinese history who had already taken note of the intercommunication of "formal thought" and "popular thought."

An example of this can be found in the second *juan* of *Guangyang Miscellany* (*Guangyang zaji* 廣陽雜記) by late-Qing to early Ming writer, Liu Xianting (1648–1695):

> In my observation of the ordinary people of this world, there has never been anyone who did not like to sing and watch plays, such is the "poetry" [*Book of Songs*] and "music" [*Classic of Music*] in their nature; there has never been anyone who did not read novels (*xiaoshuo*) and listen to storytellers, such is the "history" [*Book of History or Documents*] and "the Annals" [*Spring and Autumn Annals*] in their nature; and there has never been anyone who did not believe in divination and sacrificing to ghosts and spirits (supernatural beings), such is the "changes" [*Book of Changes*] and "the Annals" [*Spring and Autumn Annals*] in their nature. Thus, the teachings of the Sages in the Six Classics were originally all based upon human feelings.[38]

This passage clearly states that the Six Classics originated from some of the daily life activities of "the ordinary people of this world" and were certainly not simply invented without any basis by the sages. Here Liu Xianting was already uniting Brinton's "two levels" into an integrated whole.

Not only did Liu Xianting argue this, but later on historian Zhang Xuecheng (1738–1801) developed the idea even further, flatly asserting that the *Dao* or the moral Way must be sought in "the daily activities in human relations" and that "to learn from the multitude [the common people], that is to be a sage." Philologist Dai Zhen even emphasized that in the human world "the daily activities in human relations [the actualities of life] and every activity in life ... are called the Way (*Dao*)."[39] From all this, we can see that the idea that "formal thought" and "popular thought" should necessarily be connected had long been established in the tradition of Chinese scholarship. This was my main motivation for auditing Brinton's intellectual history course.

Brinton was a celebrated senior professor in the history department and respected throughout the world for his studies of nineteenth-century European thought. He published many books, including *English Political Thought in the Nineteenth Century*, which had already become a classic.[40] He was one of the most esteemed scholars at Harvard and was chosen to be the second Chairman of the Society of Fellows—the most prestigious academic organization at Harvard—a position in which he served from the 1950s until his retirement in 1966.

For all these reasons, Brinton's course on European intellectual history was very popular and attracted a great crowd of students. I found auditing his course very difficult, however, because my background knowledge was inadequate and because his lectures were neither clearly arranged nor well organized. He spoke insouciantly and at random, jumping at any given time from one topic to another. At the time I thought this was due to his advanced age and his not having enough energy, but it was only after I read the memoir of his student from the 1930s that I learned that he had always lectured that way. Nevertheless, his courses and his "exasperatingly casual lectures" were full of substance, and the students who attended his lectures learned a great deal.[41] What I primarily gained from Brinton was from his reviews of the merits and shortcomings of various contemporary research orientations. That I was able to read Arthur O. Lovejoy's celebrated work, *The Great Chain of Being*, and gain a better understanding of the "history of ideas" method of research was due to Brinton's course.[42] It was only later when I wrote my doctoral dissertation that I came to realize how much Brinton's lectures had imperceptibly inspired me in my research on Chinese intellectual history.

Myron P. Gilmore's "Renaissance and Reformation"

Finally, let me explain how I came to audit Myron P. Gilmore's "Renaissance and Reformation" course. Before I came to Harvard, I had never even heard of Professor Gilmore. I audited his class mainly to complete the visiting scholar plan that I had given to the Harvard-Yenching Institute. In my research plan I wrote that if I were given the opportunity to visit Harvard for one or two years, I would like to read more Western works on the history of the Renaissance era to better understand Europe's development from the medieval to modern times. I believed that this knowledge would be very helpful for my future research on the entire process of how China made the transition from traditional to modern. After arriving at Harvard, I discovered that Professor Gilmore was an expert in this area and was offering a course that year aimed at third- and fourth-year undergraduates and first- and second-year graduate students. So I decided to check it out.

There was also another incidental factor that led to my auditing of Professor Gilmore's class. In the other classes I sat in on, I was the only Chinese student, but there was another Chinese student officially enrolled in this Renaissance course, and he had to sit for the examinations to receive his credits. This Chinese student was Professor Wang Dezhao (1914–1982) who had graduated from Peking University at the end of the 1930s. After going to Taiwan, he taught Western history at National Taiwan Normal University (formerly Normal College) and had already achieved the rank of professor. In 1955 he passed the examination to study abroad in the United States at public expense, received a two-year scholarship, and went to Harvard to study for a master's degree. Since his specialty was European history and he was my senior classmate, I felt I had the rare opportunity to seek his guidance whenever I needed it; he was also very happy to have someone to talk to. He told me that he had discovered that he and Professor Gilmore were not only the same age but also that they had both written books on the Renaissance and served as professors of Renaissance studies. This gave him the feeling that his "Way was not alone."

My relationship with Professor Wang Dezhao was not limited to this time at Harvard. From 1973 to 1975, when I went on leave from Harvard and returned to New Asia College, as fate would have it, he had moved from Taipei to the United College of Hong Kong, which was part of the Chinese University of Hong Kong, to serve as a high-ranking instructor in the history department. This time he was no longer teaching Western history; he now taught modern Chinese history. We therefore had the opportunity to be colleagues for two years at the Chinese University of Hong Kong. While he was there, he wrote *Studies in the Qing Dynasty Examination System* (*Qingdai keju zhidu yanjiu* 清代科舉制度研究).[43] It is a very comprehensive work, but unfortunately Wang Dezhao passed away prematurely and did not see his book published.

PART TWO: STUDYING FOR THE DOCTORATE

As discussed earlier, New Asia College recommended me to Harvard so that I could participate in the Harvard-Yenching Institute's visiting scholars' program for a period of one to two years. Therefore, I initially had no expectation of pursuing a degree. However, one year later, the autumn of 1956, I transferred from the visiting scholars' program to become a graduate student studying for a PhD degree in ancient Chinese history. How did this sudden change come about? Let me offer a brief explanation.

Around 1950, the United States established a semi-official, semi-civil organization known as the "Aid to Refugee Chinese Intellectuals, Inc." Its chief function was to assist scholars who had escaped from Mainland China to reestablish stable lives, including through immigrating to other countries. Early on my father had registered with the refugee aid organization and applied to immigrate to the United States, but he had not received any response, and he forgot about it. But then something fortuitous happened: not long after I came to America, my father received a notice from the organization that his application had been accepted. The only condition was that he had to have a letter from relatives or friends or some organization in America guaranteeing that if he encountered difficulties, they would provide economic assistance. Due to this extremely unexpected turn of events, the first thought that occurred to my father was that I should not return to Hong Kong within these next two years because if I did, I would be gone when my whole family came to America and because he very much needed my assistance. So he wrote me a quick letter, asking me to inquire at Harvard about the possibility of my transferring into a PhD program and extending my stay in the United States. He also told me that Professor Qian Mu already approved of the plan.

At the time I was happy for my father, but at the same time I felt it would be difficult to approach the Harvard-Yenching Institute with this request. After thinking about it for a long time, I decided to consult Professor Yang Liansheng. To my surprise, Professor Yang was quite enthusiastic about the idea of me studying for a PhD. He told me that the only thing that concerned the visiting scholars' examination committee at first was that I was too young. Most of the visiting scholars were between thirty to forty years old, but I was only twenty-five. On that account he encouraged me to put in my request to enter the PhD program directly to Serge Elisséeff, Director of the Harvard-Yenching Institute. In addition, he also told me how to submit my request convince Mr. Elisséeff. I followed his directions and very quickly received Harvard-Yenching Institute's approval. The most crucial element in all this was that Professor Yang wanted me to be his PhD student; if not for that, things certainly would not have gone so smoothly. At that time, I did not know anything about the operating procedures of the Harvard Graduate School of Arts and Sciences, and it was not until several years later when I started to teach at Harvard that I came to understand them.

The transition from a visiting scholar to a graduate student studying for a PhD was the most important turning point in my life. Quite obviously, if I had returned to New Asia College after two years as a visiting scholar, then both my future teaching and research would have followed different paths. At that time because he empathized with my family and understood our wanting to reunite, Professor Qian generously allowed me to work for a different degree, but in his heart he continued to hope that I would first return to New Asia College. He stated all this to me in an extremely frank manner in a letter dated February 22, 1956:

> It would be difficult to measure the gains and losses if you decided to return early. There is an increasing shortage of people [scholars] specializing in literary and historical studies, and we'll have to wait for the excellent and outstanding ones in the younger generation to fill these important areas.

> Academic degrees are really just empty titles, and if you could return early while my health is still fortunately not in decline, then we could investigate and discuss any problems and exchange ideas with each other. With several years accumulated of these academic experiences, I was very much hoping that you would be able to establish a broad foundation and make great accomplishments so as not to disappoint me in my long-standing expectations of you.

> To study in the United States can certainly increase one's new knowledge, but ancient [traditional or classical Chinese] texts are also profound and deep and need to be studied and mastered through intense concentration. If you study them later than at your most opportune time [your fitting age], you will have to double the effort but achieve only half the gains. Besides, there will definitely be no lack of opportunities if you plan to go abroad again.

> Thus, whether you continue your advanced study abroad or return here [to Hong Kong] to concentrate on studying the ancient texts and then go abroad again after a few years, the odds of the gains and losses are really 50/50. You should just go ahead and feel

at ease to follow the course of destiny; don't think or worry too much about it.[44]

In this letter, Professor Qian clearly expressed his desire to pass on his lifelong lessons to me before he declined. This was something that he had never said before, and I was deeply moved when I read this. To don the mantle of Professor Qian's lifelong work would be the opportunity of a lifetime. How could studying in the United States be discussed as being on a par with it? I have to point out that this was not merely a matter of choosing a scholarly path but also one that involved our bond as teacher and student. In a letter to my father dated December 21, 1959, Professor Qian wrote an exceptionally touching description of how he felt:

> I only hope that next year after I return from my long journey, I can set aside school affairs and have more leisure time, then Ying-shih and others can come over often to discuss scholarship and enjoy the outdoors. I should buy a car for my wife to drive, we could prepare family-style dishes and invite Ying-shih and others over to share a meal and stroll the grounds. My mind is focused on this. ... If Ying-shih could study with me and I could see firsthand his rapid progress, just like a horse breaking free from the reins and galloping a thousand miles in one day, nothing would make me happier than that.[45]

This letter was written in January 1960, before Professor Qian visited Yale, and that was why he wrote "next year after I return from my long journey." Three years earlier he wanted me to "return early" so that we could "carefully study and learn from one another," but this time his wording was more emotional. Unfortunately, in order for my family to reunite, I had to transfer to a doctoral program, and after I graduated, I also had to teach in the United States first. Thus, it was not until 1973 that I could take a leave of absence from Harvard and return to New Asia College to fulfill my obligation as promised, but by that time Professor Qian had already gone to live in Taipei. It is my great regret to have lost the opportunity to study with Professor Qian during his later years.

Now allow me to offer a brief recollection of the complicated process of studying in the PhD program. In the fall term of 1956, I officially became a PhD student in the Department of History at Harvard University. According to the departmental rules at that time, a PhD student had to enroll in four courses: one major and three minor subjects of study. My major had already been decided long ago: I was to work under Professor Yang Liansheng in the study of ancient Chinese history with a concentration on the Han to the Tang dynasties. For the three minors, the first course I chose was modern Chinese history, taught jointly by John K. Fairbank and Benjamin I. Schwartz. From what I had heard at the time, Western scholars who did research in this area relied primarily on Western archives and written records—Fairbank's masterpiece *Trade and Diplomacy on the China Coast: The Opening of the Treaty Ports, 1842–1854* being a most obvious example.[46] Following this path, I could happily correct the partialities of Chinese research. I felt that I should not pass up this good opportunity to use "the stones of other hills" as "grinding tools" to "polish my jade."[47] As for the other two minor subjects, I had already decided in principle to choose courses in European history. This was not just because these were my interests but also for the teaching requirements I had to fulfill when I returned to New Asia College. At the time, other than the course on "The Renaissance," I was hesitant about these courses. Fortunately, it was early, and I still had some time before I had to finalize my course selection; I could think it over without any rush.

My curriculum choices that first semester fully reflected my state of mind at the time.

Ronald Syme's "History of Rome"

For my first minor, I enrolled in a course on the history of Rome. This was because Professor Gilmore was on leave that year and there were no courses that I could take that covered the period from the Renaissance to the Reformation. Harvard did not then have any professor who specialized in the history of Rome, but luckily that year Professor Ronald Syme (1903–1989) from Oxford University was a visiting scholar at Harvard for one year, and he offered a "History of Rome" course. At that time my knowledge of the world of Western historians was very limited and I had never heard of Professor Syme, but at the course-selection meeting in the Department of History, Professor Fairbank highly recommended him, telling me that Professor Syme was a major historian of Rome and that this was a rare opportunity. I decided that Rome could be a fitting counterpart to the Han dynasty in highlighting the similarities and differences between the two unified empires of the East and the West, and so I took Professor Fairbank's suggestion. Later, after attending one semester of Professor Syme's lectures and reading his masterpiece, *The Roman Revolution*, and some of his other works, I developed a good appreciation for his erudition and the profundity of his thought and realized that he genuinely deserved to be hailed a major historian of his generation.[48]

Thirty years later, I had the occasional opportunity to interact with Professor Peter Brown (1935–). I asked him if he had studied with Professor Syme when he was at Oxford. He replied very enthusiastically that although someone else was his academic advisor in the field, he had attended Professor Syme's lectures, which he found very stimulating and enlightening. (Professor Brown's advisor was Arnaldo Momigliano [1908–1987], also a major figure in the same field.[49]) Peter Brown today is himself the most respected scholar of Roman history; he initiated the field of "Late Antiquity" and has received innumerable academic honors, including the Library of Congress John W. Kluge Prize. Later when I wrote *Trade and Expansion in Han China: A Study in the Structure of Sino-Barbarian Economic Relations*[50] and touched on the communications between China and Rome, what I learned in Professor Syme's course was of great benefit, which was an unexpected stroke of good fortune that I could not have anticipated.

Morton White's Philosophy of History

For my second minor, I chose philosophy of history taught by Professor Morton White in the Department of Philosophy. I already mentioned earlier that in October of the previous year at the Harvard-Yenching Institute dinner, I had become extremely interested in Professor White's philosophy of history; now that I was a graduate student, I decided to enroll in his "Nature and Function of History" course. This was a new course that Professor White had been preparing for a long time; the students who took the course (both senior undergraduates and graduate students) were mainly from the history department while students from the philosophy department were the minority. Ever since the beginning of the 1950s, Morton White and Russian-born British philosopher Isaiah Berlin (1909–1997) were of the same mind and were planning to coauthor a book on the philosophy of history, which was clearly expressed in their mutual correspondence.

We have to remember that the period from the 1950s to the 1970s was the era British and American analytic philosophy (including the philosophy of language) flourished. The discussion of historiography from the points of view of analytic philosophy and linguistics was also in vogue at the time, and Berlin and White were the pioneers of this new trend. In 1953, Isaiah Berlin's celebrated lecture entitled "Historical Inevitability" (later published in a book) caused quite the sensation. White's views were essentially the same as Berlin's in this area, and he was also inspired by Berlin, so their motivation to coauthor a book was very strong. White offered this new course at Harvard to facilitate this, but a short time later he discovered that there were some fundamental differences between his views and Berlin's, and they were hard to reconcile. In the end, he published his own original, single-authored book, *Foundations of Historical Knowledge*.[51]

Because Professor White was aware that he was opening up a new field in the humanities, he often expressed in his lectures his passion for promoting a new current of thought. His enthusiasm was contagious, making his audience, myself included, feel as if they were also participating in this, which probably corresponds to what was called "joining the flow" (*yuliu* 預流), *sotâpanna*, or entering the first stage of Buddhist enlightenment. Due to its wide influence, I felt that I had to do an in-depth, comparative study of the similarities and differences between Western and Chinese historiography in order to identify where particular characteristics of Chinese history and culture stood. On that account, I proposed a comparison of the historiographic thought of Zhang Xuecheng and R. G. Collingwood (1889–1943) as the theme of one of my midterm papers in Professor White's class.[52] By a fortunate coincidence, in 1953 David S. Nivison (1923–2014) had just completed his Harvard PhD dissertation "The Literary and Historical Thought of Chang Hsüeh-Cheng, 1738–1801."[53] Professor White knew that there was this English source for reference and accepted my proposed topic. My April 1957 essay "The Historical Thought of Zhang Xuecheng and R. G. Collingwood" ("Zhang Xuecheng yu Kelingwu de lishi sixiang") was a revised and enlarged version of this midterm paper.[54]

This particular class of Professor White's greatly influenced the direction of my subsequent academic research. The unfolding of my research into the intellectual history of the Qing dynasty with Zhang Xuecheng and Dai Zhen as its central focus began at this point. Later in my academic career, Professor White and I met again. In 1987 when I moved to teach at Princeton University, I discovered that he had already left Harvard for Princeton's Institute for Advanced Studies, and so I had many opportunities to dine and converse with him. Often joining our dinner conversations were my Chinese studies scholar friends at Princeton, Willard Peterson and Benjamin Elman (1946 –), and we had many happy, exuberant discussions.[55] I remember once Professor White told us laughingly that he did not understand one bit of Chinese, but quite unexpectedly because I took his course he befriended many Sinologists and became increasingly interested in Chinese thought and culture.

Professor Morton White was born in 1917 and passed away on May 27, 2016; according to the Chinese way of counting age, he lived for one hundred years.[56] In the modern history of American philosophy, his achievements, whether in philosophical analysis or innovations in

pragmatism, were all high-level breakthroughs. The reason his achievements outweighed his reputation was that, as Richard Rorty (1931–
2007) lamented, the world of philosophy neglected him, and that was
a great injustice.[57]

Carl Friedrich's "History of Ancient Western Political Thought"

For my third course, I chose "History of Ancient Western Political
Thought" taught by celebrated political scientist Carl J. Friedrich (1901–
1984) in the political science department. German-born Professor Friedrich
had done much in-depth research in political philosophy and on political
institutions, and his publications were too numerous to mention. At that
time, his excellent analyses of the differences between totalitarian systems
and constitutional democracies were extremely influential. The reason
I chose this course was that while I was in Hong Kong, I had already
investigated the distinctions between democracy and totalitarianism and
had even written on them. At the time, however, I felt quite aware that I
lacked a systematic understanding of Western political thought because
I had not received any rigorous training and because New Asia College
did not have a department of political science yet. When I encountered
difficulties, other than asking my father, there was no one else I could
look to for guidance, but now that I actually had the chance to take a
course by a celebrated scholar like Friedrich, I would certainly not pass
up this golden opportunity.

Professor Friedrich's course included attending lectures and seminar
discussions, reading original classics, and writing midterm papers, all
perfectly suited to my need to grasp the fundamentals of the field. In his
weekly seminars, Friedrich not only required that students use both the
contents of his lectures and the classic texts in their discussions, but he
also encouraged the foreign students to attempt comparisons of Western
political ideas and the thought of their own native countries. (There were
overseas students from India, Japan, China, the Middle East, and other
countries in the class.) I was thus assigned to present a brief introduction

to Chinese Confucianism and Daoism. This course provided me with very useful training, but at the same time I also felt that my background knowledge was extremely inadequate. Not only did I not know Greek or Latin but my general knowledge of ancient Western history and classics was also woefully far behind that of the American graduate students, and so I was under immense pressure from beginning to end.

Nevertheless, I had a very interesting experience in this class, one that I have not forgotten to this day. Professor Friedrich required his students to write a midterm essay in lieu of a midterm examination, and he explained that this would be a report for which we had to choose a subject and express our views; it was not a research paper and so it was not necessary to give detailed citations or footnotes to the classic texts. I had been reading Plato's (427–347 BCE) *Republic* and had come up with a question: Was this ideal of sociopolitical order truly created by Plato alone? Or was it inherited from the past and latent in the Greek tradition for a long time? I examined several popular studies of the *Republic*, but I could not find a clear answer.

In the process of thinking about these questions, I suddenly had an idea. Why not try to track down Greek thought by employing the Chinese method of searching for the origin of thought known as evidential investigation (*kaozheng xue*) on the texts of relevant Greek classics?[58] With this idea in mind, in addition to the *Republic*, I also examined Plato's *Statesman* and *Laws*, Aristotle's (384–322 BCE) *Politics* and *Nichomachean Ethics*, and even Thucydides's (ca. 460–400 BCE) historical classic *The Peloponnesian War*. I wrote a short essay of five or six pages to report that the result of my investigations was that the concepts in Plato's *Republic* certainly had pre-Platonic sources. Professor Friedrich had told his students that we did not need to provide footnotes, so in my essay I quoted the text of the classics but did not give the details of chapters and page numbers. A week later, I received a short letter from Professor Friedrich, asking me to provide detailed citations of each of the classic texts for his reference. This was certainly unexpected, but I was very happy at his unexpected affirmation that my evidential investigation had some merit and was of some value even for an expert like him. This was sixty years ago, but my memory of those events is still quite vivid and attests to the great impact his words had on me. Unfortunately, Professor Friedrich's handwritten letter and my original essay have since vanished without a trace due to our many moves.

John King Fairbank's Research Seminar

The three aforementioned courses had nothing to do with my PhD program. I selected them for two reasons. First, at the time I had decided to return to New Asia College to teach after receiving my degree, and so I felt that I needed to make the best of this opportunity to learn what I could about the background of Western history and culture, and the more the better. Second, the curriculum I chose was in fields similar to what I had studied and written about in Hong Kong, and so my interest was very strong. I took all three classes in the fall of 1956. As noted earlier, my foundation initially was very weak, and so I felt that just one of these classes required tremendous effort, not to mention three at the same time. I was also constrained by the course-selection guidelines by the history department. It stipulated that every semester, PhD students should enroll in three lecture courses and one seminar and write an original essay. I did not dare take a seminar in the field of Western literature and history, so I enrolled in Professor John King Fairbank's research seminar on modern Chinese history. This course had two parts. In the first part, the graduate students (about six or seven) were to read specially selected chapters from the collection of Qing-dynasty documents on foreign affairs entitled *The Management of Barbarian Affairs from A To Z* (*Chouban yiwu shimo* 籌辦夷務始末) and, as much as possible, use relevant Western references.[59] This part was for the first three or four weeks and constituted the preparatory stage of the whole course; the graduate students were expected to choose their essay topics at that time and begin working on their individual research papers. For the second part, students took turns every week to report the results of their research, after which the professor and their fellow students raised questions and discussed the issues. This was the first time that I had engaged with Western "Chinese Studies."[60]

My essay for the course was a fairly in-depth examination and analysis of Feng Guifen's (1809–1874) *Straightforward Words from the Lodge of Early Qing Studies* (*Jiaobinlu kangyi* 校邠廬抗議) and *Hall of Open Aspirations* (*Xianzhitang gao* 顯志堂稿) in the context of Late Qing statecraft thinking.[61] The teaching assistant for the class was Mr. Liu Guangjing (Kwang-Ching Liu; 1921–2006). He was proficient in modern Chinese history and American economic history, and Professor Fairbank relied on him heavily.[62] He and Professor Fairbank both approved my essay, but Professor Fairbank wrote a comment at the end that made me feel rather embarrassed. His original English was "Your pronunciations are all wrong!" As it turned out, at that time Western romanization of Chinese characters was based on the Wade-Giles system, but I did not even know of its existence and so I spelled out all the Chinese names in my essay in my own way according to my own pronunciation (both incorrect and inconsistent). Later, with Mr. Liu Guangjing's guidance, I began studying the romanization system with the help of a Chinese-to-English dictionary. It is obvious from all this that I was a complete outsider in both "Chinese Studies" and "Sinology."

The first semester at Harvard was most stressful for me. This was mainly because I adhered to the history department's guidelines completely and did not seek advice from experienced classmates or even consult my advisor. In reality, it was very common for first-semester graduate students not to enroll in a seminar, and they could substitute one reading course without any examinations for one of the three lecture courses. Starting out this way meant that one could have the pleasure of being calm and collected.

Studying Japanese

In my second year (1957–1958), I made a fundamental adjustment to my doctoral program, with the greatest change being that I substituted a course in Japanese language for one course in European history. Thus, my final program consisted of ancient Chinese history, modern Chinese history, Renaissance and Reformation, and Japanese language. This program was accepted by the history department and the Department of Far Eastern Languages, and my studies and writing for the next three years were focused on these areas.

I made these changes primarily because of Professor Yang Liansheng's influence. In the second semester of the first year, I took his "Chinese Institutional History" course. This was the focus of his teaching and research; his first book was *Studies in Chinese Institutional History*.[63] In this course he used his own *Topics in Chinese History* as the textbook.[64] In it the subjects were not only organized into categories but also under each category he listed the most important and most fundamental original sources and contemporary studies. I had been very familiar with the original sources, but the contemporary studies were a complete blank to me, as I mentioned earlier in connection with asking Professor Yang's advice on the great families of the Eastern Han. Now that I was formally enrolled in a class, I could finally systematically and rather completely study the works of Western and Japanese Sinologists. In *Topics in Chinese History*, Professor Yang was, of course, not able to mention many Sinological works, but in his lectures he reviewed a select number and attached particular importance to the newest accomplishments.

As the semester went on, I discovered that Japanese research on various aspects of Chinese history was not only very perceptive but also so bountiful that it greatly exceeded my imagination. I felt that reading Japanese was probably necessary for my specialty. I asked Professor Yang for his advice, and he agreed completely with me. He told me it would be best for me to take one less course on European history and replace it with the Japanese-language course by the Department of Far

Eastern Languages, which was an "intensive course." It was taught by the Department Chair Edwin O. Reischauer (1910–1990, who would become the American ambassador to Japan in 1961); the class met five times a week and I would have to make an all-out effort to pass.[65] This was how it came to be decided that I would study Japanese. By coincidence, Mr. Yan Gengwang (1916–1996) was a visiting scholar at the Harvard-Yenching Institute that year.[66] After perusing the Chinese and Japanese collections in the Harvard Library, he discovered that there were innumerable Japanese books and other research publications on the Tang dynasty that he had to consult. When he heard that the Department of Far Eastern Languages had a Japanese-language curriculum, he promptly enrolled in Professor Reischauer's course. He did not have to take the examinations, so he was much more relaxed than I was.

It was probably in the autumn of 1958 that I satisfied all the university's requirements for both lecture courses and seminars that a doctoral student had to take. Right after that, I consulted with the advisors of my three specialized subjects on how to prepare for my PhD oral examination, my biggest hurdle in the entire doctoral program. The basic way of preparing for this comprised the "reading course" format and fixed meetings with the advisors, usually once every one or two weeks. Through these meetings, graduate students gradually developed the focus of their questions and the scope of their reading.

My three advisors were Professors Yang, Fairbank, and Gilmore. Unfortunately, Professor Yang, who was the advisor for my major, suffered a serious anxiety disorder at the end of 1958 and needed a rather long time for treatment and recuperation. Thus, the reading courses could only begin for two of my minors. The course on modern Chinese history went very smoothly, but the Renaissance and Reformation course was the one in which I had the weakest foundation, and so I should write briefly about it.

Following Gilmore and Reading the Renaissance

Let me begin with my advisor Myron P. Gilmore. At that time, he was one of America's most distinguished historians of early modern Europe. In 1952 in response to an invitation from William L. Langer, Harvard's authority on modern history, Professor Gilmore wrote *The World of Humanism, 1453–1517* for the prestigious book series, "The Rise of Modern Europe."[67] It was a history of the most important period of the Renaissance. He was most highly regarded because he had earlier published many essays that opened up new horizons in the study of Renaissance humanism. As mentioned earlier, the first year that I was a visiting scholar at Harvard, I sat in with Wang Dezhao on Professor Gilmore's lecture course. At that time, I was only auditing and did not finish reading the assigned texts, so I gained only a general gist of the subject. By the time I became a doctoral student the next year, Professor Gilmore first went on leave and then took the position of Chair of the history department from 1957 to 1962, and he did not offer his "Renaissance and Reformation" course again. In my third year, however, I did take a lecture course on Renaissance history taught by Visiting Professor Felix Gilbert (1905–1991).

Professor Gilbert was born in Germany and immigrated to the United States in 1936 from Italy and taught at Bryn Mawr College in Pennsylvania. He was not only one of the Renaissance scholars who had made the greatest contributions to that field, but he was also widely recognized as the most knowledgeable expert on historiography. (In 1962 he was given a permanent appointment as Professor of History at Princeton's Institute for Advanced Studies.) After I heard the history department graduate students' introduction of Professor Gilbert, I decided to enroll in his class as my optional course.

Professor Gilbert's lectures and his assigned readings certainly stirred my interest; and due to my strong interest, in 1959 at the request of New Asia College *Academic Annual* (*Xinya xueyuan xueshu niankan* 新亞書院學術年刊), I wrote a long essay entitled "The Renaissance and

Humanist Thought" ("Wenyi fuxing yu renwen sichao"), in which I cited several of Professor Gilbert's journal articles. (Later, this article, with some revisions, was included in my book *History and Thought*.[68] The article is a commemoration of my course with Professor Gilbert. When I went to Princeton, he had already retired in 1975 and was over eighty years old. I never had the opportunity to see him again, but I did read the book he wrote in his last years, *History: Politics or Culture? Reflections on Ranke and Burckhardt* and benefited greatly from it.[69]

Before I enrolled in Professor Gilbert's reading course "Renaissance and Reformation" in the spring of 1959, I had had no personal contact with Professor Gilmore. I had listened in on his course and read his *The World of Humanism*, so he was not unfamiliar to me, but he knew nothing about me. He accepted me as his graduate student (i.e., allowed me to participate in his "reading course") mainly because I had already taken Professor Gilbert's course, and it was only one of my minor fields. Thus, although Professor Gilmore was clearly aware that my background knowledge was limited, he still treated me leniently in allowing me to take his course. He was very busy with departmental duties at the time and also had eight or nine graduate students, so in our two-hour or so group meetings every two weeks to discuss problems arising from our "readings," he did not offer any long comments and usually only added some of his responses to the most difficult questions arising from our deliberations. I did not have much opportunity to communicate with him directly. During the semester, we had no more than two one-on-one discussions; each one lasted no more than twenty minutes, consisting mostly of my reporting on the state of my "readings" and then listening to his instructions. As such, in my preparations for my PhD oral examination, Professor Gilmore's course was the one I had least mastered.

In my preparation process, however, I truly did make some important improvements, even though they had no direct relation to the upcoming examination, and to this day I still remember two things.

The first is that in 1958, psychologist Erik H. Erikson (1902–1994) published a study of the young Martin Luther (1483–1546), in which he studied Luther's "life history" based on psychoanalysis and made some new, extremely original observations on the origin of the Reformation. It was from the discussions with other graduate students in the reading course that I learned of this book and its originality in historiography. It was very stimulating for my later study of the history of Chinese scholarly thought.[70]

The second is that Professor Gilmore's research on the Christian humanist Erasmus (1466–1536) was exceptionally perceptive, and he was publicly acknowledged as an authoritative Erasmus scholar. He wrote an article, "Fides et Eruditio, Erasmus and the Study of History," that explored how Erasmus employed his erudition (*erudito*) to reestablish Christian faith (*fides*). I was exhilarated after reading this essay because this was very much the same as the Qing-dynasty debates about "philology" (*xungu* 訓詁) and "moral principles" (*yili* 義理). For me, this opened wide the gateway to a comparison of Chinese and Western intellectual history.[71]

In conclusion, I certainly did study very conscientiously for this course on the Renaissance and the Reformation, and I benefited greatly from it. In my PhD oral examination on that subject, however, my performance was far from ideal. Professor Gilmore did not even touch on the areas that I had most carefully prepared for; rather, he brought up some concrete issues that I could discuss only in a general way but was unable to be thorough. Although I passed the oral examination, I could not help feeling somewhat disappointed.

PhD Dissertation

Lastly, allow me to explain briefly my PhD dissertation, "Views of Life and Death in Later Han China, A.D. 25–220." In 1959 I wrote a long essay of 100,000 characters entitled "The New Consciousness and New Thought Trends of Scholars Between the Han and the Jin Dynasties" to commemorate Professor Qian's birthday.[72] Unlike the essay on the great families of the Eastern Han mentioned earlier, for this work I collected and consulted innumerable relevant modern works, including those of Chinese, Japanese, English, and French scholars. After I completed the draft, I asked Professor Yang to read it and provide feedback. He basically agreed with my thesis and concurred that I should use this essay as the foundation for writing my PhD dissertation.[73]

Later, as I was outlining the dissertation, my way of thinking changed. First, I felt that translating my previously published Chinese essay into English and building on that lacked a sense of freshness and intellectual stimulation. I would rather work a little harder and start from scratch on a new path. Second, since 1956, because I was influenced by the discussions of "formal thought" and "popular thought" by Crane Brinton and others, I wanted to make a new attempt to approach my topic from that angle. The so-called "formal thought" referred to systematic learning or theory developed by cultural elites, like the ancient Greek philosophers and the various philosophers of pre-Qin China (before 221 BCE), while the so-called "popular thought" referred to the various kinds of consciousness expressed by the general population in the course of their daily lives. (See the earlier section "On First Visiting Harvard.")

The greatest difficulty in doing research on "popular thought" is that the historical sources are few and scattered. Fortunately, *Annotations on the Scripture of Great Peace* (*Taipingjing hexiao* 太平經合校) by Wang Ming (1911–1992)[74] was published in 1960, and it contained many examples of popular thought in the late period of the Eastern Han (the question of periodization has already been thoroughly researched by experts in the field). During this period, mainland Chinese and Japanese scholars had also published a number of articles on the *Scripture of Great Peace*. On this account, I thought of connecting other relevant source materials, using the *Scripture of Great Peace* as the thread to construct the outline of "popular thought" in the Eastern Han and then further investigating its negotiations and intersections with the "formal thought" of the same period. My original idea was to select some common ideas or concepts that a few elite intellectuals and ordinary people were interested in and conduct a detailed examination of the written materials found in the extant classic texts and popular reports in an attempt to discover their interactions, differences, and similarities. "Life" and "death" were obvious everyday concepts.

At first then I picked "life" and "death" only for my first chapter; there would be other common concepts that I could continue to discuss as the topics of subsequent chapters. After I presented these ideas to Professor Yang, he agreed that this might be a potentially acceptable, innovative plan, but he wanted me to write the first chapter as an experiment; if it was not successful, then I could come up with another plan. The twin concepts "life" and "death" turned out to be extremely complicated, and the range of areas they covered was unexpectedly broad. After I had written about half the chapter, Professor Yang looked over the first draft and told me to expand this first chapter into my entire thesis; there was no need for other concepts. This was how "Views of Life and Death in Later Han China" came to be my PhD thesis. I have provided this explanation to clear up the misconception that my doctoral thesis was on the *Scripture of Great Peace*.

Professor Yang was my thesis supervisor, but I also had two outside readers, Professors John King Fairbank and Benjamin I. Schwartz. Professor Yang was very familiar with every aspect of my thesis, and Professors Fairbank and Schwartz read it through—and they did not have any concerns. In the beginning of January 1962, after the three professors held an examination committee meeting, Fairbank, as the chairman of the doctoral committee, announced that my thesis did not require any major revisions. With that, my requirements to earn a degree were completed.

I would like to mention here Professor Benjamin Schwartz's concerns about my thesis. After the thesis had been approved, he wrote me a two-page letter of comments and pointed out some areas that merited further discussion as well as some that were praiseworthy. What needed to be discussed more was my translation of Chinese concepts into Western terms—the connotations were usually not very appropriate and could easily lead to misunderstandings; for example, the Chinese *chushi* 出世 (literally "go out of the world") and *rushi* 入世 (literally "enter the world") being translated as "otherworldly" and "worldly." In the process of rewriting my thesis later into journal articles, I corrected all these problematic issues.

Professor Schwartz praised as perceptive my discussion of Chinese concepts such as form or body (*xing* 形), spirit (*shen* 神), *hun*-soul or soul that can detach from the body (*hun* 魂), and *po*-soul or soul attached to the body (*po* 魄) that demonstrated that the Chinese had the concept of the binary separation of body and soul (or spirit) before the transmission of Buddhism into China. Regarding the evidence I provided in my thesis, he stated that "it conclusively proves [Joseph] Needham wrong …" Professor Schwartz had published many works on recent and modern Chinese history, but his true interests and contributions were in the area of Chinese intellectual history, as evidenced by the work of his later years, such as *The World of Thought in Ancient China*.[75] So when he read my thesis, it was very easy for him to see its merits and faults.

An interesting thing about this discussion is that when Joseph Needham (1900–1995) wrote about my 1964 essay "Life and Immortality in the Mind of Han China" and claimed that there was no *bishi* 彼世 ("otherworld"), he persisted in his previous opinion that China's native thought only had the concept of "this world" (*cishi* 此世) and naturally could not have had the concept of the binary separation of body and soul.[76] On this issue, I later wrote another essay, "O Soul Come Back—A Study in the Changing Conceptions of the Soul and Afterlife in Pre-Buddhist China," in which I gave a detailed discussion of changing Chinese understandings of the afterlife before the introduction of Buddhism.[77]

**PART THREE: HISTORICAL DEVELOPMENT OF CHINESE
HUMANITIES SCHOLARS AT HARVARD**

In the final section of this chapter, I would like to discuss the interactions
between the Chinese scholars (including graduate students and visiting
scholars) who came to Harvard during this period to conduct research in
the humanities as well as the general situation at Harvard then concerning
the exchange of study and thought. From this we can discern the locus
of a generation's trends in academic learning. (Note that "Chinese" for
the aforementioned "Chinese scholars" only refers to their ethnicity and
culture; that is, it has an "ethnic-cultural" connotation and has nothing
to do with their nationality [*guoji* 國籍] and even less so with politics).

When I came to Harvard as a visiting scholar in 1955, I unintentionally
arrived during a crucial new period. The mid-1950s was the beginning
of a new period when Chinese scholars (including visiting scholars and
graduate students) started coming to Harvard for advanced studies. Let
me first explain how this came to happen. After the end of the Anti-
Japanese War of Resistance in 1945, China was immediately plunged into
the throes of civil war between the Chinese Communist Party and the
Nationalist Party. The economy was deteriorating rapidly, and the number
of scholars and students coming to America to pursue their studies
naturally declined drastically. Moreover, after the end of the Northern
Expedition against local warlords (discussed earlier), the Tsinghua system
of overseas study in America had changed; it was replaced by publicly and
privately funded overseas-study examinations. It is common knowledge
that after 1949, Mainland China and the United States had completely
isolated each other, and so the main stream of Chinese students coming
to America dried up. As a result, when I arrived at Harvard in 1955, the
Chinese history and literature scholars that I met were all around ten
years older than I; most of them had already attained their degrees and
were working as teachers or researchers. In contrast, there were only
two Chinese humanities graduate students who were about my age, and
they had just arrived from Taiwan (more on this shortly). Therefore,

from the end of the 1940s to the middle of the 1950s, humanities graduate students from China had already stopped coming to Harvard. However, every year there were two or three humanities graduate students from Taiwan and Hong Kong coming to Harvard—some for an MA, but most for a PhD. This is what I mean by calling it a crucial new period.

What made this period "new" was not only that Chinese students coming to Harvard were now from Taiwan, Hong Kong, and other places, instead of Mainland China, but also that the humanities graduate students made completely different cultural contributions from their predecessors. To clarify this, we have to take a look back in time.

The First Period: Beginning of Modern Chinese Humanities Research

There were two periods when Chinese humanities scholars came to Harvard for advanced study that deserve our attention. The first period lasted about ten years, from 1915 to 1925; the second period was also roughly a decade, from the late 1930s to the middle of the 1940s. Both periods brought forth many first-rate academics who produced extremely high-quality scholarship. The scholars from the first period were especially important because they initiated a new era in thought and learning, and their influence was wide and profound. To illustrate this, I only have to name a few of these scholars. From what I have read, the earliest scholars appear to have been Mei Guangdi and Zhao Yuanren, who both enrolled at Harvard in 1915. Mei studied literary criticism under Irving Babbitt, and Zhao received his PhD from the Department of Philosophy in 1918 under the direction of the two renowned scholars William E. Hocking (1873–1966) and Henry M. Sheffer (1882–1964).[78] Zhao Yuanren was especially interested in linguistics, and he remained at Harvard from 1921 to 1923 because he was hired to teach Chinese language and culture for a year and a half. After he left his position and returned to China, as his replacement he recommended Mei Guangdi, who returned to Harvard and taught there for many years.

Wu Mi entered Harvard as an undergraduate in June of 1918 and returned to China in July of 1921 after three academic years. In his diary entries of those three years, he recorded in detail the various activities of his friends studying the humanities at Harvard at the time.[79] This diary is a most valuable resource. In his diary, Professor Wu Mi mentioned the following friends who were studying the humanities (listed in the order in which they appear): Mei Guangdi, Chen Yinke, Wei Tingsheng (1890–1977, who first studied economics and in his later years moved into historiography), Tang Yue (psychology), Tang Yongtong (1893–1964 [historian of Buddhism]), Yu Dawei (philosophy), Gu Tailai (history and politics), Hong Shen (1894–1955, drama [one of the founders of modern Chinese spoken drama]), Zhang Xinhai (English literature; he later changed the *xin* 鑫 in his name to *xin* 歆), Lou Guanglai (English-literature translator and Shakespeare expert), Lin Yutang (1895–1976, [scholar, humorist, and well-known popularizer of Chinese culture in the United States], the *yu* 玉 in his name was later changed to *yu* 語), and Li Ji (1896–1979), archaeology and anthropology [considered the founder of Chinese archaeology]). These twelve men were the friends most closely associated with Wu Mi, so while other names were mentioned, I have not listed them. When these scholars returned home to China, they all became leaders in their various fields. Here is one such example. In 1925 when the Institute of Chinese National Studies (Guoxue Yanjiuyuan 國學研究院) of Tsinghua University was established, they hired the "four great tutors" (*si da daoshi* 四大導師), who were Liang Qichao, Wang Guowei, Zhao Yuanren, and Chen Yinke. In addition, an instructor was also hired, and this was Li Ji; and Wu Mi handled the institute's administrative affairs. From this, we can appreciate the pioneering foundational work in modern Chinese humanities studies by these scholars who did their advanced studies at Harvard in the first period.

One major characteristic distinguishing the interactions of these scholars is their mutual, collaborative learning. A passage from Wu Mi's diary for August 17, 1920, reads:

Chen Yinke and Tang Xiyu returned from New York, and Zhang Xinhai also returned earlier. So the seven stars, the 'Pleiades,' met together and it was extremely lively. (Note: this refers to seven people: Chen Yinke, Tang Yongtong, Zhang Xinhai, Lou Guanglai, Gu Tailai, Yu Dawei, and Wu Mi.) Everyone gathered at [Wu] Mi's place to discuss books and scholarship and exchange witticisms. Outsiders would not really understand the joy we felt in these discussions.

Because I hadn't the time to study philosophy, I asked Yu Dawei to teach me the main principles of the history of philosophy. We met for one hour per day for a total of ten days from the fifteenth to the twenty-fourth. Next [I] asked Xiyu (that is, Tang Yongtong) to teach me the main points of Buddhism and Indian philosophy. We settled on some books and I read the most important ones.[80]

This passage vividly captures how these scholars interacted.

The diary also includes many detailed records of their "talking about books and scholarship." Here is an example from an entry on December 14, 1919, when Chen Yinke compared Chinese and Western culture:

Chinese philosophy and fine arts are far inferior to those of Greece, and it is not only [Chinese] science that is inferior to that of the West. But the ancient Chinese were always good at politics and practical ethics, and in that they most resembled the Romans. When they spoke of morality (*daode* 道德), they only valued practical utility and did not investigate abstract principles; this was where both their strong points and their shortcomings lay. Their strong point was their teaching of the path of "cultivating one's self" (*xiu* 修), "ordering one's family" (*qi* 齊), and "regulating the state" (*zhi* 治) in order to "bring peace to all under Heaven" (*ping* 平). Their shortcomings were that they paid excessive attention to practical advantages and disadvantages or successes and failures, but lacked profound and far-reaching thought. In the past, most scholar-officials all studied for the eight-legged essays [of the examination system] to achieve glory and riches while the number of scholars who studied moral virtue were always an extremely small minority.

Today, as well, all of the overseas students study engineering, industry, and commerce in hopes of achieving riches and honor; they are all similar in being unwilling to exert themselves and study for the true meaning of knowledge. Furthermore, they do not understand that science is the foundation of industry. They do not even grasp its foundations but only apply themselves to its trivialities, and so at most they only become inferior craftsmen or artisans. If they encounter some slight changes in the principles they have studied, then their technical skills can no longer be used, and that which was of the so-called most practical utility will turn into something of minimal practical use.

As for the knowledge of the Principle of Heaven and human affairs that are profound, extensive, and mysterious and that run without change all the way through all antiquity and cross the nine boundaries [the center and eight directions in classical Chinese thought], these can be employed at any time and in any place ... for statecraft to save the nation, we especially have to use [such] spiritual knowledge (what is called metaphysics) as the foundation.

This is exactly what our nation's overseas students do not study, but rather disdain, and they do not feel ashamed of their ignorance and backwardness. It is all because they have not changed their old habit of emphasizing practical utility.

If later, China's enterprises develop, our lives become affluent, and our financial resources are well established, then the Chinese people's characteristic business and commercial skills will come into use, and the Chinese should be able to become rich merchants of the world.

If, however, you hope that the Chinese can surpass others in the mastery of learning and the arts, then, that would definitely be very difficult indeed.[81]

Widely regarded as a conservative who stood up for Chinese traditional culture, the previous passage shows that Professor Chen Yinke nevertheless had a very clear understanding of not only the strengths but the weaknesses of Chinese culture (i.e., Chinese thought, fine arts, and other related facets). His was an understanding that could only be achieved through comparative research on Chinese and Western cultures, not from subjective speculation. For example, when he wrote that "the ancient Chinese were always good at politics and practical ethics, and in that they most resembled the Romans," he was clearly influenced by Hegel's assessment of "Chinese philosophy" in *Lectures on the Philosophy of History*, but Chen also elaborated on it more deeply.[82]

Some of Chen Yinke's observations have proven to be astonishing predictions that have come true. Today, a century later, the Chinese people's "lack of profound and far-reaching thought," "disdain for spiritual knowledge," and "excessive attention to the practical or utilitarian" are no less but much greater than before. Due to various changes, "China's enterprises" and the "Chinese people's specific business and commercial skills" have been developed to the highest level, and the Chinese have become "rich merchants of the world." In contrast, when we speak of "surpass[ing] others in the mastery of learning and the arts," however, China today has not only not made any progress since Chen Yinke's 1919 pronouncement but has fallen behind even more. From time to time, we hear of incidents of plagiarism in Chinese essays submitted to scientific journals outside of China. Merely from these incidents alone, we can clearly see that the spirit of "knowledge for the sake of knowledge" has not been imparted to the sacred land of China (*shenzhou dadi* 神州大地).

The Second Period: Discussing Traditional Learning to Cultivate New Knowledge

Next allow me to offer a brief introduction to the second period.

In his diary entry for October 14, 1943, Hu Shi wrote:

Had dinner at Zhou Yiliang's [1913–2001] home this evening. Also present were Yang Liansheng, Wu Bao-an, and Ren Hua; all of them are the people here who are most deeply knowledgeable about the history of Chinese writing. Mrs. Zhou is also very learned ... In New York there was no one I could discuss textual research on Chinese writing with, and so every time I wrote an essay I would mail it to my friend Wang Zhongmin [1903–1975] and ask him to read it first. Here there are so many people, and among the young people, there are quite a few with whom I can talk at length about Chinese history and literature.[83]

After Hu Shi stepped down as ambassador to the United States in September 1942, he lived for a long time in New York, but he often accepted invitations from Harvard to lecture or teach there. As such, he was at Harvard for almost twelve months during the span of three years from 1943 to 1945, during which he had many intellectual interactions with the younger generation of history and literature scholars who were studying there at the time. The October 14, 1943, diary entry was made when he accepted a position at Harvard to lecture on "The Historical Culture of China." The lecture was given six times over two weeks. From the tone of the diary entry, one can infer that he was friendly with Zhou Yiliang, Yang Liansheng, Wu Bao-an, and Ren Hua. A letter, "Yang Liansheng to Hu Shi," dated June 17, 1944, describes their intellectual discussions:

I received your June 16 letter and your writing about Quan, Zhao, and Dai. This "Note" does such heavy lifting with such wondrous ease; reading it was just like watching a very neat and skillful magic trick; it made me feel extremely good. (This refers to Hu Shi's "A Note on Ch'uan Tsu-wang, Chao I-ch'ing and Tai Chen" that is in the appendix of *Eminent Chinese of the Ch'ing Period, 1644–1912*, edited by Arthur W. Hummel.[84] ... This evening Wu Bao-an and Ren Hua invited Zhou Yiliang and his wife (to congratulate Zhou on receiving his PhD degree after completing his exams on Thursday the fourteenth) and also to welcome Li Baoqian. Zhang Longyan and I will be there to meet them, and we plan to circulate your essay and let them read it; will probably be able to return it in three to five days. ... We are all waiting to read your two important essays. We heard that you were originally coming in September, but later changed it to November—we are very anxiously waiting to see you.[85]

This letter not only confirms that Hu Shi often "talk[ed] at length about Chinese history and literature" with the younger scholars at Harvard but also further demonstrates that Zhou, Yang, Wu, and Ren were the four people whom Hu thought most highly of at that time. The statement at the end of the letter that they were "very anxiously waiting" for Hu Shi to come to Harvard refers to Hu having already accepted Harvard's invitation to come as a Visiting Lecturer for the next academic year. Hu took up his post in Cambridge on October 22, 1944, and returned to New York on June 17 the next year. During these eight months, Hu Shi's intellectual exchanges of ideas with younger scholars at Harvard were even greater than his earlier ones.[86]

Zhou, Yang, Wu, and Ren were indeed the most outstanding, brilliant, up-and-coming young scholars of that time. Some have proclaimed that in the 1920s Chen Yinke, Wu Mi, and Tang Yongtong were "the Three Heroes of Harvard," and Zhou Yiliang's "The 'Three Heroes' of Harvard University's Chinese Overseas Students" confirms this in the passage in which he notes:

At that time there were three humanities students who sought both learning and the PhD degree. In private, I give them the title of the "three heroes." They were Yang Liansheng, Wu Bao-an, and Ren Hua.[87]

Professor Yang Liansheng has already been discussed earlier, so I will write about the others. Wu Bao-an (1913–1993) was from Xiuning County in Anhui Province. From 1939 to 1941, he was a graduate student in the Economic Research Institute of Nankai University in Kunming; his graduate thesis was "Scholars and the Collapse of the Ancient *Fengjian* System" ("Shi yu gudai fengjian zhidu zhi jieti" 士與古代封建制度之解

體). After graduating, he passed the Tsinghua University examination to qualify for the publicly funded study-abroad program and went to Harvard to study history and politics. His doctoral dissertation was entitled "A Comparative Study of Eastern and Western Political Systems in the Medieval Era" ("Zhong shiji dong-xi fang zhengzhi zhidu de bijiao" 中世紀東西方政治制度的比較). After he returned to China in 1947, he had taught in the history department of Wuhan University.

Ren Hua (1911–1998) was born to an influential family in Guizhou. His father, Ren Kecheng (1878–1946), was a *juren* (a successful candidate in the imperial examinations at the provincial level) during the late Qing dynasty; he participated in the establishment of the Republic of China and the overthrow of Yuan Shikai's imperial regime, and then he served successively as the Provincial Governor and the Minister of Education of Yunnan. In 1931 Ren Hua entered the Department of Philosophy at Tsinghua University and became the favorite pupil of Jin Yuelin (1895–1984).[88] At Harvard under the supervision of the major philosopher of pragmatism, Clarence Irving Lewis (1883–1964), he completed his doctoral dissertation entitled "Three Types of Phenomenalism in Contemporary Philosophy."[89] Although their research specialties were in the areas of Western historiography and philosophy, both Wu Bao-an and Ren Hua were deeply knowledgeable about Chinese literature, history, and philosophy, and both were highly accomplished and could write outstanding ancient-style poetry.

A modest person, Zhou Yiliang did not include himself in the group of "three heroes" in "The 'Three Heroes' of Harvard University's Chinese Overseas Students," and his friend commented:

> People say that at that time your work was also pretty good. Why don't you join the "three heroes" and make it "four spirits"?[90]

The "three heroes" should indeed be "four heroes" or "four spirits," especially because in "The History of the North-South Dynasties and

Me" ("Wo he wei-jin nan-bei chao shi" 我和魏晉南北朝史), Zhou Yiliang did note that:

> When I was at Harvard, my fiend Yang Liansheng encouraged me by saying that in the future I could inherit the mantle of Chen Yinke.[91]

I also heard this from Professor Yang himself. In the 1940s at Harvard, then, there is no denying that there were "four [Chinese] heroes" studying the humanities.

According to Zhou Yiliang, there were more than fifty Chinese overseas students at Harvard in the 1940s. About twenty of them were in the humanities, and they had close intellectual exchanges in the fields of Chinese literature and history. This was probably due to three factors.

First, Zhao Yuanren transferred from Yale to the Harvard-Yenching Institute in 1941 to begin editing a Chinese dictionary. Later, he also taught Chinese for the "Army Special Training Program" at Harvard. Zhao and his wife liked entertaining and therefore had frequent contact with Chinese students. They also needed to meet as many Chinese students as possible to learn about the different Chinese dialects and ways of pronunciation for teaching the language. From almost the start of their time in Cambridge, the Zhaos made their home a hub for Chinese students, and many of them would gather there for holidays and Chinese New Year.[92]

Second, from 1943 to 1945, Hu Shi taught and gave many lectures at Harvard. He had a great influence on the Chinese students, especially those in the humanities, and led them to develop considerable interest in Chinese history, literature, and thought (as noted in the earlier discussion about the "four heroes"). In addition to intellectual exchanges with the "four heroes," he also interacted frequently with the Chinese overseas students. While at Harvard, Hu Shi often talked to the Chinese students about his research in Chinese literature and history, and he "lectured in an easy-to-understand way that fascinated people."[93] Due to a lack of historical records, I am unable to determine how many Harvard students Hu Shi met at that time. However, I can give some idea from Hu Shi's diary entry on December 17, 1944:

> Mr. and Mrs. Zhao Yuanren invited a group of old and young friends who knew it was my birthday to their house for lunch— altogether there were forty-four people.[94]

The "old and young friends" included many humanities graduate students, and it is impossible to find out who they are, but from the historical records I have seen, the following five are likely part of this group: Zhang Longyan (1909–2009), a notable calligrapher; Chen Guansheng (Kenneth K. S. Chen; 1907– ?), a well-known scholar of Buddhism; Wang Minyuan; Liu Guangjing (K. C. Liu); and Wang Yitong (Yi-t'ung Wang; 1914–2016), a notable scholar of the Six Dynasties. Hu Shi was a mentor to many; and even though he particularly valued the "four heroes", especially Yang Liansheng and Zhou Yiliang, he had many contacts who were certainly not limited to these few people. I would like to emphasize this specifically to avoid any misunderstandings.

Third, after the sneak attack by the Japanese on Pearl Harbor on December 7, 1941, the United States and China officially became allied nations. To strengthen their relationship with China, from 1942 to 1947 the United States government hired Chinese scholars, especially in the humanities and social sciences, to visit various American universities for durations ranging from a month to a year. Harvard was, of course, the most highly regarded institution for visiting scholars. Due to Harvard's unique position, many visiting scholars from other universities often liked to come for a visit. According to the sources I've seen, from 1943 to 1947, visitors to Harvard from the older generation included Jin Yuelin; Feng Youlan (1895–1990), a noted historian of Chinese philosophy; Zhou Gengsheng (1889–1970), a jurist and educator; Lo Changpei (1899–1958), a scholar specializing in the history of Chinese phonology; Dong Zuobin (1895–1963), a leading authority on oracle bone inscription; Liang Sicheng (1901–1972), regarded as the father of modern Chinese architecture; Li Fanggui, an important scholar of Chinese linguistics and linguistic reconstruction; and Qian Duansheng (1900–1990), a notable legal studies scholar known as a founder of modern Chinese political science. From the middle and younger generations, there were Zhang Qiyun; Liang Fangzhong (1908–1970), a historian of Chinese economy, especially the financial history of the Ming dynasty; Wang Xinzhong (1909– ?), a specialist on Japanese history; Quan Hansheng (1912–2001), a notable Chinese economic history scholar; and Ding Shengshu (1909–1989), a well-known linguist. This list is far from complete, but it is extremely impressive. During their time as visiting scholars, they primarily interacted with Chinese overseas students in the humanities and had great influence on broadening the intellectual horizons of these younger scholars.[95]

In terms of talented humanities students, the Chinese overseas students at Harvard in the 1940s were just as good as those in the 1920s, and there were more of them. In terms of their contributions to Chinese scholarship after graduation, however, the scholars of the first period left the ones of the second period in the dust. Just as Zhou Yiliang wrote:

> As anyone can see, the "three heroes" of the 1920s made a great impact on academic and cultural circles. Of the "three heroes" of the 1940s, some returned home and some stayed abroad. Due to changes in generation and times, the impact of those who returned home was very different. Generally speaking, they were rather far behind the "three heroes" of the 1920s. Those who did not return home and remained "strangers in a strange land" were, on the contrary, able to put their talents to full use and make some contributions.[96]

As noted previously, Professor Zhou Yiliang's "three heroes" should be read as the "four heroes" or "four spirits." Of the "four heroes," Zhou Yiliang, Wu Bao-an, and Ren Hua returned to China, and only Yang Liansheng remained in the United States to teach. He is one who, as Zhou wrote, "remained 'strangers in a strange land,' [and one of those] able to put their talents to full use and make some contributions." That

Zhou Yiliang expressed such deep regret [about the second generation who "were rather far behind" the first] not long before his death cannot but elicit our sympathy. Be that as it may, in the final analysis the second generation embodies the spirit of Zhu Xi's (1130–1200) poetic lines "in discussing the old learning, [my understanding of] it becomes increasingly profound and precise, and in cultivating the new knowledge it also develops and turns progressively deeper."

Here is a little more information to conclude this section. At first, Professor Yang Liansheng had decided to return to China. He did not only because his family was in straitened circumstances and he wanted to earn a little more money to supplement their income, and so in September 1946 he decided to work in the languages department of the United Nations for a year. He had already accepted an invitation from Peking University and told his friend at the United Nations that "whenever Mr. Hu tells me to return, I will return."[97] Then, Harvard's East Asian department offered him a five-year teaching position; he still intended to return to China and asked Hu Shi to decide for him. It was not until Hu Shi sent him a telegram on March 5, 1947, stating "Advise accepting Harvard" that he finally decided to stay on. He ended up receiving an agreement from Harvard to stay for two or at most three years, and he never gave up the idea of returning to China.[98]

The Third Period: A Completely New Turn
Now having discussed the first two periods, I can explain the historical significance of the third period in the 1950s and how it was a completely new stage. As noted earlier, when I first arrived at Harvard as a visiting scholar, there were only two Chinese graduate students who were about my age, and both were from Taiwan. The first one was Gao Yougong (1929–2016), who entered the Department of Far Eastern Languages as a graduate student in 1954. (A few years later the department's name was changed to East Asian Languages and Civilizations.) The second was Zhang Guangzhi (or K. C. Chang; 1931–2001), who began his PhD degree in the Department of Anthropology on the recommendation of

Professor Li Ji. Most unfortunately, both Gao and Zhang have passed away, so I can only offer details based on what I can recollect. Fortuitously, their scholarly trajectories represent two typical examples of the main intellectual patterns of this new period, which I will describe further.

Gao Yougong Studies to "Improve Himself"

In 1947, Gao Yougong (Kao Yu-Kung) passed the examination to enter the Faculty of Law at Peking University, but a year later, his family moved to Taiwan because of the civil war. He transferred to the Chinese department of National Taiwan University and majored in Chinese linguistics and literature. Gao had always had a deep interest in Chinese literature and had taken Professor Zhou Zumo's (1914–1995) course at Peking University.[99] At National Taiwan University, Professor Dong Tonghe's courses on Chinese linguistics were Gao's favorite, and he soon became Dong's favorite disciple. Gao's interest in Chinese literature was stoked by [the celebrated] Professors Wang Shumin (1914–2008) and Zheng Qian (1906–1991). Gao once told me that he had audited Professor Mou Zongsan's course on the *Zhuangzi* at then Teacher's College, and although he could not accept his overall theory, he greatly appreciated many of Professor Mou's original ideas. From this we can see that Gao had torn down the barriers between Chinese literature, history, and philosophy and was on a path to integrating them, from structure to thought.

When Gao Yougong came to Harvard, he explored the spiritual and intellectual worlds of the West in the same manner. He not only audited courses on Western literary theory, literary criticism, and analytic philosophy but also enrolled in classes on Greek history and ancient Greek language, making a conscientious effort to understand the origins of Western civilization. One minor subject in his PhD program was the history of Rome, which attests to his determination in understanding classical Western civilization.

At the time, there were a couple of things about Gao Yougong I regarded as somewhat unexpected: his major subject was Chinese history—not Chinese literature—and the topic of his dissertation "The Rebellion of Fang La (?–1121)" was chosen and assigned by Professor Yang Liansheng. A work of very high quality, it was later published in the *Harvard Journal of Asiatic Studies* and opened up research on "people's rebellions" in the American study of Chinese history.[100] Gao once told me an interesting story: Many years after his dissertation, a specialist in the study of "Chinese peasant rebellions" wanted to discuss with him some of his assertions in his "A Study of The Fang La Rebellion," and he had to tactfully but resolutely refuse. He laughingly said, "I had completely forgotten everything about the Fang La incident," implying that his real interests were not in the study of history, as confirmed by his later research that was solely in the area of Chinese literature.

Although Gao Yougong attained a high level of mastery in the field of Chinese literature, he did not suffer from what we call "scribomania," writing a great number of specialist books. He would only write when he felt that he had the necessary insights and opportunities, and he did so only in essay format for both Chinese- and English-language journals. As such, he does not have many publications, but everything he put forth was definitely valued by his peers in the field. His many Chinese essays on the cannon of literary aesthetics and the lyric tradition have been collected and anthologized by the younger generation and have had such a great influence that there is no need to detail them here.

My perspective on Gao's work is that the most important motive behind his wide-ranging reading and study on Chinese and Western arts and literature (including music, drama, and dance) was to reveal the distinguishing characteristics of Chinese culture using the comparative method, and thus I especially appreciate his emphasis on the Chinese "lyric tradition." His 1991 essay, "Chinese Lyric Aesthetics" compared Chinese "lyric aesthetics" (*shuqing meixue* 抒情美學) with Western "narrative aesthetics" (*xushi meixue* 敘事美學) and asserted that the former is intended to present people's inner nature and emotional states while the latter is intended to describe the external world. According to his observations, Chinese arts and literature emphasize the "lyric" or "emotional" feelings (*shuqing*), but Western arts and literature emphasize "narrative."[101] He elaborated on this thesis in a more thorough and detailed manner in later Chinese essays. Although Gao Yougong was not the first one to present this thesis (Chen Shixiang [1912–1971] did it before him), it was more concretely established by him.[102] I have always believed that Chinese culture emphasizes "inward transcendence" (*neixiang chaoyue* 內向超越) and Western culture emphasizes "external transcendence" (*waixiang chaoyue* 外向超越), and Gao's arguments have strengthened my conviction from the realms of literature and the arts.[103]

Since the teachings of Confucius, the Chinese have always paid attention to the difference between "to improve oneself" and "to impress others" in learning and study. (In chapter 14 of the *Analects*, it is reported that "the Master said, 'Men of antiquity studied to improve themselves [*weiji* 為己]; men of today study to impress others.'")[104] In his *Collected Commentaries on the Four Books* (*Sishu zhangju jizhu* 四書章句集註), Zhu Xi quoted the following from Master Cheng (Cheng Yi): "'To improve themselves' means to want to obtain learning for oneself; 'to impress others' means to want to show off knowledge to others." Most readers of later generations accept this interpretation. Of all of the Harvard Chinese scholars I met, Gao Yougong can be said to have practiced this mantra "to improve [himself]" to the highest level. The chief purpose of his research was indeed "to obtain learning for himself" and not at all "want[ing] to show off [his] knowledge to others." I was a student with him at Harvard for six years and then a colleague of his at Princeton for twelve years until he retired. I never once felt that fame or status was of any concern to him. He never showed disdain toward anyone nor considered himself to be exceptional; his demeanor was completely natural and unassuming. On December 18, 1998, when he gave his last class lecture, I wrote the following seven-syllable poem for him:

Ten years we were together in Princeton,
Every mention of Cambridge is filled with emotion.
Today the song ends and we hear elegant music,
Still a great scholar loves the clear springs.

Every word came straight from the heart, and here's why.

When I first arrived at Harvard, I did not know anyone, but after I'd known Gao Yougong for only a short time, he came to visit me at my residence. We both lived on the same street (Shepard Street in Cambridge); he lived with Dong Tonghe and Zhang Guangzhi, and they looked out for one another. He came to visit me not so much to socialize, but because he saw that I was all alone and wanted to check on me. I soon realized this from our conversation and was very touched.

Here is another example of Gao Yougong's kindness. In 1962 I was hired to teach at the University of Michigan, and the university wanted to apply for my permanent residence status. I did not know anything about this process, so I wrote a letter to Gao, asking him about it because he had just completed the process not much earlier at Stanford University. What I never expected was for him to write back with a densely packed, long five-page letter, telling me about every single relevant detail in the process of his application and making it a point to alert me to the areas that required special attention. This shows how Gao would do his utmost when it came to helping a friend. By the time I finished reading his letter, I couldn't help but tear up.

I had countless conversations with Gao Yougong; sometimes some other friends were there, but most of these conversations were just between the two of us, and they were especially frequent during my later years at Princeton. Occasionally we would discuss topics that were serious, touching on intellectual issues and the exchange of ideas, but our chats always ended happily with much laughter. Unfortunately, after he retired in 1999, these conversations came to an end because he moved to New York, which meant that we no longer had the opportunity of getting together frequently. This being the context of our last conversation makes it all the more meaningful.

On the afternoon of October 26, 2016, my wife Chen Shuping had occasion to telephone Gao regarding a small matter. In recent years, his health was not too good, so we tried not to bother him too much. We might phone him occasionally just to exchange a few words. Just before she hung up, Shuping asked him, "Do you want to talk to Ying-shih?" and he cheerfully said he did, and so I took the phone from her. To my surprise, once he started talking he went on a mile a minute just like before; he was full of energy, and his voice was very clear. Initially, I was afraid of tiring him out, but our conversation was so interesting that I could not stop. We went on talking without any concerns, frequently breaking into laughter. We talked for almost twenty minutes, and it was only due to Shuping's reminder that I took advantage of a pause to conclude our conversation.

After I hung up, I was confident that in Gao's health was improving, so it was a great shock when we received news of his death just three days later (October 29). It seemed as if Heaven had set up that long conversation as a way for me to bid him farewell. Had Gao's mental sharpness three days earlier been what is medically known as "terminal lucidity" or the "rally before death"? Was our conversation indicative of an unconscious premonition of eternal parting? I will never know, but I can confidently say that this was one of the most unforgettable, fortuitous moments of my life.

Zhang Guangzhi (K. C. Chang): Friendship and Reflections on Learning

Next, I want to talk about Zhang Guangzhi, who passed away in 2001 In May 2002 the Sanlian book company in Beijing published a memorial volume, *The Four Seas as One Family: Recollections of the Anthropologist Zhang Guangzhi* (*Sihai weijia: Zhuinian kaoguxuejia Zhang Guangzhi* 四海為家：追念考古學家張光直), and I was invited to contribute a commemorative essay. I wrote an encomium entitled "A Volcano that Did Not Erupt: Lamenting My Departed Friend Zhang Guangzhi," which offered my general understanding of him.

To avoid repeating the essay, I will focus on our friendship, supplementing my account with a few relevant details about his scholarly research.

Before I met Zhang Guangzhi, I had already heard that he was not only the most outstanding graduate of the archaeology and anthropology department at National Taiwan University but also Professor Li Ji's most prized disciple. Later I discovered that he had taken courses at National Taiwan University taught by scholars such as Dong Zuobin (1895–1963), Shi Zhangru (1902–2004), and Gao Quxun (1909–1991), who had participated in the excavation of the Yinxu ruins at the Yinshang site in Anyang in Henan [the Shang dynasty, 1600–1027 BCE, site]. Zhang Guangzhi thus had many good teachers from whom he inherited genuinely modern ways of studying Chinese archaeology. He was also a teaching assistant for Professor Ling Chunsheng (1901–1981), which helped and further develop his methods of applying anthropological concepts to archaeology.[105]

Zhang Guangzhi's career clearly demonstrates the very important role the Institute of History and Philology of the Academia Sinica played in nurturing talents in a short period after it moved to Taiwan. In fact, Gao Yougong's career also attests to this. Earlier, I mentioned Dong Tonghe and Wang Shumin, two of the elite scholars in the second generation of the Institute of History and Philology, who also taught Zhang Guangzhi. Through National Taiwan University, the Institute of History and Philology's tradition carried on the teachings of many talented scholars of literature and history, but that is another story that I will not go into here.

At Harvard in the Department of Anthropology, Zhang Guangzhi was also an outstanding graduate student; not only was his academic foundation strong but his competence and diligence were beyond imagination. During my first year, I often went to see Dong Tonghe and Gao Yougong. Zhang Guangzhi lived with them, but he would only come out of his room for a minute or two to greet me and then return to his room, shut the door, and resume his studying. At the end of the year, all his grades were exceptional.

In 1960 Professor Chen Bozhuang (P. C. Chun) visited Harvard in connection with his translation project (discussed earlier); his goal was to discuss it with the authors of the original books. The people he wanted to interview included Talcott Parsons of the sociology department, Wassily Leontief of the economics department, and Clyde Kluckholm (1905–1960) of the anthropology department. I made a few phone calls for him and arranged the interviews. Chen later told me that Professor Kluckholm had the highest praise for Zhang Guangzhi and declared him the most talented and exceptional student he had seen in the department for many years. They had mentioned Zhang in connection with the possible translation of Kluckholm's new book, *Mirror for Man: The Relation of Anthropology to Modern Life*.[106] Kluckholm believed that Zhang Guangzhi would be the ideal translator. Zhang accepted this translator's job, but unfortunately Chen Bozhuang passed away after his return to Hong Kong, and this project also came to an end, which to this day I still consider a great pity. I bring up Zhang being asked to translate Kluckholm's book to show that even in his student years, Zhang's brilliant academic future was already fully apparent.

After passing his PhD oral defense in 1958, Zhang Guangzhi finally had time to socialize with his schoolmates, and I began to get to know him. As far as ancient Chinese archaeology was concerned, I was a complete outsider. However, because my major was Chinese intellectual history, I always kept my eye on trends in the study of pre-Qin economic and historical documents, and archaeological excavations frequently turned up unexpected new material. Thus, our common ground was much greater relative to other graduate students on the Harvard campus at the time. We often discussed works such as *On the Yin Zhou Political System*

(*Yin Zhou zhidu lun* 殷周制度論) by Wang Guowei, *Theories of Yi Xia East West Origins* (*Yi Xia dong xi shuo* 夷夏東西說) by Fu Sinian, and *The Legendary Era of Ancient Chinese History* (*Zhongguo gushi de chuanshuo shidai* 中國古史的傳說時代) by Xu Xusheng, among many others.[107]

We interacted most frequently from 1960 to 1961. Zhang Guangzhi was an instructor in the Department of Anthropology that year, and his family of three lived across from my place on Harvard Street. At that time, I was living with my father and mother. We had a rather large living room, and Zhang Guangzhi, his wife Li Hui, and their son Bo Geng came over to visit with us for two or three hours almost every weekend; it felt like one big family gathering. When Zhang Guangzhi saw that many fellow students often came over to chat, he started an informal seminar that convened about once every two weeks. A dozen or so history and literature students and visiting scholars (from Taiwan and Hong Kong) would attend, and each time one would choose a topic to speak about, and this would be followed by discussions and even debates. This informal seminar continued for a while and had a positive impact on the exchange of ideas.

After Zhang Guangzhi and I became well acquainted, he constantly brought up the idea of collaboration. As early as our Harvard days, he had suggested that we collaborate on researching the formation and transformation of the "Mid-Autumn Festival" (the 15th of the eighth lunar month); he would look at it from the standpoint of cultural anthropology, and I would be responsible for the history. I was too busy with other projects at the time, and we were not able to discuss it any further. In the spring of 1973, he phoned me from Yale and asked me about the vicissitudes and cultural significance of "food" (*shi* 食) in Chinese history and again asked me if I wanted to collaborate with him. There were probably two factors that inspired this research project. One was that in the process of his research into ancient Chinese implements, he had come upon countless utensils related to food and drink, which led to his inclination to investigate the subjects of food and drink themselves. The second was that at the time many Western anthropologists had begun to have a great interest in the cultural connotations of food, and many studies were published; Zhang could not avoid being influenced by them. We discussed this for a long time on the phone, and, because I did not want to disappoint him again, I agreed to write an essay on food in the Han dynasty as a chapter in his book.[108]

Immediately following that, we had two more interactions concerning "collaboration." The first was in 1976 when a position to teach the history of China before the Qing dynasty became available at Yale, and Zhang made great efforts to get me to come over and take it. He had a very powerful argument: this was the best opportunity for us to carry out long-term collaboration. I was moved by his ardent request and said I was willing to consider the Yale history department's offer. Most unexpectedly, however, at the same time the Harvard Department of Anthropology was working to have Zhang Guangzhi come and teach at Harvard, but he did not reveal this. As a result, by this strange turn of events we changed places at Harvard and Yale (more on this later). This was how I completely changed the trajectory of my career due to my "collaboration" with him, and it had no small impact on me.

The second occasion was in 1978. Between the spring and summer of that year, the Committee on Scholarly Communication with the People's Republic of China in Washington, DC, suddenly sent a representative, Alexander P. DeAngelis, to Yale to see me. He told me that the committee had decided to organize a Han Dynasty Studies Delegation to visit the central ancient Han-dynasty archaeological sites in Mainland China to carry out a month of onsite observations. The committee had already drawn up a list of ten members, of which I was one, and they recommended that I serve as president of the delegation. This was a complete surprise to me. I had no plans to visit Mainland China, and I had no idea what sort of an organization the Committee on Scholarly Communication with the People's Republic of China was. Regardless, this assignment should not have been given to me, but then I soon received a phone call from Zhang, who told me that he was also going to be a member of the delegation and urged me not to decline the leadership appointment. I then realized that Zhang was behind the arrangement. He knew I always maintained an anti-communist position and often criticized the Chinese Communist Party, and so he probably wanted to take advantage of this opportunity to visit to make me change my mind. I knew that his motivation had nothing to do with the Chinese Communist Party's usual "united front" activities but rather was intended to dismantle the barriers to our academic "collaboration." I will discuss the Han Dynasty Studies Delegation later.

I have to point out that our differences in political thought inevitably had some impact on our academic relationship and even on our friendship. We were clear early on about where our differences lay, and we never engaged in political arguments. This was because neither of us were political activists. I really do not know why Zhang avoided arguing with me about politics. As far as that is concerned, I have always respected an individual's freedom of thought and belief and never tried to arugue with or persuade those who disagreed with me. Besides "goodness is not easy to explain, and reason is not easy to discover"—I always feel that what I personally think and believe is a value system that can be continuously modified, and it is not some absolute truth that everyone has to accept. This value orientation, however, does make it impossible for me to accept the Chinese Communist Party regime's "one-party dictatorship."[109]

Zhang's value orientation was clearly different from mine. From his *Stories of a Sweet Potato Man* (*Fanshuren de gushi* 蕃薯人的故事), we can see that from the time he was a teenager he was already inclined to believe in the ideals of communism.[110] He never joined the party and never accepted the party ideology, and as far as I know, he believed that the Chinese Communist Party's "Anti-Rightist Campaign," "Cultural Revolution," and suppression of the "June Fourth" 1989 Democracy Movement were all wrong. Nevertheless, he never abandoned the ideals from his youth because of these political campaigns and events. He seemed to believe that all man-made "mistakes" could be corrected. If we use Mao Zedong's statement that "the road is winding, but the future is bright" to describe his basic attitude, we would not be far off.[111] I have to add one more point here, and that is that his ideals for society were intimately tied up with his feelings of patriotism. A fellow Chinese archaeologist summarized the life of Zhang Guangzhi in a single truly accurate sentence: "With his mind on our motherland, he worked diligently all of his life."[112]

For many years, Zhang and I kept our opinions to ourselves and did not argue, so things were peaceful between us. From 1994 to 1996, however, when he became the vice president of the Academia Sinica, problems arose. I remember that at the time the president of Academia Sinica, Li Yuanzhe (1936 –), phoned me in America to tell me that he was preparing to appoint Zhang Guangzhi as vice president and make him responsible for all matters related to the humanities.[113] He asked me my opinion. Without hesitation, I replied that "he is the best choice, and I approve one hundred percent." This was the truth and not just polite talk. In two years as vice president, Zhang spared no effort in promoting integrated research in the Division of Social Sciences and Humanities and its internationalization. To achieve these goals, he proposed comprehensive plans for reforming every humanities research institute. Such a large-scale reform necessarily met with various forms of resistance; those two years were extremely difficult, and he was unable to achieve the desired results. What disheartened him most was his failed attempt to separate the archaeology section from the Institute of History and Philology and make it an independent Institute of Archaeology.

In principle I supported Zhang's plans to reform, but I did not participate in them because I was in the United States and busy writing. I only learned about the various setbacks he suffered in their aftermath, but from the firsthand reports I heard, I also discovered that Zhang regarded me as an obstacle to his efforts. This was not only tremendously shocking to me but also very difficult to accept emotionally.

One or two years after Zhang Guangzhi stepped down from his position, the soon-to-be Director of Planning of the Literature and Philosophy Institute, Dai Lianzhang, came to America and visited me at my home. As soon as we met, he told me that he had come to "confess his crime" and I was completely in the dark about what he meant.[114] It turned out that in order to reorganize the Chinese Literature and Philosophy Institute, Zhang Guangzhi wanted to bring in a Taiwan scholar who was supported by the Chinese Communist Party's United Front Work Department to be one of the candidates for the position of director of the Institute. Appointment by the Academia Sinica, however, required that the applicant satisfy two prerequisites: appraisal by specialists in the applicant's field and approval by the Academia Sinica's consultative committee. I was a member of this consultative committee, and my specialty was very close to that of the applicant's. Zhang believed that my political leanings did not support his plan, and so he urgently urged Professor Dai not to allow me to become involved in the selection process. This appointment did not materialize because the candidate was not approved by the evaluating specialists, but I knew nothing about the process from beginning to end. Professor Dai was regretful, and now that this was in the past and the situation had changed, he decided to tell me the whole story. In addition to his oral recounting of the event, he brought the complete dossier of documentation for me to look over.

When I heard about this case, I could not help feeling disturbed. I had always thought that there was mutual trust between Zhang Guangzhi and me, such that even when we had disagreements it was not difficult to clarify them face-to-face. Now that I discovered that to put his plan into operation, Zhang had proceeded in secret and excluded me, I felt that our friendship of several decades had been destroyed in one moment. Not much later, however, I realized that my reaction was somewhat extreme. From its inception, Zhang's overall plan had one important aspect, which was to link up with research trends in the humanities and social science on the mainland and effectively combine them with Taiwan's. The most obvious example of this mission was Zhang's plan to set up an independent Institute of Archaeology, for which his list of members now reached a hundred. At that time, he had just received permission from the Chinese State Administration of Cultural Heritage to carry out excavations with the Beijing Institute of Archaeology at Shangqiu City in Henan Province. Undoubtedly, his idea was that the chief mission of his new Institute of Archaeology was to conduct excavations in Mainland China because Taiwan was unable to accommodate such a large number of professional archaeologists. Later, the leadership of the Institute of History and Philology actually used this as their official reason for rejecting his proposal for a separate Institute of Archaeology.

After the events surrounding the Han Dynasty Studies Delegation, Zhang Guangzhi knew that my position about the Chinese Communist Party was not going to change, and so he was somewhat on his guard against me from then on; although this was regrettable considering our friendship, it was nevertheless understandable. He did not understand me well, however, because what I could not approve of was the Chinese Communist Party's totalitarian political regime, not the Mainland Chinese academic circles, let alone individual scholars. In fact, quite a few Mainland Chinese archaeologists were our mutual friends, and I expended much effort to raise the funds to help underwrite the enormous expenditure of the Shangqiu excavations.[115] Zhang truly did not understand me at all, but when I recall his lifetime of contributions to Chinese archaeology, especially his ceaseless struggles when his health was extremely bad, it all outweighs this incident. I have long since stopped feeling bothered about it.

In the final analysis, our differences and disagreements arose from Zhang Guangzhi having his "mind on his motherland." This was not only a major driving force for his archaeological research but also what led to the events that he regretted most in his academic career. I feel that I need to give a clear explanation of this issue, but I can provide only a synoptic outline.

First let us look at the description of Zhang Guangzhi having his "mind on his motherland." In his essay "Sacrificing to Guangzhi in the Autumn Wind and Rain" ("Sanqiu fengyu ji Guangzhi" 三秋風雨祭光直), Shi Xingbang [a noted archaeologist and Chinese Communist Party member] wrote the following description:

> Guangzhi's feelings for his motherland were extremely strong. … I hear that he once told Professor Xia Nai [1910–1985] that he wanted to return to the mainland to work in archaeology, and I think he was genuinely sincere.[116] … I saw that he was very friendly and completely at ease with younger mainland scholars; he had the aspiration to assimilate himself into this swiftly rising academic group. One time in a discussion in the conference room of the Beijing Institute of Archaeology when everyone was calling each other comrade (*tongzhi* 同志) and someone said, "Comrade so-and-so [says] such-and-such," he also said "I agree with Comrade Huang Zhanyue's [1926–2019] opinion!"[117] … This was certainly a true expression of his feelings. Guangzhi had already unconsciously integrated himself into this academic community.[118]

I think that this passage is written in an extremely cordial manner, and it vividly presents Zhang Guangzhi's "feelings for his motherland." As far as I know Guangzhi revealed this attitude as soon as he began to associate with mainland archaeologists.

On November 27, 1973, Guangzhi wrote a letter to Guo Moruo in very neat Chinese calligraphy in which he expressed the following wish: "I would very much wish to have the opportunity at the soonest possible time to return to our country (*fanguo* 返國) to learn from the archaeological colleagues in our country." He further explained, "A month ago the American Academy of Sciences invited me to participate in their archaeology and fine arts delegation that is currently visiting our country. The main reason that I did not participate is because I want to return [to our country] (*huiqu* 回去) as an individual. (This letter is included in the 2002 book *Four Seas are One Family*.) He refused to join an American delegation but "wanted to return [to our country] as an individual." This very clearly indicates that he hoped that "*guonei* 國內, those inside our country/China" would accept that he was one of them living in "*guowai* 國外, outside of our country/China."[119] At the same time he sent a copy of this letter to Xia Nai together with a personal letter to him. The two letters, however, sank like stones thrown into the ocean and received no reply. In the end, Zhang joined the American anthropology delegation and finally returned to China for the first time in May 1975. As soon as he arrived with the delegation in Beijing, he immediately requested a one-on-one personal meeting with Xia Nai.

The *Diary of Xia Nai* (*Xia Nai riji* 夏鼐日記) records that on May 23, 1975, Zhang Guangzhi wrote an archaeological report, and when the meeting ended at five o'clock: "I agreed to his request and stayed behind to talk with him until six o'clock when I returned to the Institute." I believe Zhang wanted to explain face-to-face why he had sent that letter to Guo Moruo. After that, almost every time he went to the mainland, he would try to have a one-on-one talk with Xia Nai. When we read the *Diary of Xia Nai*, we know why, and there is no need to say any more here. Zhang Guangzhi later said this publicly: "He raised with Xia Nai the idea of his working at the Beijing Institute of Archaeology, but Professor Xia was noncommittal about it."[120] He undoubtedly made this request during his talks with Xia Nai. The main reason he was willing to leave the United States and go to Beijing to work at the Institute of Archaeology was, of course, to fulfill his lifetime dream of carrying out archaeological excavations in China. Xia Nai being "noncommittal" was his way of rejecting of Zhang's application to enter the Beijing Institute of Archaeology.

Xia Nai understood Zhang Guangzhi's accomplishments in the fields of archaeology and anthropology far better than any of the other Chinese archaeologists in the institute. As early as August and September 1963, he spent ten days carefully reading Zhang's newly published *The Archaeology of Ancient China*.[121] The September 12, 1963, entry in the *Diary of Xia*

Nai notes that "this book employs the concepts of cultural anthropology to introduce the archaeology of ancient China; most of it concerns developments from after liberation [that is 1949] and it can well be viewed as a unique expression of opinion, but some of its arguments are too hurried." Subsequent entries in the *Diary of Xia Nai* record that he read Guangzhi's major Chinese and English works in succession. In a normal academic environment (whether inside or outside of China), Professor Xia, being the director of the Beijing Institute of Archaeology, would certainly try to recruit such an outstanding, talented archaeologist like Zhang lest he lose him to other organizations. What possible reason could there be for closing the door on him? Xia Nai was not moved by Zhang's "feelings for his motherland," and the door to the Institute of Archaeology remained closed to him.

Zhang Guangzhi then settled for the next best thing and transferred his hopes to a Sino-American archaeological cooperation. Immediately after the Chinese Communist Party and the United States government officially established diplomatic relations on January 1, 1979, he put forth a plan for such an arrangement. In a January 22, 1979, entry, the *Diary of Xia Nai* records, "Suggestions regarding the proposal for cooperation sent by Professor Guangzhi." The next day's entry reads, "In the morning, I went to the Ministry Office of Foreign Affairs to confer with them regarding ... Zhang Guangzhi's proposed archaeological cooperation, and discussed it with Bureau Chief Tang Kai ..." This proposal was discussed among the leaders of the Chinese Academy of Social Sciences for a month, and then on February 20, the *Diary of Xia Nai* has the following extremely important statement:

> I went to the Ministry and discussed the matter of Sino-American archaeological cooperation with Liu Yangjiao and Bao Zhenggu. I proposed that we tactfully decline the offer.

Zhang's plan for cooperation was also thwarted by Xia Nai, but it was what happened to his plan for cooperation with Sichuan University that hurt him the most. After Zhang had completely lost hope in the

Beijing Institute of Archaeology, he did not give up and shifted his attention to trying to find possibilities for cooperation with various universities in different regions. In the early 1980s, he received support from Sichuan University where Professor Tong Enzheng (1935–1997) was to cooperate with him in carrying out archaeological investigations in the upper reaches of the Yangzi River.[122] Not only did both parties sign an agreement for this project, but the Ministry of Education also officially approved it. Universities belonged to the Ministry of Education system and were not controlled by the Chinese Academy of Social Sciences. When Xia Nai got wind of this agreement, however, he immediately phoned the Minister of Education personally and used all his influence in successfully getting the agreement thrown out.[123]

Xia Nai was the most prominent expert in the mainland Chinese archaeological world, but his position was not that of an individual's but rather a collective one—his actions embodied the will of the Chinese Communist Party government. In relation to Zhang Guangzhi's heartfelt lifetime desire to return as an individual to "*guonei*, his country of China" to carry out archaeological excavations, we cannot help remembering some often-encountered lines from Ming- and Qing-dynasty fiction: "I originally wanted to face the bright moon, but the bright moon, alas, shone on the ditch." Eventually the times and circumstances changed, and in 1994 Zhang finally obtained an opportunity to collaborate with the Beijing Institute of Archaeology in the Shangqiu Henan excavations, but time was not on his side and his health no longer permitted him to carry out any field work. Without a doubt, this was what he most regretted in his entire life.

The Distinctive Features of the New Period

The experiences of Gao Yougong and Zhang Guangzhi that I have just related represent only a brief synopsis of events, but they reveal some unique characteristics of this new period, which I will summarize next.

The first noteworthy point is that after 1949 the modern Chinese humanistic tradition was no longer able to thrive on the mainland, but it moved to Taiwan; although it was not as widespread there, it still achieved a high level of success. That was why National Taiwan University was able in four or five years to cultivate students like Gao Yougong and Zhang Guangzhi who immediately performed exceptionally well when they entered Harvard.

The greatest difference between the Chinese overseas students at Harvard during the new period and the ones from the earlier period was that after the former graduated, most of them remained and worked in the United States, whereas the earlier overseas students returned to China immediately after graduation. This difference was brought about primarily by general circumstances and cannot be completely attributed to the individual choices of these students. To have a clearer understanding of what I mean by general circumstances, we need to look at Chinese and American conditions during that time. On the Chinese side, the entire mainland had already become a closed-off world. The other choices of Chinese societies available to the Chinese overseas students were Taiwan, Hong Kong, and Southeast Asia, where there were very few high-level research and teaching institutions. It was not until after the 1970s and 1980s, because of the economic takeoff in these countries, that this situation began to change. On this account, for those students who went back to China after graduation, even if they had no problem finding a professional position, they would find it very difficult to keep abreast of new research developments.

The situation in the United States was the complete opposite. Due to the Cold War and especially the Korean War, from the 1950s on, an intense desire to understand China emerged at all levels of the American government and society. This was reflected in the education and scholarship in the United States; there was a significant rise and spread of research on China in many American universities, among which Harvard University was the leading pioneer. With this new trend, the development of Chinese history and culture (including, ancient, medieval, recent, and modern) was seen as particularly important and Chinese humanities scholars studying in America were given a hitherto unprecedented scope for their work.

When this new period began, the Chinese overseas students in the humanities, whether from Taiwan or Hong Kong, did not seem to have had ideas of remaining in the United States after graduation. In fact, they did not quite understand the American situation at the time, and it was hard for them to conceive that they could develop their own specialties, such as Chinese history and literature, in the United States. As for me personally, I did not even know about Professor Yang Liansheng teaching premodern Chinese history at Harvard, let alone this big picture. At that time, my only thought was to return immediately to New Asia College to teach after completing my advanced studies at Harvard. Zhang Guangzhi had similar thoughts. From his letters to Li Ji, we can see that up till 1957 he "resolved to return to Taiwan after finishing his degree."[124] If my memory is not mistaken, it was only three to four years later that we finally became aware of the possibility of remaining in the United States to carry on our research.

That Chinese overseas humanities students were inclined to remain and work in the United States mostly because of the research conditions. The United States not only offered freedom of thought and freedom of expression but also could provide the highest level of research resources. At that time, the Chinese Communist Party was in the process of systematically imposing their Marxists-Leninist ideology onto their grand narrative of Chinese history. They were also compiling and printing on a large scale various resource materials from ancient to modern Chinese history to accord with their views. Specialist scholars studying Chinese literature, history, and philosophy outside of Mainland China naturally could not simply ignore this and do nothing. However, those materials used by scholars in China could not be imported into Taiwan. Research scholars were therefore unable to read those documents, and even if they could, they still could not discuss them openly. (According to my understanding, due to funding problems, New Asia College library did not systematically collect mainland source materials until after it joined the Chinese University of Hong Kong.)

In stark contrast, the East Asian libraries of various American universities started to collect mainland publications right from the beginning, and their collections were generally comprehensive. At the same time in American classrooms and publications and at scholarly conferences, there were constant examinations and criticisms of mainland Chinese research materials as well as debates that allowed researchers to understand the overall dynamics of the field. This was the main reason that many Chinese humanities scholars chose to remain in the United States in the 1980s and 1990s. Zhang Guangzhi is a good example. His specialty was Chinese archaeology, and virtually all his research materials came from archaeological excavations held on the Chinese mainland after 1949. If he had stuck with his original idea of returning to Taiwan after completing his degree, his entire scholarly life would have taken a totally different path.

The number of Chinese overseas students who remained in the United States continued to grow steadily, and the nature of their scholarly contributions in the new period was very different from that of the scholars the previous two periods. They had no opportunity to make a direct impact on the Chinese academic world, but after they graduated, they made important contributions to American (and Western) China Studies or Sinology. Through publishing in English and teaching, they expanded and deepened Westerners' understanding of China. Before this new period, only a handful of Chinese humanities scholars participated directly in the development of Sinology in the United States, but after the 1960s, there were many more Chinese participants, who spread into every field of study. Due to their participation, these scholars unwittingly gave a completely new face to American China studies because they not only mastered large amounts of original resource materials but also introduced their own original ideas and different visions to the field.

The achievements of Gao Yougong and Zhang Guangzhi discussed earlier are clear evidence of this trend. Gao Yougong elucidated thoroughly the distinct characteristics of the Chinese literary tradition, and, while he was at Princeton, mentored many outstanding students who went on to teach Chinese literature at important American universities like the University of Michigan, Yale, and Harvard. Zhang Guangzhi is an even more special case. The study of Chinese archaeology began in the United States because of his efforts, and the archaeologists whom he trained fanned out even more widely across the world.[125]

These achievements that were initiated in the new period by Chinese scholars in America eventually went on to inspire a new orientation in humanities research in various regions of China because these US-based Chinese scholars' research methods and their style of writing gradually came to serve as exemplary models. This can be clearly seen in the specialist journals and monographs on Chinese literature, history, and philosophy published in Taiwan and Hong Kong since the 1970s and 1980s. After Mainland China opened up, mainland Chinese scholars in various fields of the humanities anxiously sought the exchange of ideas with the West, and Chinese scholars in America and their writings very logically served as points of introduction and connection. The full story of the influence of the Chinese overseas scholars of the new period on their native China is extremely complex, and only specific research could explain it clearly, and so I'll end my discussion of the topic here.

Harvard Only Part of a General Trend

I should note here that the Chinese humanities scholars' research in the new period in America I just discussed is centered on Harvard University, but this is in no way due to any desire to brag about Harvard. The focus is on Harvard because I'm writing about past events that I personally witnessed or heard about at the time. In fact, at that time the presence of

Chinese humanities scholars was a common trend in first-rate American universities all over the United States. Harvard is simply one example of this major trend. There are many Chinese humanities scholars from other American universities throughout the country who have made outstanding contributions to China Studies or Sinology. Obviously, I am not able to write about them in my personal memoir. I just want to clarify this point lest readers misunderstand my intentions.

NOTES

1. Yü Ying-shih note: Qian Mu, "Shiyou zayi" [Random recollections of friends and teachers], in Qian Binsi xiansheng *Quanji* [Complete works of Mr. Qian Binsi], vol. 51, pp. 320–321.
2. Talcott Parsons, *The Social System* (Glencoe, IL: Free Press, 1951).
3. Yü Ying-shih note: See *Hu Shi quanji*, vol. 25 (Hefei: Anhui jiaoyu, 2003), 558. For Professor Chen's life and thought, see his *Sa-nian cungao* [Thirty years of collected manuscripts], with a preface by Hu Shi (Hong Kong: Dongnan yinwu, 1959).
4. Fang Zhaoying was a well-respected historian of the Ming and Qing dynasties. He and his wife, Du Lianzhe, worked in the libraries of Chinese, American, and Australian universities and helped edit many works on the Ming and Qing dynasties, including the *Dictionary of Ming Biography, 1368–1644* (New York: Columbia University Press, 1976). *Water Margin* is one of the most famous Ming-dynasty novels; it relates the exploits of Song Jiang and his Shandong bandits (108 "heroes"). See Nienhauser, William H., *The Indiana Companion to Traditional Chinese Literature* (Taipei: SMC Publishing, 2003), 712–716.
5. John Campbell Pelzel was a major in the United States Marine Corps during World War II; he served as chief of the Public Opinion and Sociological Research Division under General Douglas MacArthur during the reconstruction of Japan. Pelzel later received his doctorate from Harvard; his thesis was entitled "Social Stratification in Japanese Urban Economic Life," which he published along with other works on Japan and China.
6. Francis Woodman Cleaves founded Sino-Mongolian studies in the United States and translated *The Secret History of the Mongols* (Cambridge, MA: Harvard University Press, 1982).
7. Morton White was a philosopher and intellectual history scholar at Harvard and the Institute of Advanced Studies at Princeton. He published many books including *A Philosophy of Culture: The Scope of Holistic Pragmatism* (Princeton, NJ: Princeton University Press, 2002).
8. Chen Yuan was a major figure in modern Chinese historiography that was closely associated with the Qing-dynasty school of philology. He was an expert in Yuan-dynasty history and religion. His letter to Hu Shi expressing the Chinese Communist Party view on the "liberation" of Beiping can be read at https:// www.douban.com/group/topic/88702751/.

9. Wang Hao received his Harvard PhD in 1948. In the 1950s he studied in Zurich and then taught at Oxford University, Harvard University, and Rockefeller University. He authored many books and made important contributions to the study of computers as well as to the study of the philosophy of mathematics by Ludwig Wittgenstein and Kurt Gödel.

10. Li Fanggui was a Chinese linguist known for his reconstructions of Tai languages (including that of the Zhuang people) and revision of Bernhard Karlgren's reconstructions of ancient Chinese.

11. Dong Tonghe, *Shanggu yinyunbiao gao* [Table of ancient Chinese phonetics (draft)] (Taipei: Zhongyang yanjiuyuan lishi yuyan yanjiu suo,1944).

12. See Dong Tonghe, *Zhongguo yuyinshi* [Chinese historical phonetics] (Taipei: Zhonghua wenhua chuban shiye weiyuan hui, 1958).

13. Yü Ying-shih note: See my essay "Wo zouguo de lu" [Roads I have travelled], in Chen Zhi, *Yü Ying-shih fangtan Lu* [Record of an interview with Yü Ying-shih] (Beijing: Zhonghua shuju, 2012), 1–11.

14. Friedrich A. Hayek's *The Road to Serfdom* (Chicago: Chicago University Press, 1944) was, of course, enormously influential in arguing for individual freedom and classical liberalism versus the Soviet communist system. Yang Zhu (c. 440–360 BCE) was a Chinese philosopher who advocated egoism but was taken here by Xing Muhuan to stand for individualism.

15. Yü Zong Xian's "First Preface," *Selected Poems by Academician Xing Muhuan*, 7.

16. James T. C. Liu (Liu Zijian) was a leading scholar of Song-dynasty history who taught for over twenty years at Princeton University and published many important works on the Song dynasty.

17. The first quote is from the *Lunyu* VII.2, Lau, *Analects*, 86. The second quote is from *Mengzi* 7A.20 in which Mencius said that "a gentleman delights in three things" and teaching the best students in the world was the "second delight." See Lau, *Mencius*, 185; we have changed his translation to fit the context here.

18. *Xue yi zhi yong* 學以致用, "to study something (to perfection) for practical application" is a combined allusion to ideas of Confucius and the *Book of Changes* (*Yijing* 易經). *Xueyi* is from *Lunyu* (Analects) 19.7, and *zhiyong* is from the "Commentary, One" (*Xici* 繫辭) of the *Yijing*.

19. Zhou Hongjing was a mathematician and educator. As secretary-general of the Academia Sinica, he helped plan the academy's new location in Nangang in Taipei.

20. The quoted passage is from the *Book of Rites* (*Liji*), "Random Records (*Zaji*) Two #125". We have modified James Legge's translation from the Chinese Text Project, (CTP), https://ctext.org/liji/za-ji-ii.

21. Wassily Wassilyevich Leontief won the Nobel Prize in 1973 for his work on input-output analysis. Paul Anthony Samuelson was Leontief's student. He was sometimes called "the father of modern economics" and received the Nobel Prize in 1970 for his scientific analysis of economic theory. His economics textbooks were the foundation of academic study in the United States for many years.

22. Cambridge means Harvard University, and Pei Mountain refers to the town of Belmont in the western suburb of Boston where Professor Yü Ying-shih lived.

23. East Forest means New Asia College in the Chinese University of Hong Kong, and the South Sea Shore refers to Hong Kong.

24. The iris and orchid symbolize people of integrity.

25. Mo Gang and Mo Chuan refer to the hills and the river along the winding road leading up to the Han Garden, which was the presidential residence of the Chinese University of Hong Kong where Professor Yü resided then.

26. Zhang Jinghu was a celebrated geographer and climatologist. He was a research associate at Harvard from 1956 to 1958 and an editor of *National Geographic*.

27. A noted historian and the founder of the Chinese Cultural University, Zhang Qiyun (Chang Ch'i-yun) edited many works on dynastic histories and was chief editor of the *Zhongwen Da Cidian*.

28. See Yang Liansheng, *Dong Han de haozu* [Great families of the Eastern Han] (Beiping: Qinghua daxue, 1936; Beijing: Shangwu yinshuguan, 2011). "Dong Han zhengquan zhi jianli yu shizu daxing zhi guanxi" [The establishment of the Eastern Han regime and its relations with the great land-owning families] is in Yü Ying-shih, *Zhongguo zhishi jieceng shulun: gudai pian* [On ancient Chinese intellectuals: ancient volume] (Taipei: Lianjing, 1980), 109–203; it includes an afterword on Hans Bielenstein's theory of Wang Mang's fall.

29. Hans Bielenstein, *The Restoration of the Han Dynasty* (Stockholm, 1953); and Kiyoyoshi Utsunomiya, *Kandai shakai keizaishi kenkyû* 漢代社會經濟史研究 [Research on Han dynasty society and economics] (Tokyo: Kôbundô, 1955).

30. Yü Ying-shih note: Xiao Gongquan, *Wenxue jianwang lu* [Record of life-long study and rectification of the past] (Taipei: Zhuanji wenxue, 1972), 64.

31. Owen Lattimore was a well-known scholar of China and Central Asia. He was an advisor to Chiang Kai-shek during the war and later taught at several universities. The most popular of his many books was perhaps *The Inner Asian Frontiers of China* (New York: American Geographical Society, 1940).

32. Xiao Gongquan, *Wenxue jianwang lu*, 223. Quoted passage is from Wang Yangming, *Wang Yangming ji* 王陽明集 [Collected works of Wang Yangming] (Shanghai: Shanghai guji, 1992) *juan* 8, *wenlu* 5.7; https://ctext.org/wiki.pl?if=gb&chapter=95631.

33. Yü Ying-shih note: For a systematic discussion of Professor Yang Lian-sheng, see my essay, "Zhongguo wenhua de haiwai meijie" [Overseas intermediaries of Chinese culture], in *You ji feng chui shui shang lin* [Still remembering the wind roiling the waves upon the water] (Taipei: San-min shuju, 1991), 169–198.

34. During his years at Harvard, Talcott Parsons could have been considered the dean of American sociology. His most influential work is *Structure of Social Action* (Glencoe, IL: Free Press, [1937] 1949; second ed. 1967). The historian Crane Brinton's best-known work is *The Anatomy of Revolution* (New York: W.W. Norton & Company, 1938). Myron P. Gilmore was a historian of Europe and the Renaissance and the Gurney Professor of History and Political Science at Harvard. He is best known for his books *World of Humanism, 1453–1517* (New York: Harper, 1952) and *Humanists and Jurists: Six Studies in the Renaissance* (Cambridge, MA: Belknap Press of Harvard University Press, 1963).

35. *Xiangtu Zhongguo* [*From the soil*] (Shanghai: Guancha, 1948. Fei Xiao-tong, *From the Soil: The Foundations of Chinese Society: A Translation of Fei Xiaotong's Xiangtu Zhongguo*, translated by Gary G. Hamilton and Wang Zheng (Berkeley: University of California Press, 1992). Fei Xiao-tong and Chang Chih-I (Zhang Zhiyi), *Earthbound China: A Study of Rural Economy in Yunnan* (Chicago: University of Chicago Press, 1945).

36. Jin Yaoji (Ambrose King Yeo-chi) is a well-known Hong Kong professor of sociology who was president of New Asia College (1977–1985) and vice chancellor of the Chinese University of Hong Kong (2002–2004).

37. Yü Ying-shih note: On this issue, see Crane Brinton, *Ideas and Men: The Story of Western Thought* (New York: Prentice-Hall, 1950), 9.

38. Liu Xianting, *Guangyang Zaiji* [Guangyang miscellany] (Shanghai: Shangwu, 1941), *juan* 2.152 in the Chinese Text Project, https://ctext.org/wiki.pl?if=gb&chapter=246590. The traditional Chinese Six Classics are the *Book of Songs* (*Shijing*), *Book of Documents* or *Book of History* (*Shangshu*), *Book of Rites* (*Liji*), *Classic of Music* (*Yuejing*), *Book of Changes* (*Yijing*), and the *Spring and Autumn Annals* (*Chunqiu*).

39. Zhang Xuecheng was an influential Qing-dynasty historian and philosopher of history. Dai Zhen was an influential Qing-dynasty philologist and philosopher who was prominent in the movement of evidential research. For the Zhang Xuecheng quote, see "Yuan Dao san pian," in *Wenshi tongyi* (Beijing: Zhonghua shuju, 1956). For the Dai Zhen quote, see Dai Zhen, *Xuyan* in Dai Zhen, *Mengzi ziyi shuzheng*, ed. by He Wenguang (Beijing: Zhonghua, 1961). For more on these two scholars, interested readers could consult Ying-shih Yü, "Zhang Xuecheng Versus Dai Zhen: A Study in Intellectual Challenge and Response in Eighteenth-Century China," in his *Chinese History and Culture*, Vol. 2: *Seventeenth Through Twentieth Century*, 85–112.

40. Crane Brinton, *English Political Thought in the Nineteenth Century* (London: E. Benn, 1933).

41. Yü Ying-shih note: "exasperatingly casual lectures" is from Arthur M. Schlesinger, Jr., *A Life in the Twentieth Century, Innocent Beginnings, 1917–1950* (Boston and New York: Houghton Mifflin, 2000), 172.

42. Arthur O. Lovejoy, *The Great Chain of Being* (Cambridge, MA: Harvard University Press, 1936).

43. Wang Dezhao, *Studies in the Qing Dynasty Examination System* (Hong Kong: Chinese University of Hong Kong Press, 1984).

44. Yü Ying-shih note: Qian Mu, *Sushulou yu shen* [Further notes from sushu studio] in *Qian Binsi xiangsheng Quanji* [Complete works of Mr. Qian Binsi], vol. 53, 403–404.

45. Yü Ying-shih note: Ibid., 206–207.

46. John K. Fairbank, *Trade and Diplomacy on the China Coast: The Opening of the Treaty Ports, 1842–1854*, 2 vols. (Harvard University Press, 1953).

47. The quotation is based on the *Book of Songs* (*Shijing*) poem "When a Crane Cries." The end of the first stanza is "There are other hills whose stones / Are good for grinding tools" and the end of the second stanza is "There are other hills whose stones / Are good for working jade." Arthur Waley, *Book of Songs* (New York: Grove Press, 1960), Mao shi standard edition poem number 184, Waley's poem number 281, p. 314.

48. Ronald Syme, *The Roman Revolution* (New York: Oxford University Press, 1939).

49. Arnaldo Dante Momigliano was a prolific Jewish-Italian historian who had to leave Italy in 1938. He is best known for his work on historiography as well as for studies of Greece, Rome, paganism, and Christianity.

50. Yü Ying-shih, *Trade and Expansion in Han China, A Study in the Structure of Sino-Barbarian Economic Relations* (Berkeley, CA: University of California Press, 1967).

51. Morton White, *Foundations of Historical Knowledge* (New York, Harper & Row, 1965). Interested readers can learn more about this book in White's autobiography, *A Philosopher's Story* (University Park: Pennsylvania State University Press, 1999), 231–232; 244–247.

52. R. G. Collingwood, *The Idea of History* (Oxford: Clarendon Press, 1946).

53. Yü Ying-shih note: For more on Nivison's research on Zhang Xuecheng at Harvard and its association with analytic philosophy, see my preface to the Chinese translation of his *The Life and Thought of Chang Hsüeh-ch'eng, 1738–1801* (Stanford, CA: Stanford University Press, 1966), which is included in my *Huiyou ji* [Collection of essays on friendship through writing] vol. 1 (Taipei: Sanmin shuju, 2010), 168–176.

54. Yü Ying-shih note: "Zhang Xuecheng yu Kelingwu de lishi sixiang" [The historical thought of Zhang Xuecheng and Collingwood] is in *Lun Dai Zhen yu Zhang Xuecheng* [On Dai Zhen and Zhang Xuecheng] (Hong Kong: Longmen, 1976).

55. Willard Peterson is Professor Emeritus of East Asian Studies and History at Princeton. His specialty is Chinese intellectual history of the Ming-Qing period and in early Chinese thought. He is the author of *Bitter Gourd: Fang I-chih and the Impetus for Intellectual Change* (New Haven, CT: Yale University Press, 1979). Benjamin Elman is Professor Emeritus of East Asian Studies and History at Princeton. His specialty is Chinese intellectual history from 1000 to 1900. His publications include *On Their Own Terms: Science in China, 1550–1900* (Cambridge, MA: Harvard University Press, 2006/Beijing: People's University Press, 2016) and *A Cultural History of Modern Science in Late Imperial China* (Cambridge, MA: Harvard University Press, 2009).

56. The Chinese count a person's age as one at birth and add one at Chinese New Year. Thus, a person who is N numbers of Chinese *sui* 歲 (years) will be regarded as N+1 numbers of years old.

57. See Herman J. Saasthamp, Jr., ed., *Rorty & Pragmatism: The Philosopher Responds to His Critics* (Nashville: Vanderbilt University Press, 1995), 214–215.

58. "Evidential studies" or "evidential investigation" is a form of meticulous philological research that flourished during the Qing dynasty whose purpose was to uncover the original meaning of the Chinese classics. See Benjamin Elman, *From Philosophy to Philology: Intellectual and Social Aspects of Change in Late Imperial China* (Cambridge, MA: Council on East Asian Studies, Harvard University, 1984).

59. According to Endymion Wilkinson, *Chinese History: A Manual, Revised and Enlarged* (Cambridge, MA: Harvard University Asia Center, 2000), 828, the *Chouban yiwu shimo*, the management of barbarian affairs from A to Z, (Gongwu bowuyuan, eds., 260 *juan*, 1929–1930) is a facsimile of three collections of foreign affairs documents compiled during the late Qing and covering the years 1863–1874.

60. Yü Ying-shih note: At that time in American academic circles, the study of "premodern China" was known as "Sinology" (*Hanxue* 漢學), and the study of China after the middle of the nineteenth century was known as "Chinese Studies" (*Zhongguo yanjiu* 中國研究).

61. Feng Guifeng was a supporter of the Self-Strengthening Movement and the major leader of Qing statecraft during the Tongzhi Restoration of 1862–1874. For more on Feng and Qing statecraft, see "Sun Yat-sen's Doctrine and Traditional Chinese Culture" in Yü Ying-shih, *Chinese History and Culture*, vol. 2: *Seventeenth Through Twentieth Century*, 152–177.

62. Liu Guangjing (Kwang-Ching Liu) was an economic historian who received his doctorate in 1956 from Harvard University, where he was a student of John King Fairbank. He later became an academician at the Academia Sinica.

63. Yang Liansheng, *Studies in Chinese Institutional History* (Cambridge, MA: Harvard University Press, 1961).

64. Yang Liansheng, *Topics in Chinese History* (Cambridge, MA: Harvard University Press 1950).

65. Edwin O. Reischauer was born in Tokyo to missionary parents and was a leading American scholar of Japanese history and culture. He was the American Ambassador to Japan from 1961 to 1966. In 1973 he founded Harvard's Japan Institute, now the Edwin O. Reischauer Institute of Japanese Studies.

66. Yan Gengwang, an early student of Qian Mu's, was a prolific scholar of Chinese history and geography, especially the Han and Tang dynasties.

67. Myron P. Gilmore, *The World of Humanism, 1453–1517* (New York: Harper, 1952).
68. Yü Ying-shih, *Lishi yu sixiang* 歷史與思想 [History and thought] (Taipei: Lianjing, 1976).
69. Felix Gilbert was a German-born Jewish American historian. He was a fellow at the Institute for Advanced Studies from 1962 to 1975. According to his obituary in the *New York Times*, (February16, 1991), "Dr. Gilbert wrote, edited or coedited more than a dozen scholarly books [... and] the American Historical Association honored Professor Gilbert in 1985 with its first award for scholarly distinction." The book referred to here is *History: Politics or Culture? Reflections on Ranke and Burckhardt* (Princeton, NJ: Princeton University Press, 1990).
70. In Erikson's book, *Young Man Luther: A Study in Psychoanalysis and History* (New York: Norton, 1958), he described Luther's rebellion in terms of psychoanalysis.
71. Yü Ying-shih note: The essay on *fides* and *eruditio* in Erasmus was later included in Myron P. Gilmore, *Humanists and Jurists, Six Studies in the Renaissance* (Harvard University Press, 1963), 87–114.
72. Yü Ying-shih, *Han-Jin zhiji shi zhi xin zijue yu xin sichao* [The scholars' new awareness and new thought tides between the Han and Jin dynasties] (Hong Kong: Xinya shuyuan, 1959). This essay is also in *Zhongguo zhishi jieceng shilun, gudai pian* [On ancient Chinese intellectuals: ancient volume] (Taipei: Lianjing, 1980), 205–327.
73. Yü Ying-shih note: Professor Yang's *Diary*, November 8, 1959, records that "part of this work could also be included in dissertation." "This work" refers to my PhD dissertation.
74. Wang Ming, *Taipingjing hexiao* 太平經合校 [Annotations on the scripture of great peace] (Shanghai, Beijing: Zhonghua shuju, 1960).
75. Benjamin Schwartz, *The World of Thought in Ancient China* (Cambridge, MA: Belknap Press of Harvard University Press, 1985).
76. Yü Ying-shih note: See Joseph Needham, *Science and Civilization in China*, vol. 5, book 2, p. 98, note c (Cambridge, UK: Cambridge University Press, 1974).
77. Yü Ying-shih note: The aforementioned two essays are included in Ying-shih Yü, *Chinese History and Culture*, vol. 1: *Sixth Century B.C.E. to Seventeenth Century C.E.* (2016), 20–84.
78. William Ernest Hocking was a major philosopher of American idealism, empiricism, and religion, who published some twenty-two books. Henry Maurice Sheffer was a graduate of Harvard who taught logic and philos-

ophy at Harvard from 1916 to 1952. His mathematical logic was highly regarded by Bertrand Russell and Alfred North Whitehead.

79. Yü Ying-shih note: See *Diary of Wu Mi* (*Wu Mi riji*), vol. 3 for 1917 to 1924 (Beijing: Sanlian shuju, 1998).

80. Ibid., vol. 2, 179–180.

81. Ibid., vol. 2, 100–101.

82. Yü Ying-shih note: See George Wilhelm Friedrich Hegel, *Lectures on the Philosophy of History* translated by E. S. Haldane (Lincoln: University of Nebraska, 1995), vol. I, 120–121.

83. Yü Ying-shih note: *Hu Shi riji quanji* (Taipei: Liangjing, 2004), vol. 8, p. 181. Translators' note: Zhou Yiliang was a history professor and an expert on the Wei-Jin North South Dynasties period. Wang Zhongmin was an expert on ancient Chinese bibliography, who worked on the Chinese collection at the Library of Congress from 1939 to 1947 and later taught in the Department of Library Studies at Peking University.

84. Arthur W. Hummel, ed., *Eminent Chinese of the Ch'ing Period, 1644–1912* (Washington, DC: United States G.P.O, 1943–1944).

85. Yü Ying-shih note: Hu Shi Ji-nianguan, ed., *Lunxue tanshi ershinian—Hu Shi—Yang Liansheng wanglai shuzha* (Taipei: Lianjing, 1998), 35.

86. Yü Ying-shih note: See *Hu Shi riji quanji* (2004), vol. 8, p. 198, and Zhao Xinna and Huang Peiyun, eds., *Zhao Yuanren nianpu* (Beijing: Shangwu, 1998), 278.

87. Yü Ying-shih note: Zhou Yiliang, *Jiaosou puyan* (Beijing: Xin shijie, 2001), 17.

88. Jin Yuelin was a notable Chinese philosopher and logician, who wrote works on logic and the Chinese Dao; he also critiqued the philosophy of Bertrand Russell.

89. Clarence Irving Lewis or C. I. Lewis was the founder of "conceptual pragmatism" and a leading American academic philosopher.

90. Yü Ying-shih note: Zhou Yiliang, *Jiaosou puyan* (2001), 43.

91. Yü Ying-shih note: Ibid., 81.

92. Yü Ying-shih note: See the records for 1941 to 1946 in Zhao Xinna, ed., *Zhao Yuanren nianpu* (Beijing: Shangwu, 1998), 258–293.,

93. Yü Ying-shih note: See Zhou Yiliang, "Zhuiyi Hu Shi Zhi xiansheng" in *Jiaosou puyan* (2001), 2.

94. Yü Ying-shih note: *Hu Shi riji quanji* (2004), vol. 8, p. 206.

95. Yü Ying-shih note: Again, all of the people mentioned in these two paragraphs were major scholars in their fields.

96. Yü Ying-shih note: *Jiaosou puyan* (2001), 17. Translators' note: The "strangers" line is from the Tang poet Wang Wei's (692–761) well-known poem "Thinking of my Shandong Brother on the Double Ninth."

97. Yü Ying-shih note: Yang Liansheng, *Lunxue tanshi ershinian* (1998), 71.

98. Yü Ying-shih note: Ibid., 75 and 80.

99. Zhou Zumo was a well-known scholar of linguistics, Chinese rhyming dictionaries, literature, and language pedagogy.

100. Kao Yu-Kung, "A Study of The Fang La Rebellion," *Harvard Journal of Asiatic Studies*, vol. 24 (1962–1963), 17–63.

101. Yü Ying-shih note: See Yu-kung Kao, "Chinese Lyric Aesthetics," in *Words and Images: Chinese Poetry, Calligraphy, and Painting*, eds. Alfred Murk and Wen C. Fong (New York: The Metropolitan Museum of Art and Princeton University Press, 1991), 47–90.

102. Chen Shixiang was Professor of Chinese and Comparative Literature at the University of California, Berkeley, for many years. See Yang Mu, ed., *Chen Shixiang wencun* (Taiwan: Zhiwen), 1972.

103. Yü Ying-shih note: See Yü Ying-shih, *Cong jiazhi xitong kan Zhongguo wenhua de xiandai yiyi* (Taipei: Shibao wenhua chuban qiye gufen youxian gongsi, 1984) and *Lun tianren zhiji: Zhongguo gudai sixiang qiyuan shitan* (Taipei: Lianjing, 2014).

104. *Lunyu*, 14.24, Lau, *Analects*, 128.

105. Ling Chunsheng was an expert in Chinese music and a pioneer of Chinese archaeology and ethnology.

106. Clyde Kluckholm, *Mirror for Man: The Relation of Anthropology to Modern Life* (New York: McGraw-Hill, 1949; London: Routledge, published 2017, copyright 2018).

107. Wang Guowei, *Yin Zhou zhidu lun* (Taipei: Yiwen yinshuguan, 1971); Fu Sinian, *Yi Xia dong xi shuo* (1934); Xu Xusheng, *Zhongguo gushi de chuanshuo shidai* (Beijing: Wenwu, 1985).

108. Yü Ying-shih note: See "Food in Chinese Culture: The Han Period (206 BCE–220 CE)" in K. C. Chang, ed., *Food in Chinese Culture: Anthropological and Historical Perspectives* (New Haven, CT: Yale University Press, 1977), 53–83. Translators' addition: This is also included in Ying-shih Yü, *Chinese History and Culture*, Vol. 1: *Sixth Century B.C.E. to Seventeenth Century C.E.* (2016), 91–121.

109. "Goodness is not easy to explain, and reason is not easy to discover" (*shan wei yi ming, li wei yi cha* 善未易明，理未易察) is a well-known aphorism of Lü Zuqian (1137–1181).

110. Zhang Guangzhi, *Fanshuren de gushi* 蕃薯人的故事 [Stories of a sweet potato man] (Taipei: Lianjing, 1998).

111. See *Mao Zedong xuanji* [Selected works of Mao Zedong], *juan* 4, "Guanyu Chongqing tanpan" [On the Chongqing negotiations] for his statement that the Chinese Communist Party's road to victory would be long and winding, but their ultimate success was assured. See https://zhidao. baidu.com/question/264954675390204085.html.

112. Yü Ying-shih note: Said by the well-known Chinese archaeologist An Zhimin (1924–2005) in *Si hai wei jia: Zhuinian kaogu xuejia Zhang Guangzhi* [Four seas are one family: Remembering the archaeologist Zhang Guangzhi], edited by Li Li (Beijing : Sanlian Shudian, 2002), 66.

113. Li Yuanzhe (Yuan Tseh Lee) is a Nobel Prize–winning chemist who was president of the Academia Sinica from 1994 to 2006.

114. For Dai Lianzhang, see http://www.litphil.sinica.edu.tw/people/ researchers/Tai, %20Lian-chang.

115. Yü Ying-shih note: See Yu Weichao, "Wangshi zhuiji" [Remembering past events], in *Si hai wei jia: Zhuinian kaogu xuejia Zhang Guangzhi* (2002), 24.

116. A student of Li Ji's, Xia Nai became a major figure in Chinese archaeology. He was an expert in Egyptology and a member of the Department of Archaeology at the Institute of History and Philology, but he remained in China when the institute moved to Taiwan. He was persecuted during the Cultural Revolution, but he later rose to become vice president of the Chinese Academy of Social Science.

117. Huang Zhanyue was a prolific archaeologist of the Han and Tang dynasties. *Tongzhi* or "comrade" is a communist term that for a period replaced terms like "Mr.," "Miss," or "Mrs." in China but should actually refer to members of the Chinese Communist Party.

118. Li Li, ed., *Si hai wei jia: Zhuinian kaogu xuejia Zhang Guangzhi*, 37.

119. The use of Chinese terms like *guonei* and *guowai* indicate that a person regards China as their country, and *guonei* can also mean people who have political authority in China. Such a person is in the United States and a citizen of the United States, but still says *guonei* (inside the country) when speaking of things that occur in China.

120. See Li Shuicheng, "Zhang Guangzhi xiansheng yu Beida," [Mr. Zhang Guangzhi and Peking University], in *Si hai wei jia: Zhuinian kaogu xuejia Zhang Guangzhi*, 100.

121. Chang, Kwang-chih, *The Archaeology of Ancient China* (New Haven, CT: Yale University Press, 1963).

122. Tong Enzheng was a noted cultural anthropologist who also wrote science fiction. After the Tiananmen Massacre, he escaped to the United States where he was visiting scholar at Wesleyan University. His essay "Thirty Years of Chinese Archaeology, 1949–79," is in *Nationalism, Politics, and the Practice of Archaeology*, edited by Philip L. Kohl and Clare Fawcett (Cambridge, UK: Cambridge University Press, 1996), 177–97.

123. Yü Ying-shih note: For the details of this incident, see chapter 9 of the *Diary of Xia Nai* as well as Zhang Guangzhi, *Kaogu renleixue suibi* [Essays on archaeological anthropology] (Beijing: Sanlian shudian, 1999), 176-180.

124. Yü Ying-shih note: See Li Guangmo, *Si hai wei jia: Zhuinian kaogu xuejia Zhang Guangzhi*, 160.

125. Yü Ying-shih note: See Luo Tai (Lothar von Falkenhausen), "Zhuiyi Zhang Guangzhi" [Remembering Zhang Guangzhi] in *Si hai wei jia: Zhuinian kaogu xuejia Zhang Guangzhi* (2002), 158–159.

APPENDIX

Figure 1. Professor Yü Ying-shih's Home in Guanzhuang County.

Source: Photo from author's personal collection.

Figure 2. Professor Yü Ying-shih, aged six (1936) and aged 14 (1944).

Source: Photos from author's personal collection.

Figure 3. Professor Yü Ying-shih, aged 16 (1946).

Source: Photo from author's personal collection.

Figure 4. Professor Yü Ying-shih, aged 19 (1949).

Source: Photo from author's personal collection.

Figure 5. Professor Yü Ying-shih with his aunt Zhang Yunhua who raised him until 1946 (1947).

Source: Photo from author's personal collection.

Figure 6. Professor Yü Ying-shih's mother, Zhang Yunqing.

Source: Photo from author's personal collection.

Figure 7. *Xiyang tongshi* 西洋通史 (General history of the West) by Professor Yu Xiezhong.

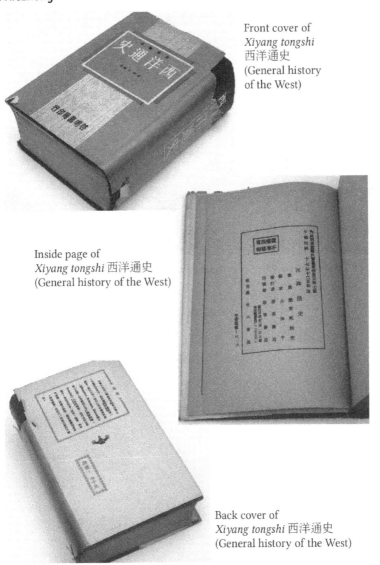

Front cover of
Xiyang tongshi
西洋通史
(General history
of the West)

Inside page of
Xiyang tongshi 西洋通史
(General history of the West)

Back cover of
Xiyang tongshi 西洋通史
(General history of the West)

Source: Photos from author's personal collection.

Figure 8. Professor Yang Liansheng and Professor Qian Mu.

Source: Photo from author's personal collection.

Figure 9. Professor Yü Ying-shih Awarded the John W. Kluge Prize for Lifetime Achievement in the Study of Humanity (2006).

Source: Library of Congress.

Figure 10. Professor Yü Ying-shih, Winner of the 2014 Tang Prize in Sinology.

Source: Courtesy of the Tang Foundation.

About the Author

Yü Ying-shih (1930–2021) was Professor Emeritus of History at Princeton University and arguably the premiere historian of Chinese social and intellectual history of the classical period. Awarded the John W. Kluge Prize for achievement in the Study of Humanity and the inaugural Tang Prize International Award in Sinology, he published more than thirty books and five hundred articles and essays on Chinese history, thought, politics, and culture. His most recent works include *Lun tian ren zhi ji* (Between heaven and the human: An exploration of the origin of ancient chinese thought; 2014), *Zhu Xi de lishi shijie* (The historical world of Zhu Xi: A study of the political culture of Song intellectuals; 2003, 2011), *Shi yu Zhongguo wenhua* (Chinese intellectuals and chinese culture; 2003, 2010, and 2013), and thirty-three of his English-language essays are published in *Chinese History and Culture Volume 1: Sixth Century B.C.E. to Seventeenth Century C.E.* and *Volume 2: Seventeenth Through Twentieth Century* (Columbia University Press, 2016), with the editorial assistance of Josephine Chiu-Duke and Michael S. Duke.

About the Translators

Josephine Chiu-Duke is Professor of Chinese Intellectual History in the Asian Studies Department at the University of British Columbia.

Michael S. Duke is Professor Emeritus of Chinese and Comparative Literature from the Asian Studies Department at the University of British Columbia.

INDEX

CPSIA information can be obtained
at www.ICGtesting.com
Printed in the USA
LVHW021457260921
698753LV00006B/374

9 781621 966258